D0571908

From Jim Baker:

To my father, who introduced me to the American Football League.

From Bernard M. Corbett:

*To a pair of friends who are diehard Pats fans: Rocco Zizza,
a football guy who brings the same passion to 1–15 as he does
to 16–0, and Michael Day, whose seat in the end zone was never
empty, mother nature be damned.*

CONTENTS

CONTENTS

Introduction

In the still-young twenty-first century, the New England Patriots have enjoyed a run of success nearly unparalleled in NFL history. If you're reading these words, chances are you know the statistics: nine division titles, five Super Bowl appearances, three championships. Future hall of famers at quarterback and head coach, and a secure place in the history books. This much you can see, and have seen, from the comfort of your couch.

But football is a brilliantly complex and interesting game, and the more you put into it, the more you get out of it. What looks like a slick, easy touchdown pass may in fact be the result of hit after relentless hit on the line of scrimmage. And whether it's the millennial, pass-happy Patriots or the hard-nosed teams of the 1960s, there is more to the story than what's printed in the papers, and we wanted to tell it.

To make this happen, we looked to the people who lived these events: the players, coaches, and executives who took part in the contests and the writers and broadcasters who enhanced the experience with their narratives and descriptions. Players representing all eras, from the obscure substitute groundskeeper Mark Henderson to all-time greats like Gino Cappelletti and John Hannah, these are the people who defined the Patriots. By asking them to share their thoughts and memories, we have brought to life thirteen games that define the Patriots' existence from the time before they were conceived up to the moment that they reached for perfection.

To their recollections we add detailed accounts of the background and events that made these games special in the pantheon of not only the franchise, but the sport itself. There are more than thirty appendices filled with facts, trivia, and analysis relevant to every game—and what games they are! You'll read about:

- The birth of the most successful new league since the NFL came to be in the early 1920s.
- The very first playoff game in team history.
- The best game by a Patriots legend.
- The birth of a new era in team history.
- A heartbreaking loss just when the team seemed on the cusp of greatness.
- One of the most improbable NFL games in history.
- An underdog team determined to break a decades-long losing streak and get to the Super Bowl for the first time.
- The team delivering its first-ever home playoff victory.
- An epic battle in the snow which turned on a legendary call.
- An upstart team given no chance to win the Super Bowl against one of the greatest offensive juggernauts of all time.
- A mismatch on paper that instead became one of the best Super Bowls ever.
- The game in which the Patriots officially became a dynasty.
- An epic battle against an opponent determined to see perfection denied.

The greatest football contests transcend their own time and become historical mainstays unto themselves, and in *The Most Memorable Games in Patriots History: The Oral History of a Storied Team,* these games are brought to life through the memories and experiences of those who were there to experience them firsthand. The result is a book that appeals to the hardcore fan and casual rooter alike as you follow a team's rise and fall repeatedly—usually in an entertaining fashion—only to attain a level of sustained greatness that few before it ever have.

The journey to that exalted place has been as compelling a tale as any in sports and here, through the voices of those who lived through it all, you are invited along for the ride.

Jim Baker
Bernard M. Corbett

Denver Broncos at Boston Patriots

AMERICAN FOOTBALL LEAGUE INAUGURAL
September 9, 1960

	1	2	3	4	F
Denver Broncos	0	7	6	0	13
Boston Patriots	3	0	7	0	10

BIRTH OF A DREAM

Given the success that the Patriots have become, it is hard to fathom that the highest levels of pro football were without a representative in New England throughout the 1950s. After a number of failed attempts, Boston ranked as the largest market in the Northeast without a professional football team. (See "The Patriots Preceders," on page 22.) This was a city that had not one but two baseball teams at the start of the decade, and yet it did not have a franchise in the National Football League after 1948 nor in the All-America Football Conference, which operated from 1946 to 1949. (Then again, who would have imagined that the NFL would one day have three teams in California but none in Los Angeles?)

Throughout those empty years, though, there were men in the city who wanted to see football return to Boston. One of them was Dean Boylan, of Boston Sand and Gravel.

Dean Boylan: In 1954 or '55, I got a call from Dom DiMaggio, who had just retired as the center fielder for the Boston Red Sox. Dom was a close personal friend of mine. He called me and said, "Dean, would you be interested in becoming one of the owners of a new

1

football team coming to Boston?" I said, "Are you going to go into it, Dom?" He said he was, so I said, "Count me in." And that was it.

Another interested party was Billy Sullivan, a former sportswriter and publicity man for Boston College, the Boston Braves, and the University of Notre Dame, who had since become an executive with Metropolitan Coal and Oil Company.

Patrick Sullivan: [NFL Commissioner] Bert Bell had promised my father an NFL franchise in 1958, if Dad could come up with a stadium plan. There was no legitimate place for football at that point in time. There was Harvard Stadium, but Harvard wasn't going to allow any pro football in there. Dad started working as early as 1958 on designs for a new stadium in Norwood, right near the 128 train station. When Bert Bell passed away, those plans went out the window. Dad was pretty discouraged about it. Then his old friend and mentor, Frank Leahy, called him and said he was involved with the then–Los Angeles Chargers. There was a new league forming and it looked pretty good. If Dad could put together some dough, he'd recommend that they get it.

Dean Boylan: They got ten people together, of which I was one, and we had to come up with twenty-five thousand dollars each. This was in order to get our certificate, which we did get. We went from there; I never really knew how Dom got involved. My guess is Billy Sullivan, who had the piece of paper with the franchise, called Dom and asked him if he was interested. And also asked him, I presume, if he knew any others who might be interested in becoming part owners. I believe, although I never did ask Dom, that's how it all came about.

Patrick Sullivan: It was in November 1959, Dad got a call in his office at our home in Wellesley, Massachusetts. It was [American Football League cofounder] Lamar Hunt on the phone, telling him if he had two hundred and fifty thousand dollars in a bank down in Dallas in the next five days, he'd be in. Then he got the eighth and final franchise in the AFL. Dad was pretty excited about it.

Dean Boylan: I'd never met Billy, but I knew who he was because I had been reading about him in the papers for a long, long time. When the ten of us got together and had our so-called first meeting, that was the first time I met Billy. I didn't know anything about anything before that, except that Billy had the piece of paper from the new league. Naturally, he was elected president. Without Billy there wouldn't have been any Boston Patriots.

Patrick Sullivan: The original ownership group was eclectic. There was Dom DiMaggio, a group of old Brahmin Bostonians, and William Haines.

Dean Boylan: We had Paul Sonnabend, who was a hotelier. Dan Marr was in the scaffolding business here in Boston, also cranes and that type of equipment. There was George Sargent, the brother of Frank Sargent, who later became governor of Massachusetts. George died very young, so Frank took his place on the board, representing Mrs. George Sargent. When Frank became governor in 1967, he resigned from the board.

Patrick Sullivan: My dad's uncle, Joe Sullivan, who was in the printing business, bought in.

Dean Boylan: We had Edward McMann, from Maine. There was Edgar Turner, who was in business in Needham. He had the 7-Up franchise. Then there was a gentleman by the name of John Ames, from Easton, Massachusetts. His family has started the Ames Shovel Company, which went back to the Revolution, and they had donated all the land for Stonehill College. Both were fine gentlemen.

Patrick Sullivan: It was a very diverse group, but the first three years were critical, and those guys hung in there.

While all this was going on, the NFL feigned nonchalance, but went about making moves that were meant to strangle the AFL baby in the crib.

Gino Cappelletti: There was supposed to be a Minnesota AFL franchise. Then the NFL jumped right in right after them. They went to Minnesota and met with Max Winter who owned the Celtics, and he was a guy who was a sports-minded individual, and he liked to own teams. They said, "If you bail out on the AFL, we'll give you an NFL franchise that starts next year. The NFL did that to two cities. They created the Dallas Cowboys, and that eventually forced the Dallas Texans, who became the Kansas City Chiefs, to move out of town. That franchise that was Minnesota's then went to Oakland. That's how Oakland became the eighth team in the AFL. They wanted an even number of teams in each division. The [NFL] tried to torpedo the AFL. They didn't want them around.

The team needed a name, and a young publicity assistant named Jack Grinold, who would later become the longtime sports information director at Northeastern University, was tasked with running a name-the-team contest.

Jack Grinold: We asked the public to write in and submit their entries. Frankly, the winning name was not Patriots, which was number two. Number one was Minutemen. At that time, the University of Massachusetts teams were called the Redmen. We thought there should be another step, get kids involved and people involved, so we decided there should be an essay contest. You had to write an essay about why the name you suggested should be chosen. Bill Orenberger, the superintendent of the Boston School Department, was the judge, and he determined that the winning essay was one that suggested Patriots. Also, our advertising agency thought Minutemen was too long. Once we became the Patriots, we went all out. Everything was red, white, and blue. Our first practice field was a playground in Concord, Massachusetts. Where else would the Patriots practice? Our phone number was Copley 2-1776. So we were in the spirit.

LOU SABAN AND THE FIRST CAMP
For their first coach, the Patriots looked to the college ranks and found Lou Saban at Western Illinois.

Jack Grinold: Saban had captained those four great Cleveland Brown teams in the old AAFC and then got into coaching. He became head coach at Northwestern for a year. That didn't work out too well [0–8–1 in 1955]. He ended up at Western Illinois. Our general manager, Ed McKeever, hired him. Saban brought with him a coaching staff that just amazes me when I think about it. There was Red Miller, who would later coach the Denver Broncos; Joe Collier, who went on to coach the Buffalo Bills; and Jerry Smith, who was an NFL lifer—he stayed in the NFL for ages. Then a fourth assistant was added. The Patriots' first hire had been Mike Holovak, who had just been let go by Boston College. Bill Sullivan had hired him as his player personnel director, but when Saban came, Mike told Lou that if it was okay with him, he'd like to be the fourth assistant. He went on to a distinguished life in the NFL, coaching the Patriots and being an assistant with the Raiders and 49ers. He was general manager of the Oilers and was still a consultant until a couple of years before he died, well into his eighties. When you look back at that original group, it was something else.

Larry Garron: We had just won our second championship at Western Illinois. I had received three letters: one from the Green Bay Packers, one from the Cleveland Browns, and one from the Chicago Bears. I went to Coach Saban to talk about it. He looked at me and said, "Well, I have another opportunity for you." That was in 1959, my senior year. He said, "I think you have a better opportunity with me." So I signed my contract and went to Boston for the first time in my life. It was the farthest I had been away from home.

Jack Rudolph: I was at Georgia Tech and we were playing in the Gator Bowl against Arkansas the day after New Year's, and after the game was over Mike Holovak came down there and approached me and talked to me for several hours about the possibilities of coming to Boston. I had been drafted by the Detroit Lions, but he talked to me and, over the next month or so, Ed McKeever came down and visited with me and we talked, and I decided that that's where I had the best chance of playing was with Boston, and I signed a contract with him in the dormitory at Tech. So, after I was done signing, my roommate came in and said, "Who is this guy in here?" I said, "Well, that's Ed McKeever—he's the general manager of the Boston Patriots, and I just signed with them." So my roommate said, "Do you think he would buy us something to eat?" And I said, "What do you mean?" and he said, "We've got no damn money. Do you reckon he'd take us up to the Varsity and feed us?" Back then at the Varsity, hot dogs were two for a quarter, French fries were fifteen cents, and drinks were a dime. So McKeever said, "Yeah, I'll take you guys up there, c'mon." So we went up to the Varsity and ate, and on the way back my roommate said, "Do you think we overdid it? We ate five dollars' worth of hot dogs!" Do you think many people would worry about five dollars today when they are negotiating their contracts?

Joe Collier: When I got out of the Army in 1956, I went to Western Illinois to get my master's degree. I was a graduate assistant all set to go into high school coaching. Lou Saban came there the year I was set to leave. We got to be pretty good friends, so he asked me to stay on as a full-time coach. Lou, Red Miller and I had pretty good success. When Lou got the AFL job in 1960, he took Red Miller and me with him to Boston and that's how I got started. I was one of those young coaches who did know what he didn't know.

Larry Garron: Lou Saban came my second year at Western Illinois. When he came in, he changed the whole system. We were using a pro system, but he modified it for college, and it was unbelievable. We went undefeated for two years. When he came to Boston, all he did was upgrade that system.

Meanwhile, the man who would become the face of the franchise in its AFL years very nearly didn't get to be a Patriot at all, owing to a missed connection.

Gino Cappelletti: In 1959, I was working in a bar owned by a former University of Minnesota teammate of mine, a place called Mack and

Cap's. He told me about this new league that was starting. We were playing touch football and flag football and representing the bar in a Minneapolis touch football league—that was the extent of my football at that time. After my career at Minnesota, I had been up to the Canadian League for one year and tried that. I had a tryout with the Detroit Lions. I had a stint in the Army, where I played as well. So he was telling me about this new league, and lo and behold, Lou Saban was coming to Minneapolis to look at some players. I knew he was going to be at the Hotel Radisson, but I missed seeing him. I called him right after and gave him the details of my playing schedule and where I'd been, and he said, "I'll get back to you." A good month went by, maybe even two months, and I hadn't heard back. So I was getting a little discouraged. All of a sudden one night, I got a phone call. A voice said, "Cappelletti?" I said, "Yeah?" He said, "This is Lou Saban. I'm sending you a minimum contract, seventy-five hundred dollars. You've got as good a chance as anyone else to make this team." Boy oh boy, I went sky high. Didn't even hear the number that he said he was gonna pay. And so I joined my pals from Minnesota—there were four of us—and we jumped on a plane and flew east.

Larry Garron: I had an advantage, because the coach had a familiarity with me, but the turnover in that camp was like a nightmare. You would wake up in the morning and there was a different guy sleeping in the bed next to you than there had been when you went to bed the night before. Then there were guys who would quit right after practice ended, or even *before* practice ended. Guys would drop all their pads and their uniforms and take off, saying, "I quit!" It was amazing. If you didn't have the integrity and the ability to have a goal or a purpose, you didn't last.

Joe Collier: A lot of our personnel problems, if you can call them that, solved themselves. Kids could see they didn't have the skill to play at that level and they'd just walk off. We had ten to fifteen kids just quit. Some injuries occurred, and the kids who had the talent rose to the top. It wasn't that difficult. It just took time.

Jack Rudolph: Saban was very intense. He was an all-work-and-no-play type of person. My mother had never seen me play football. My father died when I was young, and she had to work, so she didn't see me in high school and she didn't see me in college. When I was with the Patriots, my brother was going to New York to do some business and he was going to bring our mother with him. We just happened to be playing the Titans in the Polo Grounds during their visit. I went to Lou, said I needed to get some tickets for my family for New York, and he said, "Let me tell you something: This is not a college where we give things out. You gotta understand that your paycheck comes from the ticket sales. We don't give out free tickets like you probably got at Georgia Tech. We have to pay for the tickets and all the things that we do so we can make the damn payroll." I ended up getting a thirty-minute lecture about asking for two tickets.

About twenty-five years later, I was coaching a high school team and I got a call from Lou. He said he was coaching a semi-pro team in Macon, Georgia, and needed some help. "We're having some try-out camps at difference places, and we're going to have one at your high school in the next month, and I wonder if you could do something for me. I need a practice field. I need a couple blocking machines. I need some ropes to run through. I need the weight room so we can test them on the weights, and I need some footballs and stuff like that. Can you help me out?" I said, "Certainly, but if you want all that stuff it's going to cost you $1,125." He said, "What are you talking about? We're just getting this franchise started." I said, "How do you think we'll make our program if we don't get the money for the equipment? I've got to think about taking care of the kids. Didn't you teach me that when I asked for the two tickets for my mother?" He wanted to know if I was serious, and I said, "Well, I'll let you off the hook—it will only be five hundred dollars." I ended up not charging him, but it was a good way to get back at him after all that time.

Larry Garron: I was familiar enough with the system both on defense and on offense that I was doing a lot of coaching—teaching and coaching as well as playing. I would teach any player that came into any of the positions. I was familiar enough to pass it on. That's why I had so many different roommates. I'd go to sleep; I'd wake up the next day and there's somebody new I'd have to start training—maybe training to take my job.

New football leagues might be short on owners, they might be short on stadium facilities, and they would most probably be short on money, but one thing they never lack is would-be players.

Patrick Sullivan: There was a huge conglomeration of characters. There were pro wrestlers, firemen, policemen, and teachers. Just about anyone that thought they had a shot were there. It was pretty hysterical.

Jack Grinold: We had an Indian chief and old football players that were in their midforties. We had guys that had been playing park-league-type football. This was their chance to try and take a shot at it. It was a very unusual experience.

Jack Rudolph: The more you could do, the better you had a chance of staying, because you were told when you play on this team there are three things that might happen: You might stay, you might go, you might play . . . It was better the second year, but that first year, when we were at the training camp at the University of Massachusetts in Amherst, we had four practices—two in the morning and two in the evening. And when the group got through with the first morning practice, they would leave their equipment—shoulder pads and such—right on the field so the second group that was coming in could wear it.

Joe Collier: The players went twice a day, but we coaches had to go four times a day. It was a hard period of time but we had to get the roster down to a working number and it only took a couple of weeks to get it down to where we could go back to a regular practice schedule. We didn't have a training table, so we ate with the summer school students. They had scallops every meal and I can't even look at a scallop ever since.

Jack Rudolph: I'm going to say conservatively that they were over three hundred people that went through the first camp the first season.

Gino Cappelletti: What the Sullivan boys, who were very young at the time, were doing was going back and forth from the training camp in Amherst to Logan Airport, bringing guys that they just cut to get their flights home, and then picking up new guys they were bringing in.

Jack Rudolph: It was hard to make friends, because by the time you knew somebody, his ass might be on the bus going home. We stayed in the dormitories there at UMass with no air conditioning. We were staying on a floor with a guy who had played for the Cardinals named Harry Jagielski, who was maybe the first three-hundred-pounder I ever saw in person. You could hear him snoring all the way down the hall at night. Everybody got off the third floor except Harry, and the rest of us moved as people came and went to other floors so we could get a good night's sleep.

Gino Cappelletti: Of course, it was difficult evaluating, as Saban only had himself and four coaches. Lou Saban wanted you to be a very aggressive, active type of player. That's what he was looking for, because he was that kind of player. I went out there and threw my body around with reckless abandon to try and make an impression. He had one drill where he would give a guy the ball, and he would say that the defensive back and the ball carrier were going to run at each other in a head-on collision course. And Saban would say to the back, "You can make a cut to the left or the right, or you can go straight through the guy." I was the defender on this drill. Some of the guys who would cut and go to the side, the blow wasn't as extreme. But some of the guys really had no cutting ability. They would go straight at you and there would be a head-on tackle and a head-on hit from the running back. And when you got through with that drill, Saban could see who could tackle and who could run over people, so he picked his players from those departments. He got a feeling for who was going to be very aggressive and who liked contact.

Jack Rudolph: We had a guy that had been with the Cleveland Browns for a lifetime, and his name was Gunner Gatski. He was our center during the early part of training camp, but I think because of his age—he was over forty—he didn't make the final squad. He had great stories and helped a lot of people have the proper attitude and ideas about what you needed to do to be a professional football player.

With the 33-man rosters of the day, specialists were a luxury teams could not afford.

Gino Cappelletti: I was tried as a defensive back, and I was gonna be a quarterback or a running back, but I was having difficulty cracking the team that way. I always had great confidence in my kicking, and so I said I gotta find a way to hang around on the team long enough so that when they start looking for a kicker—they didn't start looking for a kicker until maybe three to four weeks went by— I'd still be there to show my stuff. Lou Saban had said, "You gotta make the team. Then we'll find a kicker within the guys who make the team. And a punter." And of course I could do both. I played two-way football in college. I told them I played defensive back and could be the placekicker and punter.

Joe Collier: Being a kicker, Gino became a valuable player. He played defensive back the first year. I think it was Mike Holovak who switched him to receiver. Holovak could see the talent that he had as a receiver. First year, we tried him on defense and that was it. He made the squad. You had to have a player that was a kicker and could do two things at the same time. He became a great player. When I left Boston for Buffalo later on, he drove us crazy as far as being a receiver.

The Patriots' quarterback in their inaugural season was Edward F. "Butch" Songin. He had been drafted by the Cleveland Browns a decade earlier but had never played in the NFL. Also an All-American hockey player at Boston College, he had led the Eagles football team to a 14–10–3 record from 1947 to 1949. Since then, there had been a stint in Canada, where he helped the Hamilton Tiger-Cats win the Grey Cup, but no other high-level play.

Jack Grinold: Butch was really a ton of fun. Of course, at age thirty-six, he was the grandfather of all the players. He was an incredible athlete. He hadn't played structured football for quite a while. He played in the park league. To come in and play a pro football game at that age after not playing for years was quite exceptional. We had four other Boston College athletes: Ross O'Hanley, all-league safety in 1960; Jimmy Colclough, who caught forty-nine passes; the fullback, Alan Miller; and Joe Johnson, a receiver who had come back from the Green Bay Packers. Also on the local side, from Holy Cross we had punter and backup quarterback Tommy Greene and lineman Bob Dee. With all those locals, I believe we resembled the Boston Yanks. Of course, they had to defend their jobs in training camps, and they did. It was fun to have a lot of local guys on the team.

THE FIRST PRESEASON

Jack Grinold: Before we got into the preseason we had intersquad scrimmages. I believe one was held in Lowell; another in Greenfield. They wanted to showcase themselves all around the Boston area to introduce the product to the public. Billy Sullivan was New England's answer to Bill Veeck. He was a machine gun of ideas. He was one of the most creative persons that I ever came in contact with. He had a way of trying to get out there and reach the public.

The very first preseason game in American Football League history also involved the Patriots. On July 30, 1960, they traveled to Buffalo to meet the Bills and came away with an impressive 28–7 victory. Bob Dee scored the first-ever Patriots points when he fell on a fumble in the Bills' end zone.

Denver's Broncos, on the other hand, were the punching bag of the AFL's first preseason. In their exhibition inaugural, on August 5, they traveled to Providence, Rhode Island, and got rolled by the Patriots, 43–6.

Jack Grinold: Denver looked helpless. Billy Sullivan was a league guy. He was shocked that Denver looked so shabby, so he made a suggestion to the league commissioner, Joe Foss, that each member of the league should contribute one of their players to Denver to strengthen that franchise. That never did happen, though.

The Broncos next traveled to Rochester, New York, and were beaten up by the Bills, 31–14. A trip south saw them lose to the Oilers in Houston, 42–3, and to the Dallas Texans in Little Rock, Arkansas, 48–0. Their final exhibition game was in Los Angeles, where they had their best showing to date, a 36–30 loss to the Chargers. The Patriots, meanwhile, went 4–1 in their preseason games.

Very few of the AFL teams would have a slick look for the inaugural season. The Bills' uniforms were copies of the Detroit Lions' and had no adornment on the helmet. The Raiders, Titans, and Broncos also had generic-looking uniforms, although Denver had its infamous vertical-striped stockings, which were the laughingstock of football. The Chargers had their famous lightning-bolt helmet from the beginning, and the Oilers sported the oil derrick from day one as well, while the Dallas Texans had an outline of their home state. The Patriots were also in the adorned group.

Jack Grinold: A lot of people think that the first helmets were Phil Bissell's cartoon of Pat the Patriot. That was not so. Our symbol to the world for that first football season was the tricornered hat. Phil Bissell's cartoon appeared in 1960 around Saint Patrick's Day. They had been looking around for a logo, symbol, branding—whatever they call it now. One of the younger Sullivan kids, Patrick or Billy, said, "Dad, that's what we want for our logo." And it soon became official.

OPENING NIGHT

Patrick Sullivan: A lot of people were still referring to Nickerson as Braves Field. It was a scramble to get stands on the opposite side of the stadium and to get locker rooms set up. It was like everything in those early days: Where there was a will, there was a way. Things got done.

Jack Grinold: The odds were heavily stacked for the Patriots. It was a colossal night. We had Hugo Baron and his band in the audience, which was a takeoff from Billy's days with the Boston Braves. It was a beautiful night. The setting was perfect.

Larry Garron: Opening night was exciting. We were on the bench, and the fans were right behind us. We had a chance to talk with them, and they asked, "What do you think you're going to do?" We tried to describe to them that we were going to have fun. "We're going to give you entertainment." They'd say, "But why on Friday?" We said, "We don't want to bump heads with the Giants!"

Jack Grinold: Everyone was a New York Giant fan in those days. Those were colorful teams, with [Frank] Gifford, and Kyle Rote, and Charlie Conerly. They had captured the souls and hearts of everyone in New England. It would have been suicidal to play our games on Sunday. We couldn't play on Saturday; the NFL to this day stays away from Saturdays to give way to local colleges. The only alternative was Friday night, to escape the eight-hundred-pound gorilla that was the New York Giants.

Jack Rudolph: I think playing on Friday nights was a smart thing for them to do. The only thing I think irritated people is Friday night is generally high school football night, so you don't play games to interfere with the fans of high school football. In Georgia, where I come from, football is the main blood of the world, so I don't think if the Patriots had been in Georgia they would have let them play on Friday nights. But I enjoyed having two days off. They didn't make us come in on Saturday or Sunday even if we didn't play well. I'm sure Lou would have loved to do that a couple of times.

Coaching the Broncos was Frank Filchock, a man with a storied past. He'd been the star multipurpose player of the New York Giants in

1946 and led them to the championship game against Chicago. In the final weeks of the season, he and teammate Merle Hapes were often seen out on the town in the company of Alvin Paris, a small-time bookie operating out of Elizabeth, New Jersey. He had supplied the two players, both married, with female escorts and promises of lucrative jobs. Having buttered them up, he asked if they would go easy in the championship game. While there is no proof that Filchock and Hapes ever agreed to Paris's offer, they didn't report it, either. When the league got wind of this, they called the players before Commissioner Bert Bell. Hapes was suspended, but Filchock was allowed to play, then suspended for life after the Giants lost the title game to the Bears, 24–14. (Although Filchock threw six interceptions in 26 attempts—just a bit worse than his average that year—he appeared to play his guts out, getting his nose broken for his trouble. His teammates and opponents were convinced he had tried his best.)

Filchock applied for reinstatement, but by the time it was granted, in 1950, he was 34, his career mostly behind him. He played in Canada and also coached there. One of his players was a future opponent, Gino Cappelletti. The night before the AFL opener, Filchock was involved in a bit more intrigue, an incident that is somewhat reminiscent, albeit more low-tech, of the controversy that swirled around the 2007 Patriots.

Gino Cappelletti: Thursday night we had driven in from Amherst, and Saban had us out there for like an hour and a half. He was a little nervous about it. He wanted to make sure everybody understood everything he wanted to do in the game and how you were going to play the game. I think he got carried away, and we stayed out there for such a long time. Frank Filchock and his team were staying at either the Somerset or Kenmore hotel. He just took a walk that night down Comm. Avenue from Kenmore Square. He saw these lights on and he kind of snooped around, walked over there, and of course there was no security or anything, and he walked in and sure enough, that's us practicing, and working on things that were gonna do at the game. He grabbed a seat way up in the end zone. He had a spot that would have been the bleachers for baseball, from a distance, in the nice bright light on a nice night, and he watched our drills.

Jack Grinold: He realized that no one knew he was there. He saw the Patriots go through their final drills and, therefore, knew what they were going to run. I don't know if that's ever been confirmed, though.

THE GAME

What better way to start a new league than with a bit of trickery? On the very first play in AFL history, the Broncos ran a reverse on the kick-off return. Bob McNamara took Al Discenzo's kick at the goal line and quickly handed off to Al Carmichael, who had been one of the best return men in the NFL when he played for the Packers in the mid-fifties. Carmichael took the ball up the right sideline and was swarmed under at the Denver seventeen. First blood had been drawn.

Jack Grinold: The press box hadn't been completed. The doors wouldn't close. It was open sesame. After the game started, both the Denver and Boston coaches' screaming and yelling could be heard. There were a whole lot of Denver people in there and a whole lot of Patriots people in there. I can't tell you how much information was being passed back and forth. Not only had the Patriots been scouted out thoroughly by Filchock, but anyone that was clever enough to run back and forth between the coaches' booths, they could pass information also.

Carmichael was also the ball carrier on the first play from scrimmage in league history. He took the handoff from Frank Tripucka and got 5 yards. The Broncos got as far as the 45 on their first possession before calling in George Herring to punt. The kick was downed on the Boston 29. Boston's first play from scrimmage was a handoff from Butch Songin to Jimmy Crawford, good for 5 yards. Three plays later, Songin threw the first pass in league history, an incompletion to Walt Livingston. It was nullified by a Denver offside penalty, however, so the first official pass in AFL annals came on the next play, when Songin threw to Oscar Lofton, also incomplete.

Songin would record the league's first completion on his third try after Denver had been smacked with a 15-yard penalty for roughing up punter Tommy Greene to keep the drive going. The pass was a 1-yard gainer to Jimmy Colclough as the Patriots chipped their way down to the Denver 27 before stalling.

Gino Cappelletti: I was on the sidelines because I was playing just defensive back at that point, and Saban said, "Field goal team." We ran on the field, and there was my pal Fred Bruney, holding the ball. I froze behind the ball for what seemed like a half an hour, but it was just seconds. Freddie put the ball down, and when I didn't come forward he said, "Kick the damn thing!" I kicked through it. Fortunately it was quick enough that it got over the line and through the uprights. The record books say it was a thirty-five-yarder, but if you want to be factual, it was really a thirty-seven-yard field goal; I was standing at the thirty-seven for the kick.

It is fitting that Cappelletti would score the first points in American Football League history. That field goal represented the first three of the eventual 27,912 points that would be scored during the league's 10-year existence. And Cappelletti would personally score more of those 27,912 points than any other player.

The Broncos got their first-ever points on the opening play of the second quarter. Carmichael caught a short pass in the flat and eluded two Patriots just past the line of scrimmage. After he got free of a third defender, he took off up the left sideline, now with a full escort. Left guard Ken Adamson threw a key block at the Boston 30, leaving the way clear for Carmichael. The rest of the second quarter was ball exchange, with neither team getting any closer than the other's 47. The Patriots had a chance to get into field goal range in the waning moments of the half, but Songin fell victim to the first of Goose Gonsoulin's league-leading 11 interceptions at the Denver 17, ending the threat.

It's been a long time since the man kicking off also returned kicks, but the Broncos had such a man in this game: Gene Mingo.

Gene Mingo: Bobby McNamara had gotten hurt, and Coach Filchock came up to me during halftime and said, "Mingo, you're going to be running back, punts, and kickoffs." I had been kicking off, kicking extra points. I was on the coverage team for punts—did everything I was supposed to.

Larry Garron: Mingo and I both ran track in college. We'd bump heads at Drake relays. Before that first game he said to me, "If I get an inch, I'm going to fly by everybody." I said, "No way."

Mingo's first return came when he took the opening kickoff of the second half out to his own 27, but it was undone by a penalty that set them back to the 12.

Neither team could move the ball in the third quarter. Saban had relieved Songin with Tommy Greene, but he was just 1 for 4 passing. After his second series at the helm came up fourth and 4 on the Boston 26, Greene dropped back to punt.

Larry Garron: I kept telling the guys, "Keep Mingo to the inside; don't let him get to the outside. If he gets to the outside, he's gone." And unfortunately, he got to the outside, and that's the score that beat us.

Gene Mingo: I went back for the Boston punt. I caught it and ran it back seventy-six yards, and that was the first scoring punt return for the American Football League.

Mingo's sprint up the right sideline put the Broncos up 13–3. Perhaps winded from his ordeal, Mingo missed the extra point. Songin was brought back in and, after Crawford rushed for a 15-yard gainer, he hit Colclough for another 19—except that Colclough fumbled and Denver took over on their own 38. Tripucka hit J.W. Brodnax for 12 yards on first down. For the second play in a row, Tripucka went to the air on first down. This time, Chuck Shonta stepped in front of it at the Boston 38 and headed in the other direction. He was finally hauled down from behind at the Denver 10.

On the first play of their stolen possession, Songin found Colclough in the right side of the end zone for the score. Cappelletti's kick made it 13–10.

Boston was handed an excellent opportunity midway through the fourth quarter when a Greene punt bounced up and hit a Denver player. Charley Leo fell on it and Boston was ready to go at their own 47. When Songin dumped a screen pass to Crawford, he sprinted for 40 yards. Now at the Denver 13, the Patriots were bound to come away from this possession with at least a tie. Or so it seemed.

After Crawford was stopped for no gain, Songin tried the screen-pass route, soft-tossing the ball to fullback Alan Miller. The Broncos ate right through the screen, however, and ripped him down back at the 20. Now facing a third and 17, the Patriots could have tried a draw to keep the ball in the middle of the field for a game-tying field goal attempt by Cappelletti. Instead, Songin went for pay dirt and was picked off by Gonsoulin again.

With the ball on the Denver 2 and plenty of time left on the clock, all Boston had to do was hold them in place for another shot at tying or winning the game. Instead, Denver simply would not relinquish the ball. Forward they ground until a 15-yard clipping penalty brought the ball back to their own 26. On second and 18, this would have been the perfect moment for the Patriots to hold firm and regain possession. Instead, Mingo killed them with a devastating 39-yard run. Denver never did give up possession. They kept the final drive going for 17 plays to finish off the upset.

In the end, winning or losing wasn't really the story; it was that the game was played at all.

THE REST OF THE WAY

The 1960 Broncos turned out to be somewhere between their atrocious showing in the preseason and the promise they displayed on opening night. They finished the year at 4–9–1 and had the worst point differential in the new league. The Patriots' 10 points turned out to be the fewest they allowed in any game. They could have very easily finished 3–11, except they mounted two of the greatest comebacks in football history in a little over a month. On October 23, the Patriots traveled to Denver for their rematch and built a 24–0 lead. There were three minutes to go in the third quarter when the Broncos finally got on the board, scoring two touchdowns in short order. They pushed across 17 more points in the final frame to secure the 31–24 victory. On November 27, the Buffalo Bills came in for a visit and had their hosts on the ropes, 38–7, late in the third quarter. Tripucka threw three touchdown passes, and Gene Mingo kicked a field goal with four seconds left to cap a 24-point fourth quarter and notch the 38–38 tie. No team has ever come back from a larger deficit in the regular season. (Three decades later, the Bills erased a 32-point hole to beat the Oilers in the playoffs.)

The Patriots would fare little better, finishing 5–9 and scoring the fewest points in the AFL. Boston appeared to have things figured out when their record stood at 5–5, but four convincing losses to close the season sent them to the bottom of the Eastern Division. The highlight of their first year, aside from the fact that it was taking place, was a 35–0 road win over the eventual Western Division champion Los Angeles Chargers. The Pats also pasted a very good Dallas team 42–14, the worst loss of the season for the Texans.

Another season highlight came at the turnstiles. The team's ticket office at Kenmore Square was working overtime during Thanksgiving week as the Patriots recorded the first-ever sellout in American Football League history on Friday, November 25. A crowd of 27,123 was on hand to see the future champion Houston Oilers beat the home team, 24–10.

But it is the first game that lingers longest in the collective consciousness of the upstart league.

Joe Collier: We didn't know we were making history at the time. We had a hard time making it financially. In the off-season the coaches would work on football in the mornings and in the afternoon we'd work at Suffolk Downs. It was an exciting time and I think the organization did as good a job as they could at the time getting things going for the American Football League. Looking back on it, I'm very happy I was part of it. I'd like to do it all again.

Larry Garron: History was made that night. One of the security guys at the gate said to me, "There's a little kid here who wants to get in." I said, "Well, he's my son." My sons were still in diapers at that time, but the guard didn't know that, so he let him in. Believe it or not, twenty years later I got a card from that kid and his family. I didn't even know the kid. We were just trying to let people in to watch the game. The kid had walked all the way from Cambridge. I said, "He may as well watch the game."

The inaugural game turned out not to be predictive of what the AFL would be in its early seasons: a wide-open confederation of high-scoring teams. (See "The Highest-Scoring Seasons Ever," on page 25.) In fact, this game would prove to have the third-fewest points of the 1960 season. The lowest-scoring game would come two weeks later when the Patriots were shut out by the Bills, 13–0. On September 25, the Chargers visited the Texans and were blanked, 17–0. In fact, the league got higher scoring as it went along. In September, the teams averaged 19.9 points per game. The next month it was 23.1. In November it was 26.4, and for December, 27.2.

In another case of reverse foreshadowing, it turned out that the two teams that opened the AFL would be the only two of the original eight franchises that would *not* win a title during the 10-year existence of the league. The Broncos wouldn't finish over .500 until 1973, their fourth season in the NFL. The Patriots, at least, did get to play for the AFL title once, as we will see in the next chapter.

APPENDICES

The Patriots Preceders

The nascent NFL was a primarily Midwestern and provincial affair. (The Chicago Cardinals, for instance, played only one game outside of the state of Illinois from 1920 to 1925.) Most regions of the country, including New England, were not part of the mix. It wasn't until the sixth year of operations that an NFL team came to the area. The Providence Steam Rollers gained membership in 1925 and won the league title in 1928. They soon fell on hard times and played their last league game in 1931. The other NFL entry in the region was the Hartford Blues. They were an independent team that employed all of Notre Dame's famous Four Horsemen (Jim Crowley, Elmer Layden, Don Miller, and Harry Stuhldreher) in 1925. By the time they entered the NFL the next year, however, none of the four were around, and the team went 3–7. They left the league and went back to the independent wars.

Before the Patriots, a variety of Boston-area teams toiled in the adolescent NFL or in various upstart professional leagues that came to nothing. By the time the Patriots came along, New England had spent half of the first 40 years of the history of professional football without a representative team at that level. In view of the ongoing rivalry between the cities, it's interesting that almost all of these teams had some kind of tie to New York City.

Boston Bulldogs (American Football League, version I; 1926)

An entire football league built around one player is an odd enterprise, but that's what the first congregation to bear the name American Football League was: a place for Red Grange to showcase his talents (although Wildcat Wilson of the traveling Los Angeles club was also considered a draw). Grange and his team, the New York Yankees, had to play against somebody, so a roster of clubs like the Boston Bulldogs were assembled for the purpose. Boston played only two home games. The first was a 13–0 loss to the Grangemen at Fenway Park, the second a 21–0 beating by Los Angeles at Braves Field. The Bulldogs did not finish the season, ceasing operations after going 2–4. Only four of the league's nine teams played a full schedule, and 1926 marked its only year of existence.

Boston Bulldogs (National Football League; 1929)

This squad started life in Pottsville, Pennsylvania, in the early twenties as an independent club. By 1924, they were known as the Maroons and were the terrors of the Anthracite League. The next season, they joined the NFL and won the championship with a 10–2 record, only to have it stripped for violating the territorial rights of Philadelphia's Frankford Yellow Jackets. They were kicked out of the league, too, but reinstated because it was feared they would align themselves with Red Grange's AFL. Another good season was followed by two increasingly dismal ones, and the club was sold and moved to Boston for the '29 campaign. Five players—inaugural Hall of Famer Pete Henry not among them—made the move with the club. The team's exposure in Boston was very brief. Only three of their eight games were played there. Two of their "home" games took place at their old stomping grounds in Pottsville. They went 2–1 in Boston, 2–0 in Pottsville, and 0–3 on the road.

Boston Braves/Redskins (National Football League; 1932–36)

The first serious attempt by the NFL to place a team in Boston finally came in 1932 when a new franchise was awarded to George Preston Marshall and three other owners. Called the Braves because they used the field owned by the National League baseball entry of the same name, they started off well enough on the field, posting .500 records in each of their first three seasons. But the teams' finances worsened, and Marshall's co-owners soon sold their stakes, forcing Marshall to soldier on alone. By 1936, when the Braves won the Eastern Division, attendance was flagging at Fenway Park (where Marshall had moved the team after its first season, renaming it the Redskins). So, fearing another weak gate, Marshall moved the Championship Game to the Polo Grounds, in New York, where Boston lost to the Green Bay Packers, 21–6. For Marshall, there could be no going back to Beantown after that decision, so he moved to Washington before the 1937 season. Boston fans missed out on a golden age of Redskins football as they added Sammy Baugh in the draft just as they were leaving and finished with winning records in each of the next nine seasons, winning two championships in the process.

Boston Shamrocks (American Football League; 1936–37)

The second AFL was started by another man with deep New York ties: former Giants personnel director and minority owner Dr. Harry March. Although he was once generally referred to as "the Father of Professional Football" (in 1936, *Time* magazine credited him with helping to organize the NFL), March has never been enshrined in the Pro Football Hall of Fame and today is largely forgotten.

After writing what is generally considered the first history of pro football, based almost entirely on his recollections about being present at the creation in Ohio at the turn of the century (one that has since been discounted by diligent modern football historians for its gross inaccuracies), March, now divested of his Giants holdings, set about creating the upstart American Football League, a bold undertaking in the midst of the Great Depression.

The most successful team on the field in March's new enterprise was the Boston entry, the Shamrocks, who went 8–3. When the season was over, they embarked on a barnstorming tour of the Southeast with one of the league's other strong teams, the New York Yankees. The Shamrocks' success helped convince Marshall to take the Redskins south.

Heading into the second AFL season, Boston lost one of its top players, Hank Soar, to the Giants. Soar, best known to history as a National League umpire, caught the game-winning touchdown pass in the 1938 Championship Game for the Giants and is the only member of the '36 champion Shamrocks to carve out a significant career in that NFL. The second season of the AFL consisted of a grand total of 19 games. The Shamrocks played in seven of them, winning two. Their season ended on the West Coast with a 45–26 loss to the undefeated Los Angeles Bulldogs, followed by a 41–0 exhibition whitewashing at the hands of the Salinas Packers. The league did not answer the bell for a third season, at least not in any kind of previously recognizable form, though there would soon be yet another try.

Boston Bears (American Football League; 1940)

The Bears were a decent team on the field (going 5–4–1), and they had their moments at the gate, drawing 8,000 and 10,000 in back-to-back wins over the New York Yankees and Buffalo Indians on consecutive Sundays in October. Still, it was not enough to keep the team solvent, and they opted out of the loop for the 1941 season with the proviso that they might return in 1942. America's entry into World War II put an end to any thoughts of continuing the league, however.

Boston Yanks (National Football League; 1944–48)

New England got another shot at the NFL with a franchise that morphed out of the Brooklyn Tigers during World War II and then into the New York Yanks after they left Boston in 1949. It was a team of little accomplishment, winning just 14 games in the five years it was affiliated with Boston. Such was the qualitative nature of its roster that, after the team went to New York, its main players averaged only 12 games apiece for the remainder of their careers. Not only that, but the bulk of those games were spent with the Yanks in New York, where they performed just as poorly as they had in Boston. Only one member of the '48 team, Mike Jarmoluk, would carve out a genuine career in the NFL. The big lineman won a championship with the Eagles in 1949 and played a total of 93 games with them. Other than a handful of games, the rest of the most active members of the '48 Boston club held no appeal for anyone beyond the team's successor in New York—a club that ceased to function after the 1951 season.

The Highest-Scoring Seasons Ever

As early AFL games would go, Patriots–Broncos turned out to be a low-scoring affair—one of the dozen or so lowest of the league's first three seasons. It's no wonder, since the first two years of the American Football League were the highest-scoring in major league professional football history. In fact, half of the AFL's 10 seasons are in the top 10 highest-scoring seasons ever. There are a number of reasons why the AFL succeeded when so many other nascent leagues failed, but what happened on the scoreboard was certainly a factor.

This list details the average number of points scored per team per game in the 10 most prolific scoring years in football history.

Points	Year	League
24.2	1961	American Football League
24.0	1960	American Football League
23.2	1948	National Football League
23.1	1965	National Football League
23.1	1964	American Football League
23.0	1963	American Football League
23.0	1962	American Football League
22.9	1950	National Football League
22.8	1948	All-American Football Conference
22.6	1958	National Football League

The recent seasons closest to making this list are 2008 and 2010, when teams averaged 22.0 points per game, and 2011 with 22.2.

Pro Football Leagues: The Inaugural Games

Below are listed the debuts of nine leagues apart from the Patriots–Broncos opener for the AFL in 1960. Some went on to glory, but most never built on their opening-day excitement.

National Football League (October 3, 1920, or October 1, 1922)

For a long time, 1920 was considered the first season of the NFL, even though the league was then called the American Professional Football Association. It became known as the National Football League in 1922, and began play that year on October 1 with a slate of eight games. In the three contests involving franchises that survive to this day, the Chicago Bears beat the Racine Legion, 6–0, in Racine, the Chicago Cardinals hosted the Milwaukee Badgers and shut them out, 3–0, and the Green Bay Packers visited the Rock Island Independents and were beaten 19–14.

A good reason to treat the 1920 season as something apart from the

NFL is that games against nonleague teams were counted in the members' win-loss records. Fully 55 percent of the games played came against these independent teams, and APFA members racked up a 34–6–10 record against them. However, there are also good reasons to consider this the first season of the NFL. For one thing, that's how the NFL itself sees it. The first AFPA contests that featured league members versus other league members took place on October 3, 1920, with the Columbus Panhandles visiting the Dayton Triangles and losing, 14–0, and the Rock Island Independents pasting the Muncie Flyers, 45–0.

Which of these games kicked off first? As Bob Braunwart and Bob Carroll wrote in *The Coffin Corner,* "A glance at a map of the Midwest will show that Dayton is in the Eastern Time Zone and Rock Island is in the Central. We might then guess that the Dayton game began an hour earlier—making it the first. And we might be right. But we might also be wrong. Kickoff times were far from standardized in 1920, and, as yet, no researcher has come forward with the exact kickoff time for either game. And we don't even want to think about Daylight Saving Time!"

American Football League I (September 26, 1926)
Some 22,000 fans were on hand to see Red Grange and the Yankees come up empty against the hometown Cleveland Panthers—a team that played its games in an amusement park and would fold after only five contests. Between his stint with the Bears in 1925 and his time as the centerpiece of the new AFL in 1926, Grange was asked to play an incredible number of games. His biggest moment in this game, a 10–0 loss, was a 21-yard punt return. He was riding the bench in the second half when New York mounted its biggest threat. In other inaugural-day AFL action, the Newark Bears tied the Chicago Bulls, 7–7, and the Rock Island Independents downed the Los Angeles Wildcats, 7–3, which means that Rock Island was present at the creation of two different leagues.

American Football League II (September 20, 1936)
The league was still playing a bit of musical franchises right up to the start of the season before finally settling its erstwhile Rochester franchise

in Brooklyn. The New York Yankees were supposed to travel to Cleveland to open on September 20 as well, but that game was pushed back, leaving the Syracuse Braves as hosts of the league inaugural. Their star attraction was former New York Giant and future Hall of Famer Red Badgro. Two years before, he had led the NFL in receptions with 16. He could do little to help in this game, though, as the eventual champion Boston Shamrocks came away with the 14–3 victory.

American Football League III (September 15, 1940)
In a game that would prove to be a contest against the league's two best teams, the Columbus Bullies hosted the Milwaukee Chiefs and lost, 14–2. It would be their only defeat of the season as they went 8–1–1 and won the league title, while the Chiefs went 7–2–0 and claimed second place. Boston's entry, the Bears, didn't debut until three weeks later, downing the Cincinnati Bengals, 29–7, at Fenway Park on October 6.

All-America Football Conference (September 6, 1946)
The opening game of the AAFC presaged the next four seasons: utter dominance by the Cleveland Browns. In this 44–0 destruction of the visiting Miami Seahawks, Mac Speedie scored the first touchdown on a pass from Cliff Lewis. Speedie would go on to become the most successful receiver in the short existence of the AAFC. By halftime, the Browns were up 27–0. They would score two defensive touchdowns in the fourth quarter and eventually win all four AAFC championships.

Canadian Football League (August 14, 1958)
By the time the Canadian Football League came into existence, most of its members already had long, rich traditions going back many years. As the professional game evolved in the fifties, the CFL was formed by joining the eastern and western leagues, although they did not meet in the regular season until 1961. In the first game under this new arrangement, the host Winnipeg Blue Bombers (coached by Bud Grant) downed the Edmonton Eskimos, 29–21. The two clubs would later play in the Western Finals, with Winnipeg winning two games to one, earning the chance to play the Hamilton Tiger-Cats for the first

Grey Cup awarded under the new arrangement, which they also won, 35–28.

World Football League (July 10, 1974)

The first glimpse most of the nation got of the new challenger to the post-merger NFL came on Thursday, July 11, 1974, when the New York Stars traveled to Jacksonville and lost to the Sharks, 14–7, on national television. The other 10 teams had opened the season the night before, with the host clubs winning all five contests. The Philadelphia Bell beat the Portland Storm, 33–8, the Florida Blazers nipped the Hawaiians, 8–7, the Birmingham Stallions downed the Southern California Sun, 11–7, the Chicago Fire blanked the Houston Texans, 17–0, and the Memphis Southmen routed the Detroit Wheels, 34–15. The initial pleasant surprise that the early large crowds generated soon gave way to dismay as it was learned that a number of the teams—especially Philadelphia—were generously handing out free tickets. It was a surprise that the league made it through its first season, and an even bigger surprise that it answered the bell for year two, though it ultimately lasted only 60 games into the second campaign.

United States Football League (March 6, 1983)

The first game to finish on the league's opening Sunday was the Tampa Bay Bandits–Boston Breakers contest, which also featured the league's first touchdown. That score came when the Bandits' John Reaves, who threw for 358 yards on the day, connected with Ricky Williams for a six-yard TD pass. The Bandits eventually prevailed, 17–14. Both teams went on to finish 11–7.

XFL (February 3, 2001)

There were two games scheduled on the opening night of the ill-fated XFL. The one that most people saw was telecast from sold-out Sam Boyd Stadium in Las Vegas, where the Outlaws downed the visiting New York/New Jersey Hitmen, 19–0. In the backup game, which NBC switched to in the fourth quarter because it was closer, the Orlando Rage got past the Chicago Enforcers, 33–29. The first-night ratings were excellent, but the reviews were not so promising. A typical response was that of Richard Sandomir, who wrote in *The New York Times*, "It was bad football called by bad announcers backed by bad entertainment." Perhaps, but the XFL's main problem was failing to grasp the obvious: People like scoring. For all its other failings, the XFL did not deliver many points, averaging just 17.3 points per game. Only once since World War II (1977) has the NFL had such a paucity of scoring.

Other Boston-Area Sports Inaugurals

These are the humble beginnings of sporting endeavors that have gone on to become institutions.

Harvard Football (June 4, 1875)

Harvard lost to Tufts, 1–0, at Jarvis Field. It has been argued that this, not the Rutgers–Princeton game of 1869, is the actual first intercollegiate football game, an argument based on this game's stronger resemblance to modern football.

Boston Braves (né Red Stockings, né Red Caps) (May 5, 1871)

Beginning life in the National Association as the Red Stockings, they opened the season with a 20–18 win over the Washington Olympics at the Olympics Grounds. On May 16, they played their first home game, hosting the Troy Haymakers at the South End Grounds and losing, 29–14. In 1876, the association was supplanted by the National League. By then more generally known as the Red Caps, Boston would go through many names before settling on Braves and moving to Milwaukee in 1953 and then Atlanta in 1966. Their debut in the new National League came on April 22, 1876, when they beat the Philadelphia Athletics, 6–5, at the Jefferson Street Grounds in Philadelphia. Their National League home opener was a 3–2 loss to the Hartford Dark Blues at the South End Grounds.

Boston Marathon (April 19, 1897)

John J. McDermott won the inaugural race, besting a field of 14 other runners.

Boston Red Sox (April 26, 1901)

Long before the Red Sox name stuck, Boston opened the first American League season with a 10–6 loss to the Baltimore Orioles (who would move to New York two years later and eventually come to be called the Yankees) at Oriole Park. Their first home game came two weeks later when they hosted Connie Mack's Philadelphia Athletics at the Huntington Avenue Grounds and punished them, 12–4.

Boston Bruins (December 1, 1924)

The Bruins made their NHL debut with a 2–1 win over the Montreal Maroons on opening night. They would lose their next 11 games and 18 of their first 20.

Boston Braves/Redskins (October 2, 1932)

They would become known as the Redskins the following season and then move to Washington in 1937, but to start things, the Braves hosted the Brooklyn Dodgers and lost, 14–0.

Boston Celtics (November 2, 1946)

The Celts dropped their first-ever game, to the Providence Steamrollers by the score of 59–53 at the Rhode Island Auditorium, while they were members of the Basketball Association of America. The first regular-season game they played at Boston Garden was a 57–55 loss to the Chicago Stags. Their NBA inaugural was a 98–83 loss to the Sheboygan Red Skins at the Sheboygan Municipal Auditorium and Armory on November 3, 1949. A week later, they also lost their first Garden appearance as an NBA team, falling to the Minneapolis Lakers, 98–84.

The Beanpot (December 26, 1952)

The annual showdown for bragging rights to college hockey in Boston features Harvard University, Boston University, Northeastern University, and Boston College. The two-round tournament began at Boston (now Matthews) Arena and moved to Boston Garden for the second installment, remaining there until the building was brought down in 1995. Harvard nabbed the first Beanpot with a 7–4 victory over BU, but since then the Terriers have dominated the tournament.

New England Revolution (April 13, 1996)

One of Major League Soccer's original franchises, the Revolution lost their opener to the Tampa Bay Mutiny at Tampa Stadium, 3–2. Their first home game turned out much better as the Revs beat D.C. United, 2–1, in a shootout at Foxboro Stadium.

Boston Patriots at Buffalo Bills

AFL EASTERN DIVISION TITLE GAME
December 28, 1963

	1	2	3	4	F
Boston Patriots	10	6	0	10	26
Buffalo Bills	0	0	8	0	8

It is a bit ironic that, in their first five seasons, the Patriots rang up three excellent records and never made the playoffs but, in a season where they just scraped over .500, they got to play for the championship. Such was life in the small divisions of the early NFL.

THE PATRIOTS

After going 9–4–1 in both 1961 and 1962 and being outdistanced by Houston Oilers teams with much better point differentials but only slightly better win-loss records, the Pats found themselves in a tight race in 1963, when Houston dropped back to the pack. The Eastern Division was populated with four solid teams, but none was consistently able to remain on top. In those years, the standard wisdom held true: Any team could win on any given Sunday. (See "The Most Tightly Bunched Divisions of All Time, on page 54.)

In the end, the Kansas City Chiefs of the Western Division would play a major role in determining the outcome of things back east. It was the Chiefs who made spirited comebacks against two of the top teams in the Eastern Division and stepped up in the Patriots' last game of the season to force the first tiebreaker in AFL history.

The Pats had changed coaches five games into the 1961 season, promoting Mike Holovak to the job after cutting Lou Saban adrift. Holovak is not well known today, but those who observed him and played for him came away impressed.

Will McDonough wrote of Holovak: "Billy Sullivan founded the Patriots, but the guy who saved them was Holovak. It was his personality, and the love his players had for him, that kept the team afloat in its first decade of existence."

Larry Eisenhauer: When Mike took over, there was kind of a settling down. He reinforced the fact that "these are my guys. You are my guys. We're going to play with you. We're going to win with you." The team kind of relaxed a little bit. We played better. Mike was a player's coach. He was very knowledgeable as a defensive coach but also as an offensive coach. He had his own ideas, but he also listened to what the players had to say about offensive plays, et cetera, and worked them into the offense.

Larry Garron: Mike changed it around because Mike was a people person. Lou was stern. He was an executive. If you didn't get it done, you'd hear a couple of *bleep-bleep-bleeps* and that was it. Mike would go, "Okay, guys, this is what we need to do. If you have any problems, you come and see me." He knew the personalities of the players, and this is what he played on. Once he did that, everybody started to fall into place. He'd say, "This is what you're capable of doing—know it." It was fantastic. He kept a lot of the system that we had, half of it [left over] from Lou Saban, which was good. Then he introduced his method of coaching and leadership. More than anything else, his leadership was what made the difference.

Patrick Sullivan: What a terrific coach Mike Holovak was. He put together some great football teams. Mike really knew the players and knew the game. He was a marvelous guy. I worked for him for years and I never heard him use a foul word.

The '63 Patriots had a middle-of-the-pack offensive unit matched with a defense that was, arguably, the best in the AFL. It is also one of the best in team history.

Ron Hall: We had Fred Bruney and Marion Campbell coaching that defense in '63. They put in the safety blitz. We had Bob Dee, Larry Eisenhauer, Houston Antwine and Jimmy Hunt in the front line, and they were outstanding. Quick. We had Nick Buoniconti leading linebackers. With Jack Rudolph and Tom Addison, we led the league that year in rushing defense. We were very hard and tough to run against that year. We enjoyed going into the defensive meetings every week to see what Bruney and Campbell were going to cook up for us. We were using some of the 3-5 defense that they use today. We were dropping Bob Dee off the line, using him as a linebacker. It was an exciting time for us defensively with those guys coaching us.

The Patriots opened the season by hammering the Jets at home, 38–14. A stretch of four straight road games followed and, while all were close, Boston lost three of them, including a tough 17–14 contest in San Diego. They got back over .500 with consecutive home wins against the Raiders and Broncos before having a tough time in Buffalo against the Bills in their eighth game.

Jack Kemp scored from the 1-yard line on three different occasions, and the Bills had a 21–7 lead with less than a quarter to play. The Patriots roared back, though. When Babe Parilli hit Art Graham for a 77-yard scoring strike to tie the game at 21, it seemed as if Boston had done enough to at least come away with a tie—especially when the Bills found themselves on their own 28 with just 28 seconds to play. But Kemp faded back and lofted a 47-yard pass to Charley Ferguson, who caught it in stride at the Patriots' 25 and streaked into the end zone for the winning touchdown. Had the tie held, Boston would have won the division outright; but it was not to be.

Boston took it out on Houston the next week, humbling them 45–3, and followed that up with an excellent defensive showing against the league's highest-scoring offense when the Chargers visited the Fens. Although the Patriots lost both regular-season games to San Diego, they held them to just 24 points in the process. Against the other six teams in the league, the Chargers averaged 31 points a game, which made Boston's performance against them in the AFL Championship Game that much more surprising.

Their next game was against the Chiefs, who decided that their regular quarterback, Len Dawson, needed a game on the bench. In his place, Hank Stram put Eddie Wilson, who was making his first big-league start. As it turned out, it would be one of only two he ever made—the other one playing for the Patriots. Both his starts ended in ties.

Aside from getting dumped in the end zone for a safety, Wilson acquitted himself fairly well, throwing two touchdown passes and setting up the Chiefs' other two scores with his arm as well. The second TD pass came with the Chiefs trailing 24–17 in the fourth quarter, once again costing the Patriots a late lead and a clean win of the division.

The Patriots had another fine defensive outing in their next game, shutting out the Bills in the second half and holding Jack Kemp to a 19–for–46 day. The 17–7 win moved them to 6–5–1. They improved to 7–5–1 when they went to Houston and dismantled the Oilers, 46–28, as the defense put 16 points on the board. Nick Buoniconti returned a fumble for a touchdown, and Bob Suci did the same with an interception. Oilers quarterback Jacky Lee was brought down in the end zone for the other two points.

With a game to go, the Patriots controlled their own destiny.

THE OPPONENT

The 1963 Buffalo Bills were a team on the verge of a mini-dynasty. The year before, Lou Saban, late of the Patriots, had taken over for the team's inaugural coach, Buster Ramsey, and had gotten off to a 0–5 start. After that, though, his charges went 7–1–1 and had continued to play well in '63. They would go on to win the league title in both 1964 and 1965 under Saban and miss going to the first Super Bowl after the '66 season by one game, a loss to the Kansas City Chiefs in the AFL Championship. By then Joe Collier was at the helm.

Quarterbacking the Bills was Jack Kemp, whom they had been able to claim off waivers from San Diego in 1962; the Chargers had foolishly tried to stash him there because he had broken two fingers. The future congressman had led San Diego to Western Division titles in both 1960 and 1961 and was well regarded for his leadership. In '63,

Kemp threw 13 TDs and 20 interceptions—an unappealing stat by today's pass-happy standards. But in the early days of the AFL, those were the numbers of a confident, talented quarterback with the ability to throw the ball and open up the offense. Kemp's yards-per-pass rate of 7.6 was second-best in the league behind Tobin Rote of the Chargers, as were his 2,910 yards in the air.

Backing Kemp was Daryle Lamonica, the rookie from Notre Dame who would start two games in 1963 and win both, the first of his remarkable 66–16–6 career starting record. He was also the team's primary punter. The busiest Bills back by far was the enigmatic Cookie Gilchrist. He had gotten his start as a professional in the fifties when he went right from high school to pro football in Canada. He was a free spirit who infamously took himself out of a game against the Patriots in 1964 because he thought he wasn't getting enough carries. He had played both ways in the Canadian Football League and was known as an excellent blocker. Banged up to start the 1963 season, he was still third in the AFL with 979 yards rushing and also scored 14 touchdowns.

Jack Rudolph: Cookie Gilchrist, a 250-pound running back for Buffalo, was hard to tackle when it was warm, and I could imagine what it was going to be like to tackle him with the damn weather the way it was in Buffalo.

Houston Antwine: Cookie was a doggone monster of a runner. On a kickoff one time, I was on the kicking team and Cookie was an up back. I was coming down the field and I saw him. He was smoking right down the middle. All of a sudden it was like no one was there but him and me. He was coming at me and I was coming at him, full steam. I had made it up in my mind, I said, *This guy cannot run over me. I can't let him do that. I have to really turn loose on him.* So I hit the man. I saw white stars. I know he did, too. We both fell down on the ground. I think both of us were knocked out for a second or two. He was the one big challenge to me. As he was smoking down the field I remembered that old song they'd sing about him: "Lookie, lookie, here comes Cookie!"

Tom Yewcic: When we played them at Fenway Park in a big game earlier in the season, we had Ross O'Hanley playing strong safety and Ron Hall playing free safety. So Buffalo ran a draw in the middle of the field. And they opened up the hole and Cookie went right up the middle. Hall and O'Hanley both converged and hit him head-on. He split both guys, knocked them out, and ran for a big gain. They brought Hall and O'Hanley to the bench, and they were pretty woozy. Coach Holovak came over and said, "You guys better quit getting knocked out on me."

The Pats' primary receiver was Bill Miller, who caught 69 passes, including 12 in one game against Oakland. Flanker Elbert Dubenion led the team with 959 reception yards on 53 catches, his career high. Ernie Warlick was a highly regarded tight end who was an AFL All-Star in each of his four seasons with the Bills. Anchoring the offensive line was five-time All-Star Stew Barber, who manned left tackle, and left guard Billy Shaw, himself an All-Star in eight of his nine seasons in the league and a Hall of Fame inductee in 1999.

The Bills' defensive standouts were Mike Stratton at right linebacker, Tom Sestak at right tackle, and Willie West at left cornerback. Up front, Buffalo also had Ron McDole, playing in the third year of a career that would stretch all the way to 1978.

As they had in 1962, in their first year under Saban, the Bills got off to a rough start in 1963. By week four, they were 0–3–1. Their tie had come in the home opener against Kansas City, when they blew a 17-point third-quarter lead. Two missed extra points and a safety caused by a muffed punt could have made the difference for Buffalo, not only for the game but for the entire campaign. When a season ends in a tiebreaker game, such incidents take on greater significance. The Bills finally got in the win column in their fifth game, a 12–0 shutout of a Raiders team that would later score more than 40 points three times in the 1963 season. In their next game, the Bills built a late lead on the Chiefs that they did not allow to get away. They won three of their next four. Along the way, they lost promising rookie halfback Roger Kochman—who was averaging almost five yards per carry—to a career-ending knee injury that was so horrific, he very nearly lost his leg.

At 5–4–1, the Bills were just a hair behind the 6–4 Oilers for the lead in the Eastern Division, but losses to the Chargers and Patriots put them in a bad spot with two weeks left in the season. On Sunday, December 8, the New York Jets came to town, and Cookie Gilchrist made them pay for coming upstate. He rushed for 243 yards and scored five touchdowns, and would have had even more but for a motion penalty that nullified a 65-yard run. The Bills prevailed, 45–14, and were right back in the thick of it with one game left to be played.

THE DOGFIGHT

Down the stretch in 1963, the AFL Eastern Division was as tight as could be. At the conclusion of play on Sunday, December 8, any of the four teams still had a chance at the title or, at least, a chance to participate in a tiebreaker game. The standings looked like this:

	W	L	T
Boston Patriots	7	5	1
Houston Oilers	6	6	0
Buffalo Bills	6	6	1
New York Jets	5	6	1

Boston had one game remaining in Kansas City, while Buffalo had one left against the Jets. The Jets also had to travel to Kansas City a week after Boston went there. Houston was scheduled to close out against San Diego at home and Oakland on the road.

With the four teams so close together in the standings, anything seemed possible. The Patriots knew all they had to do was win against Kansas City and the division was theirs. But they couldn't pull it together.

The Chiefs had won the league title as the Dallas Texans in 1962, but had a midseason swoon in their first year in Kansas City that pushed them out of the playoff picture. They had seven winless games that took them from 2–1–1 to 2–7–2. In the season's final weeks, though, they played championship football, crushing the Broncos, 52–21 (after having destroyed them, 59–7, on opening day), and then derailing the Pats, 35–3, on Saturday, December 14. With a windchill factor below zero, Boston couldn't get anything going, while Len Dawson, long since reinstated after the Eddie Wilson interlude, threw for three touchdowns and scored another on a 43-yard run. It was also in this game that Parilli had the very worst outing of his entire career. He was just 7 for 22 and threw five interceptions. His passer rating on the day was an abysmal 1.5.

Meanwhile, the Bills eliminated the Jets with a 19–10 victory in the last professional football game ever played at the Polo Grounds. Buffalo and Boston were now finished with their schedules, ending up with identical 7–6–1 records, while Houston still had two games to go, leaving both the Pats and Bills to sweat out the result of the next day's Oilers game against San Diego.

The Western Division–leading Chargers obliged by intercepting three George Blanda passes in the second quarter, each of which set up a score. They led at the half 17–7 and won going away, 20–14, eliminating the Oilers from the playoffs for the first time since the AFL was formed in 1960. The stage was set for the league's first tiebreaker playoff.

THE GAME

Ron Hall: The previous two years, we felt we had the best team in the East; our record just didn't show it. We had just finished out of the money. We felt like here we were with a third opportunity to win the championship. We went in there really ready to play. We'd always matched up well with Buffalo. We felt like we had a great opportunity to win.

Larry Eisenhauer: They had a fantastic team. They were just loaded. We didn't have a lot of those name stars like they had. You may call us the ragtag bunch of Patriots. That's how we view ourselves to this day. We wanted to kick the crap out of them. We had a fierce rivalry against them.

Patrick Sullivan: We were staying at the Statler Hilton hotel, in Buffalo. The night before the game, Bills owner Ralph Wilson paid a visit. The AFL regulations at that time said that if you placed a guy on injured reserve, he was out for the balance of the calendar year. Ron Burton had been out with a back injury, but he was cleared to play in this game. Ralph was livid. He knew what a threat Burton could be, so he didn't want him playing. I had just turned 10. I was standing there in the lobby with my dad, and Ralph is screaming at him. Next thing you know there's some pushing and shoving. A bunch of the ballplayers had to jump in between them. It got pretty hot, pretty close to a fistfight between my dad and Ralph.

Buffalo in late December is an icy, snowy, frigid place, and 1963 was no exception. There were 50 tons of hay on the field to keep it in playable shape.

Jack Rudolph: We flew over Niagara Falls, and maybe the bottom ten feet of the falls were not frozen. I'm going to say that 90 percent of that falls was frozen over. We knew then we were going to be in for a cold game.

Houston Antwine: The first thing I noticed when we went out on the field to warm up was that the fans were in the stands shoveling snow. I mean big shovels full of snow. I said, "Man, they paid to come and sit here to see this." But the weather wasn't that bad apart from the snow.

Gino Cappelletti: Whenever you got to whatever city you're playing, first thing you do is go on their facility and have a light workout. So we go out there, and there's no place to run. All they did is they had a track around the field and then they pushed off some snow in the end zone. So all we had was a 10-yard area, and then the bowl of the track, maybe another 12 yards, and that was it. We tried to run a little practice, and couldn't do it. So now they're coming in with the plows and the shovels and start bringing in a lot of hay to put on the sideline.

Jack Rudolph: We had regular cleats, and they sent out thirty-three pairs of tennis shoes so we could get a little bit better traction than what we were getting with the cleats, because that was just no traction at all.

Larry Eisenhauer: Bob Dee tried on all different footwear. First, he had cleats on and they didn't work. Then he tried sneakers, and they didn't work. Then he tried one cleat and one sneaker. That didn't work.

Babe Parilli: Any time you go to Buffalo that time of year, you got to expect snow, ice, or whatever. And I think we had a combination of everything. I remember Jack Kemp warming up, and he had sneakers on. And I watched him warm up. He went back, he was dropping back, and I noticed he was slipping. Well, I had sneakers, and I went in and changed to cleats because I had a little more traction. So I started out and I thought, This has got to help me out a little bit— and it did.

Jack Rudolph: I know that had to be one of the coldest games that we ever had because it snowed during the ballgame. They had big piles of snow on the sidelines they had taken off before the game started. They had these plumb bobs that people held ten yards from where the last ball was stopped, and they put a purple plumb-bob line across the field. A crew was brushing off the yard markers. People in the stands were making snowballs and throwing them at the players. It was just kind of a surreal experience for me because, being from down south, I had never played a game in the snow before.

Houston Antwine: If you wanted to play football, that was the game to be in. Because you really had to dig down deep and bring out everything that you had.

Oddly, it was the Bills who felt like they were out of their element. As Buffalo linebacker Mike Stratton recalled in Jeffrey J. Miller's *Rockin' the Rockpile,* "Boston came in to a frozen field and they were dressed for it and had the right kind of shoes and everything."

Bills players tried tennis shoes but could get no traction. Then they put socks over the tennis shoes and found that did not remedy the situation. Their safety, George Saimes, even resorted to wearing street shoes on the field.

Despite the teams' identical records, Buffalo was installed as 2½-point favorites. Their two strong performances against the Jets had certainly informed that decision, as had the Patriots' no-show effort against Kansas City on the last weekend of the season. Mostly, though, it was the perceived home-field advantage enjoyed by the Bills. They certainly didn't go out of their way to make visiting teams feel welcome at War Memorial Stadium.

Larry Garron: They did everything to shake our confidence. The locker room was a small, crampy place. Windows were open, and it was freezing. Even before that, we were told we're going to be sleeping overnight and we were told don't mess up the beds! Then, when we got to the locker room, we were cramped in there. The windows were out, broken, and we were saying we're going to have to do something about this. I said, "The only way we can do that is on the field." When we got back to the locker room after the half, some kids had broken in and stolen our money and goodies that we had with us. That was never reported.

Patrick Sullivan: War Memorial Stadium was not a modern stadium. The stairway the visiting team used was so narrow, you couldn't get up there with shoulder pads on. Down in that tunnel, it had to be below zero in there. When the guys finished at halftime, they had to take their pads off to get up there. They had to do the same at the end of the game.

The Bills won the toss and elected to receive. Their talented speedster El Dubenion took the ball at the 15 and had made great progress out to the 33 when he was hit by a host of Patriots who had penetrated the Bills' wedge. Dubenion coughed up the football.

"I was getting ready to make a move, and the next thing I know

43

those guys are down there killing me. That's what caused me to fumble." Reserve running back Billy Lott came up with the ball, and the Patriots set up shop in excellent field position. In the Boston backfield was a surprise.

Ron Hall: Ron Burton had been out all season. He had been one of our leading ball carriers the previous two seasons. We had missed him the whole season. That was the first game we had him back. He had a back problem. On the first play from scrimmage, he broke a fourteen-yard run. He looked like his old self. We were off and running after that. That just picked everybody up when they saw Ron was ready to go. He had one of his best games as far as we were concerned, because it was such an important game.

Burton had been missing since the first quarter of the Patriots' exhibition game against Oakland way back in August. Doctors performed a spondylodesis (spinal fusion) to relieve his pain. After four months of recovery, he was ready to come back, so the Pats asked permission for reinstatement on December 16. The Bills protested later, but AFL commissioner Joe Foss gave his approval. So Burton's first action of the 1963 season came in the playoffs.

Larry Garron: Ron Burton being allowed to play was a key to that championship game; we could work in tandem. Ronnie and I talked about it—just like Jim Nance and I would a few years later. They'd say, "Hey, you got to help me here." I'd say, "Okay. I'd hook you there." Ronnie was the same way. I'd say, "Whenever these guys come over here, we'll switch and block." The only time that he'd block, which was a key time, was when Babe needed time to get a pass off to myself or Gino. That was a key time overlooked by many people. Even in his condition, Ron was able to give a lot of good blocks to allow Babe to get those passes off.

Ron Hall: When I saw that, I had a very confident feeling. Up until that point I wasn't sure, but when I saw that with him and Garron in there and Babe throwing the ball, I felt we were really going to move the ball.

Larry Eisenhauer: Mike ran him a couple of times, and he had some significant yardage, and Buffalo was surprised. Buffalo keyed on Ron Burton, which opened up lanes for Larry Garron. Larry had a terrific game.

The first drive ended abruptly when Parilli was picked off by safety Ray Abruzzese at the 7. Now it was time to see what Cookie Gilchrist could do on the winter turf. On second and 8 from the Bills' 18, Kemp turned and put the ball in Cookie's gut. He'd barely taken a step when he was driven to the ground by Nick Buoniconti. It was a harbinger of things to come for both Cookie and the Bills. On the next series, Gino Cappelletti set up his own field goal with a 22-yard reception that put the ball on the Bills' 22.

Larry Garron: One of the scariest parts of the game was sitting on the bench. The people were sitting right behind us. Mike says, "Keep your helmets on." We couldn't figure out why. Mike said, "Keep your helmets on," and we did. Five minutes after we sat down, beer cans came flying, left and right.

Buffalo's next series ended with a 22-yard Daryle Lamonica punt, giving Boston the ball at their own 41. On second and 10, Parilli dumped a short pass to Garron on the left side. Linebacker John Tracey got his hands on the Pats' running back but couldn't hang on. When Garron broke out of Tracey's grasp, the stampede was on. He raced 59 yards for the touchdown, with most of the Bills' defensive unit in pursuit. Ten minutes into the game, the Pats were up 10–0.

And still the Bills could not get untracked. Two more times they punted the ball away, and both ensuing possessions resulted in Cappelletti field goals. Saban tried to shake things up by inserting Lamonica in Kemp's place, but the half ended with the two of them having completed just 5 of his 18 passes for 32 net yards. The Bills had just six yards on the ground and had been outgained 217 to 38 overall.

The third quarter turned into a battle in the middle of the field. Neither team could get into scoring position, although the Pats did have a fourth and 1 at the Buffalo 31 and went for it. Rookie defensive tackle Jim Dunaway met Garron at the line of scrimmage and denied him forward movement, giving the ball back to Buffalo. Mostly, the teams just traded punts: Yewcic kicked it away three times and Lamonica twice, while throwing an interception to Bob Dee to end their other possession. Meanwhile, the elements continued to be a factor.

Jack Rudolph: They had snowbanks piled up where they had taken snow off the field with machines, and they did that before the game started and they did it at halftime. Our defensive captain, the man who called the plays, was Tommy Addison. We were huddling up for a third down, and we noticed that Tommy is nowhere to be found. Everyone was saying, "Where the hell is Tommy; is he hurt?" What had happened was he had been run into one of those snow banks and he was almost up to his waist, and his feet were kicking out! It was amazing he didn't suffocate, but we had to go over and pull him out to get him back on the field.

Leading 16–0, the Patriots would have been happy to trade punts for the rest of the game. With just under two minutes to go in the third quarter, Yewcic seemingly buried the Bills when his punt rolled dead at the 7-yard line. It wouldn't be until the next decade that Howard Cosell would hang the "Mad Bomber" nickname on Lamonica during a *Monday Night Football* telecast, but what he did next certainly gave an indication as to what inspired that appellation.

"I just looked at him [El Dubenion] in the huddle and said, 'Can you go?'" Lamonica recalled. On first and 10, Lamonica aired one out to Dubenion at the 45. He grabbed the ball and sped away from safety man Dick Felt for the 93-yard score.

On the extra-point attempt, Lamonica knelt to take the snap while kicker Mack Yoho swung his arms in anticipation. Lamonica snared the ball, but instead of spinning the ball under his finger, he leaped up and began rolling right. He found John Tracey in the end zone for the two-point conversion.

Suddenly, after an afternoon of futility, the Bills had pulled to within a score of tying the game in a matter of moments. The 33,000 stalwart fans who had braved the elements only to watch their team denied now came alive, grateful that the AFL had adopted the collegiate-inspired two-point conversion as a post-touchdown option, while the more staid

NFL continued to use only the one-point conversion. The two-point conversion would not survive the 1970 merger; it would not be until 1994 that the NFL adopted the practice once and for all.

For those keen on the concept of "momentum," this was just the sort of play that would have created some for Buffalo. Instead, their next two possessions were reminiscent of most of those that had come before the big play. That is, they both ended in punts after three failed plays. On Boston's second possession of the fourth quarter, Parilli hit Cappelletti for 51 yards, moving the ball to the Buffalo 17. On the very next play, the Babe dumped a flare out to Garron, who brought it home for the 23–8 lead.

Babe Parilli: But the guy that made the job a lot easier for me was Larry Garron. He was one heck of a guy coming out of the backfield. He made some good little swing passes, and he made people miss, and it was instrumental in us winning the game.

Tom Yewcic: Babe had a good game, but Larry Garron had a terrific game. We had a controlled passing game. Babe was hitting guys with short passes.

Larry Garron: I used to play baseball. I pitched. On muddy, muddy days, we used to put on the baseball rubber cleats. I didn't wear my regular shoes that day. I put on little cleated baseball shoes. It gave me a better grip. I didn't slide like all the rest. I had traction. The guys kept telling me it was a dumb move. I kept saying, "Hey, guys, I used them before in college; I'll use them again."

Garron's old teammate from Western Illinois, Booker Edgerson, was the Bills' right cornerback.

Larry Garron: Booker and I always used to tease each other because we ran track together. He'd always say how he was faster than me, and I'd remind him that I qualified for the Olympics three times! But I couldn't afford to go—in those days you had to pay.

The Patriots then made things extremely difficult for the Bills when Dee picked off Lamonica at the Buffalo 33. Cappelletti soon converted his fourth field goal of the day, pushing the advantage to 18 with a little less than eight minutes to play. Kemp was brought back in and got the Bills moving. He drove them to the Boston 3-yard line before Felt and Ron Hall slapped away his next three passes. Kemp fumbled the ball away on fourth down.

The Pats brought in reserve back Harry Crump to crash the line three times and kill the clock before punting it away one last time. On their last possession, Kemp's drive to save face ended when Ross O'Hanley intercepted him in the Boston end zone.

Jack Rudolph: I think we were a little concerned about Cookie because the cold weather would make him harder to tackle, but it worked out the other way. We did a great job on defense on him in particular.

Larry Eisenhauer: Our defense was rock solid. We always had a great effort against Cookie Gilchrist. If you look at the records, he gained a hundred yards maybe once or twice against us in his entire career. We were able to bottle up him.

Gilchrist was a nonfactor on the ground. He totaled 7 yards on eight carries and caught one pass for 11. Thanks to Lamonica's bomb to Dubenion, the Bills' final tally of 301 passing yards (279 net) looks respectable, but they were picked off four times and committed a fumble on offense, plus another on special teams.

Gino Cappelletti: When we got back to Boston, the fans were out at the airport, and they were all East Boston fans because we had developed a following by practicing in East Boston. Also, we favored an Italian restaurant there. They would recognize all of us who go there. So we came off the plane and into the terminal, and the cheering and shouting, we were really excited about that. It was a nice reception and one that we enjoyed.

Jack Rudolph: The fact still remains that the Buffalo game was probably the highlight of the first four years of the Patriots' existence.

APPENDICES

Disaster in San Diego

The joy that beating the Bills gave the team and their fans was short-lived. No sooner were they out of the freezer than they found themselves in the frying pan, taking on the best team in the league: the Western Division champion San Diego Chargers and their innovative coach, Sid Gillman.

Larry Eisenhauer: We had a big party after the game. We had a blast. I think we left everything at the party. We were continuing in basking not only in the sun but in our victory.

Babe Parilli: I think what hurt us was that we had three days to prepare for the Championship Game and then we had to fly cross-country.

Larry Garron: The Chargers did everything to distract us. You would be sound asleep and you'd get a phone call to go out or they'd just keep calling and hang up. There were many other little things that affected what we did.

Larry Eisenhauer: Now we were playing in the Championship Game. Every day and night besides practice was filled with revelry. I think we were just floating on clouds when we went into that game. It was like we weren't even there.

Ron Hall: Sid Gillman, as everybody knows, was somewhat of a genius as a football coach. While we were playing in that playoff game, he was preparing for us.

Babe Parilli: They had the simple plays that Tobin Rote was pitching the ball out outside our containment. We were a big blitzing defense, and they were throwing the ball outside our blitzes. We had no containment, and they were just running a track meet. That was

49

probably the thing they prepared best at: getting that ball outside to Keith Lincoln and Paul Lowe.

Ron Hall: Gillman saw what we had done all year defensively and prepared appropriately. He used motion with Paul Lowe and handed off to Keith Lincoln. Keith Lincoln was off and running, and we hadn't had anyone run on us like that all year. We were leading the league in rushing defense, but every time I looked up in that game, Keith Lincoln was busting off a long one.

Gino Cappelletti: No question about it; they had a big advantage because they had an explosive offense that year. A lot of people during the course of the season were admiring the Chargers. They had a tremendous team. They had another week to prepare for us and practice what they wanted to do. All those things we were doing in trying to get to the Championship Game were pretty basic as far as what the strategy was. We were a blitzing team; we relied on the blitz. When you blitz, you can get burned. This particular game, they just threw pitchouts to Lowe and Lincoln, and when they turned the corner, all the defensive backs and linebackers were already across the line of scrimmage blitzing the quarterback, who threw these swing passes or quick tosses out to these backs. They turned the corner, there was nobody else left.

Larry Eisenhauer: We immortalized that San Diego Charger team, which was good enough without us. But our defense was just terrible. We left it all back in Buffalo and we really never showed up for that game.

Lincoln ran for 206 yards on just 13 carries, and Lowe added 94 more on the ground. Both had long touchdown runs: 67 for Lincoln and 54 for Lowe. In all, the Chargers rolled up 610 yards on their way to the 51–10 victory. It remains the most yards ever totaled by an offense in a playoff game.

Ron Hall: We had a horrible day. A lot of it might have been that we had prepared for this big Eastern Division championship with Buffalo. I don't know if we were mentally worn out or whatever. It was a long day for us.

Gino Cappelletti: It was just a game we didn't play up to our standard. I think we had been so excited with that playoff win, we finally crashed mentally and physically and just couldn't get ourselves back up to fly out there the day before and play the game the next day. It just all happened so fast, I don't think we could get ourselves ready for it, which is no excuse, and it shouldn't be, but at that particular moment in history, that's what I would say happened.

Dean Boylan: I wished I had stayed home.

The History of the Tiebreaker Game

In days of yore, men settled their differences on the field, not with esoteric tiebreaker rules. From the inception of the playoff system, in 1933, to the coming of the Super Bowl and slightly beyond, when two teams finished with identical records they played an extra game to determine who made the playoffs. These are the eleven other such games from the annals of the NFL, AAFC, and AFL. The home team is marked by an asterisk.

1941 NFL West: Chicago Bears 33*, Green Bay Packers 14
(tied at 10–1)

Green Bay and Chicago split the regular season, but the Bears (249) had a much better point differential than Green Bay (138). The Bears would beat the Giants, 37–9, in the championship.

1943 NFL East: Washington Redskins 28, New York Giants 0*
(tied at 6–3–1)

The Redskins had been 6–0–1 at one point, but lost their last three games, including the final two to New York, to force the tie. When they met the following week in a tiebreaker game, it became the only incidence in NFL history of two teams playing each other in three consecutive games. Washington went on to lose to the Bears, 41–21, in the title game.

1947 NFL East: Philadelphia Eagles 21, Pittsburgh Steelers 0* (tied at 8–4)

The Eagles split the season series with Pittsburgh and had already beaten them by an identical score on November 30. The Eagles went on to lose the championship to the Chicago Cardinals, 28–21.

1948 AAFC East: Buffalo Bills 28, Baltimore Colts 17* (tied at 7–7)

Inevitably, the Bills lost to the undefeated Cleveland Browns in the championship game, 49–7. They had split with the Colts by nearly identical scores of 35–17 (won) and 35–15 (lost). The second game came on the final day of the regular season, forcing the tie. It must have really chafed the San Francisco 49ers to have to watch these two .500 teams battle it out for a chance to be in the final, stuck behind the perfect Browns as they were. The 49ers had swept their four meetings against the Colts and Bills, outscoring them 150 to 66 in the process.

1950 NFL American: Cleveland Browns 8*, New York Giants 3 (tied at 10–2)

1950 NFL National: Los Angeles Rams 21*, Chicago Bears 14 (tied at 9–3)

The Giants held the Browns to 27 points in three games—winning both regular-season contests. The Bears also took both regular-season games from the Rams, yet they, like the Giants, had to play the tie-breaker on the road. The Browns beat the Rams, 30–28, for the title.

1952 NFL National: Detroit Lions 31, Los Angeles Rams 21* (tied at 9–3)

The Lions went on to beat the Browns for the title, 17–7, becoming the first team to win two postseason road games in the same season. They had beaten the Rams twice in the first four weeks of the season, but Los Angeles won their last eight after a 1–3 start to force this encounter.

1957 NFL West: Detroit Lions 31, San Francisco 49ers 27*
(tied at 8–4)

The Lions scored 31 points three times against the 49ers in 1957 and were answered with 35, 10, and 27 respectively. In this tiebreaker game, Detroit was down 27–7 in the third quarter and scored 24 unanswered points for one of the greatest comeback wins in postseason history. The Lions went on to crush the Browns, 59–14, for what remains their last NFL title to date. The 49ers, meanwhile, would have to wait another 24 years to play in a league title game.

1958 NFL East: New York Giants 10*, Cleveland Browns 0
(tied at 9–3)

The Giants had forced this playoff in the final moments of the regular season when Pat Summerall kicked an improbable 49-yard field goal in a blizzard for a 13–10 win over Cleveland. New York had also won their other meeting, 21–17. In this game, the Giants recorded six sacks, Jim Brown was neutralized, and the Browns were held to just 86 combined yards. New York went on to lose the so-called Greatest Game Ever to the Baltimore Colts, 23–17.

1965 NFL West: Green Bay Packers 13*, Baltimore Colts 10,
Overtime (tied at 10–3–1)

The Packers won both regular-season meetings. The tiebreaker game was forced in the final moments of the regular season when the San Francisco 49ers tied the Packers, 24–24, on a late touchdown, while down the coast in Los Angeles, the Colts overcame a late 17–10 Rams lead to prevail, 20–17. In the tiebreaker, the Colts were forced to use running back Tom Matte at quarterback when both Johnny Unitas and Gary Cuozzo were hurt. They led 10–0 at half, but a last-minute Don Chandler field goal forced the overtime, and he kicked another with 13:39 expired in the extra quarter to win it. Green Bay then won the title game, 23–12 over Cleveland.

1968 AFL West: Oakland Raiders 41*, Kansas City Chiefs 6
(tied at 12–2)

The Chiefs and Raiders had split their regular-season meetings, but in this game Fred Biletnikoff's three touchdown catches in the first half sealed the Chiefs' fate. Oakland then lost the American Football League title game to the Jets, 27–23. The AFL, with its two divisions, was still using tiebreaker games to determine division championships, while the NFL, with four divisions, had converted to head-to-head matchups. The year before, for instance, the Rams and Colts had both finished 11–1–2 atop the Coastal Division, but the Rams got the nod in deference to their 1–0–1 record against Baltimore.

With the books forever closed on the tiebreaker era, the final accounting shows that the participants split their regular-season meetings down the middle with 12 wins apiece. The eventual winners had a slight edge in points, 480 to 465. Teams that swept the season series went 3–3, while the home team in the tiebreaker game went 6–6. The sample size isn't big enough to draw any definitive conclusions, especially when nothing about the outcome of these dozen games suggests any kind of advantage.

The Most Tightly Bunched Divisions of All Time (Through 2010)

Were the final standings of the 1963 AFL Eastern Division the closest ever from top to bottom? No, but they are right up there. The claim to the division with the least separation from first to last belongs to the 2002 AFC East—still featuring three of the four teams that got so bunched up in 1963—and the 1935 NFL Western.

1 Game

2002 AFC East	Won	Lost	Tied
New York Jets	9	7	0
New England Patriots	9	7	0
Miami Dolphins	9	7	0
Buffalo Bills	8	8	0

1935 NFL Western	Won	Lost	Tied
Detroit Lions	7	3	2
Green Bay Packers	8	4	0
Chicago Cardinals	6	4	2
Chicago Bears	6	4	2

1½ Games

1989 AFC Central	Won	Lost	Tied
Cleveland Browns	9	6	1
Houston Oilers	9	7	0
Pittsburgh Steelers	9	7	0
Cincinnati Bengals	8	8	0

2 Games

1963 AFL Eastern	Won	Lost	Tied
Boston Patriots	7	6	1
Buffalo Bills	7	6	1
Houston Oilers	6	8	0
New York Jets	5	8	1

2010 NFC West	Won	Lost	Tied
Seattle Seahawks	7	9	0
St. Louis Rams	7	9	0
San Francisco 49ers	6	10	0
Arizona Cardinals	5	11	0

3 Games

1981 NFC Central	Won	Lost	Tied
Tampa Bay Bucs	9	7	0
Detroit Lions	8	8	0
Green Bay Packers	8	8	0
Minnesota Vikings	7	9	0
Chicago Bears	6	10	0

1977 AFC Central	Won	Lost	Tied
Pittsburgh Steelers	9	5	0
Houston Oilers	8	6	0
Cincinnati Bengals	8	6	0
Cleveland Browns	6	8	0

1999 AFC West	Won	Lost	Tied
Seattle Seahawks	9	7	0
Kansas City Chiefs	9	7	0
San Diego Chargers	8	8	0
Oakland Raiders	8	8	0
Denver Broncos	6	10	0

1977 AFC Central	Won	Lost	Tied
Pittsburgh Steelers	9	5	0
Houston Oilers	8	6	0
Cincinnati Bengals	8	6	0
Cleveland Browns	6	8	0

1983 NFC West	Won	Lost	Tied
San Francisco 49ers	10	6	0
Los Angeles Rams	9	7	0
New Orleans Saints	8	8	0
Atlanta Falcons	7	9	0

Oakland Raiders at Boston Patriots

October 30, 1966

	1	2	3	4	F
Oakland Raiders	0	7	0	14	21
Boston Patriots	14	3	7	0	24

Jim Nance was arguably the best skill-position player for the Patriots in their years in the AFL, following an inconsistent rookie season with an explosive 1966: He won the MVP award and became the first Patriot to appear on the cover of *Sports Illustrated*. Jim Nance was a larger-than-life figure who punished anyone who tried to tackle him with his size, speed, and determination. Yet his flirtation with greatness was all too brief: By 1969, his best years were already behind him, and he played just seven NFL games after 1971. Yet 1966 saw Nance in full force, and the October contest with the Raiders was the most prolific of his career. It symbolized how he played the game: with his head down and his legs churning.

NANCE, THE EARLY YEARS

James Solomon "Bo" Nance was born in Indiana, Pennsylvania, on December 30, 1942, and he very nearly never participated in athletics at all. When he was four years old, his brother was boiling some water on the stove, and, when he went to move it to the sink, disaster struck. In 1966, Nance told the *Mansfield News Journal*, "I reached up and pulled his arm. I got scalded. Some of the water hit my head, and the doctors told me that if it had hit my eyes I would have been blinded. My left shoulder got the worst of it, and they thought it was burned so badly it wouldn't grow normally."

Nance spent several months in the hospital, but his doctors' fears of permanent damage were soon put to rest when he not only grew normally but did normally some better. It was only natural that a boy of his physical parameters would hear the call of the gridiron—especially a boy growing up in western Pennsylvania, a place steeped in the game's traditions. His father was a coal miner who thought football was more dangerous than going down into the pit every day. A neighborhood boy had been killed playing the game on a field near the Nance home, and young Jim was forbidden from participating. But football's pull was too strong to resist, and so, as an early adolescent, Nance was involved with organized ball on the sly. By the time he reached high school, the paternal ban had been lifted: The young accident victim had become a 215-pound beast who could run the 100-yard dash in just over 10 seconds. There was no denying him a place with a top college. Having seen Jim Brown play for Syracuse on television, Nance, a two-time high school All-American, decided he wanted to go there, too.

Like Brown, he excelled at another sport. While Brown had lacrosse (which he played only his junior and senior years; he also played basketball and threw the discus), Nance had wrestling. As a sophomore in the spring of 1963, he won the national heavyweight title when he bested Larry Kristoff of Southern Illinois University Carbondale, 2–1. (Kristoff had been preceded at SIU by Nance's Patriots teammate Houston Antwine—one of the first two African Americans to win NAIA wrestling titles.) As a junior, he lost a tight 2–1 match in the quarterfinals to a grappler named Bob Billberg of Moorhead State College. Prior to that, Nance had won 78 straight matches, many against the top competitors in the circuit. In spite of the loss to Billberg, Nance was still very much in the running for a spot on the U.S. Olympic team for the 1964 Tokyo Games, but he chose not to pursue it.

In the spring of 1965, Nance reclaimed his title by defeating Russ Winer of Oklahoma State University in a 5–3 decision. He would offer the opinion that wrestling helped his football game by improving his balance and his ability to make small cuts. Wrestling historian Jay Hammond has written of Nance that he "brought a level of speed, strength, and athleticism to the heavyweight class that had rarely been seen before on the mats."

On the gridiron, Nance might not have been the equal of Jim Brown, but he was a star in his own right. Nance scored in 10 straight games in 1964 and led Syracuse in rushing with 951 yards on 190 attempts. His blocking also helped spring sophomore Floyd Little for another 828 yards and 12 touchdowns. Nance scored 13 times himself.

Nance brought defenders to their knees with a combination of power and speed, but coaches and scouts alike worried that it wouldn't last. There was one reason: weight gain. While it was not an issue in his wrestling career, Nance's weight did keep him from reaching his full potential on the football field.

It was a problem that would define his career and, ultimately, his life.

NANCE BECOMES A PATRIOT

Nance's potential was obvious, and he had the full attention of both pro leagues. The Chicago Bears took him in the fourth round after drafting Gale Sayers in the first. As Mike Holovak would later write of their head coach, George Halas, "You can imagine how the 'Papa Bear' would have done with that combination."

Meanwhile, the AFL had held a secret phone draft in the fall of 1964 in which the Jets picked Nance. When Syracuse came to New York for a game against Army, Jets coach Weeb Ewbank went so far as to introduce himself to Nance and tell him their attorney would be in touch. The Jets already had a burgeoning star at fullback in the person of Matt Snell, so Nance's path to playing time was blocked. Sensing this would be a deal breaker, the Jets intimated that they would shift Snell to halfback to make room for him. This didn't sit well with Nance, who said, "I didn't mind the competition for the job, but thinking I was stupid and telling me Snell was going to be moved? . . . I didn't like that routine."

The Jets realized they had overplayed their hand and had lost Nance's trust. They let the rest of the AFL know that they were not going to take him in the regular draft on November 28, 1964. They assumed that Nance would sign with the Bears or whichever NFL team drafted him. When the Jets threw the pick back, it served as a warning to all the other AFL teams that Nance was destined for the other league, so they stayed away from him in the early rounds.

Given the big production the college draft has become and the effort teams now put into their choices, it seems hard to believe that it used to be held during the regular season. Coaches and administrators would call in their picks on Saturday night and then play a game the next day. In the case of the Patriots in 1964, they were in Houston to face the Oilers and were working the phones at the team hotel. Billy Sullivan and Mike Holovak came to the 19th round and saw that Nance's name was still in their ever-shrinking stack of cards for undrafted players.

"I know the stories about the Bears having signed him up," said Sullivan to Holovak. "The Jets must know something. But what the heck, this is number nineteen. We aren't going to get much anyway. Let's take a chance. Time is running out."

Sullivan wasn't kidding about not getting much with their lower selections. In rounds 9 through 18, the Pats didn't get a single player who would ever start regularly in the AFL or NFL. The most productive of these picks—and productive is a very relative term here—were LSU back White Graves, taken in the 18th round, who would back up the defensive backs for three seasons; and Bowling Green's Jay Cunningham, whom the Pats took in the 14th round, who would be their return man for three years and play in 40 games. Not that the Pats knew at the time that most of their down-draft picks were ill-fated; they just understood that the real talent was gone, save for the players like Nance who, everyone assumed, would sign for more money in the NFL.

Holovak demurred for a moment and then got on the phone to draft central and told the powers that be that the team was taking Nance with their 19th-round pick. What they didn't know was that one of their players, defensive back Thomas Stephens, had been visiting his alma mater—Syracuse University—every fall and telling the players what a great gig the AFL was. Stephens's tales of AFL glory appealed to Nance. Many thought that Nance's goal was to play in the NFL and break Jim Brown's various and many rushing records, but Stephens had really sold him on the young league, so when Holovak went up to visit him, he was all ears.

Nance was still talking to the Bears when Holovak ran into their defensive coordinator, George Allen, at a coaching convention. Allen told Holovak that the Patriots had better make their pitch. (This seems like very strange behavior given that this was the height of the AFL–NFL wars. After all, Joe Namath, the classic example of competition between the two leagues, was taken in the same draft.) Nevertheless, the Pats took the opportunity to make their bid aggressively. Nance wanted to wrestle for the Orangemen, and Holovak didn't want him partaking in a collegiate sport with a signed Patriots contract sitting in a drawer. So the Patriots agreed to wait. When the wrestling season was finished, he inked his deal with Boston. Holovak made an interesting point about doing things aboveboard: "When you don't intrigue over money, you have a better relationship."

THE TOO-BIG ROOKIE

Houston Antwine: When he first came to training camp, he came in a sports car. When he came, he was leading a bunch of highway troopers behind him.

Nance made a big entrance in more ways than one. He was gregarious and well liked, and it was soon impossible to find anyone who had a bad word to say about him. There was a problem, though, and it was that he appeared for his first training camp a much larger man than the Patriots remembered signing.

Jon Morris: In those days, we never worked out in the off-season. You showed up at training camp, and that's when you got in shape. It's not like it is today, where they work out year-round.

He was so large that Holovak came up with a unique way to motivate him to trim some ballast.

Len St. Jean: His first year, Holovak threatened to make him an offensive guard if he didn't lose weight. He was kind of a bus.

Houston Antwine: I'd say, "Hey, Nance, you better lose that weight, boy, or you'll find yourself on this line next to me." That used to upset him so badly. He thought he was going to be a defensive lineman if he put on too much weight.

Tom Yewcic: It came out that some of the players heard Mike Holovak talking in a meeting: If Jim Nance didn't lose his extra weight, he was going to start the season at guard. When Nance heard that, he went to hell and back to try and get his weight down. He no more wanted to be a guard than to have another hole drilled into his head.

His rookie year got off to a very unpromising beginning with a nine-carry, 17-yard performance against Buffalo. Neither the Pats nor Nance could get on track in 1965. His next four games had showings of 12 rushes for 26 yards, 5 for 10, 7 for 11, and 3 for 2. By the 10th game of the year, the Pats were 1–8–1 and Nance was averaging less than two yards per carry. His primary contribution to that point was three touchdown plunges.

Gino Cappelletti: Jim had a slow start to his career. He came here overweight and he just seemed to be a little bit lost.

Patrick Sullivan: Mike Holovak motivated Jim Nance. He got Jim away from the training table and got him back in shape.

"Every coach I've had has thought about turning me into a guard or tackle," Nance said at the time. "I didn't know if Mike was serious or just using psychology on me. But I knew I'd better lose some weight. My trouble is, everything I eat sticks to me, and I like pies and cakes."

Things perked up for both the rookie fullback and his team in their 11th game. Nance led the team in rushing with 66 yards, and the Pats knotted the Chiefs 10–10 with 6:07 left and then hung on for the tie when Kansas City missed a field goal with 26 seconds on the clock. Boston ran the table the rest of the way and finished 4–8–2. In two of the three final contests, Nance acquitted himself well. He improved his yards per carry to 2.89—nothing that would put him in a battle for the league lead, but certainly much better than he had displayed earlier in the season.

THE STERLING SOPHOMORE

For his second professional training camp, Nance showed up in much better shape than he had for his first. He was very close to his generally accepted ideal playing weight of 235 pounds.

Houston Antwine: He was taken over with controlling his weight. He'd lay back or slack back and he'd put on pounds. He'd come in and say, "Hey Twine, I got a new diet."

Furthermore, he seemed to be imbued with a greater competitive spirit.

Tom Yewcic: Back then, we practiced at White Stadium. We used to run plays in from the fifty-yard line. Jim would carry the ball ten out of eleven times, and every time he'd run fifty yards for the touchdown. Mike Holovak would say, "Take your time coming back, Jim, we'll wait for you." Next play: fifty more yards. "Take your time coming back, Jim, we'll wait for you." Next play: fifty more yards. "Take your time coming back, Jim, we'll wait for you." He ran a dozen plays, Jim would run fifty yards. It was incredible, the attitude he had. That was the type of player he was.

Len St. Jean: I can't say enough about his ability and his work ethic. When he came back that second year, every time we would run a play, he would run another thirty yards. Holovak would say, "As long as he's running the way he's running, we'll wait for him for as long as we have to."

Although the Patriots were shut out in their season opener, Nance looked better than he ever had. In Week 2, he had his first-ever 100-yard afternoon, accounting for half the team's yardage and scoring a touchdown in their 24–10 win over Denver. By week seven, they were 3–2–1 and Nance was really beginning to establish himself. He was averaging 90 yards per game and 4.36 yards per carry, a big improvement over his rookie year.

THE NANCE STYLE

Nance left a lasting impression on his teammates.

Larry Eisenhauer: He was huge, with big thighs, a thick body, and a thick neck, but real good speed.

Gil Santos: People didn't realize how quick and light he was on his feet until he was able to get by them and into the secondary. He had surprising agility and quickness for someone of his size.

Gino Cappelletti: He was starting to develop big-time as far as really being able to knock over tacklers and rumble and ramble down the field. He was a very explosive type of runner, a hard guy to bring down. He was a lot like Cookie Gilchrist, but maybe faster, and a little more compact. He would shake a lot of tacklers off.

Ron Hall: The writers in Boston had a nickname for him; they called him the "Wild Bull of Fenway."

Babe Parilli: He was a special type of runner and such a big back for that era; a great combination of size and speed—a rare package in those times. He made my job a lot easier.

Tom Yewcic: When he played at 232 pounds, he was virtually unstoppable. Jim had that great burst off the ball. He could hit the hole quicker than heck. He had great vision at the line of scrimmage. He could pick his holes in an instant. A glimpse of what's happening in front of him and he could make a cut right, left, or whatever he had to do. He had that great burst of speed. He had power, he had great leg strength, he could run over people—and if he ever broke in the clear, forget it. I didn't see anybody that year catch him from behind.

Ron Hall: When he had his mind made up, I used to love to watch him rip through the Kansas City Chiefs linebackers, Buffalo's linebackers, the New York Jets linebackers. He ripped people a good one every time he was up in that line. I was glad I didn't have to play against him.

"Those guys in the secondary are smaller than I am," said Nance in 1966. "They'll come in looking to tackle me head-on, but after I've tagged them a couple of times they start closing their eyes or ducking their heads. Pretty soon they're swearing when they get up. Then they'll start turning their shoulders when they come at me, and I know I've got them."

Len St. Jean: With the 238 pounds and the strength that he had, he was an unbelievable force. We blocked for him a lot of times just out of fear. If you didn't open up a hole, you didn't want that big guy running up your back, I'll tell you that. You can only do that a couple of times in the game, then you wouldn't be in the game anymore.

Jon Morris: As a lineman, you had to get the guy you were blocking out of the way and you had to get out of the way yourself, because he was going to run over everything in his sight. If I got stalemated in the middle of the line, I felt this thump in the middle of my back and there was Nance, hitting me with his helmet. There was motivation for the linemen to make sure you made your blocks right.

THE GAME

The Patriots' visitors for their seventh game were the Oakland Raiders, a team that was soon to embark on one of the best three-year runs in football history. In 1966, many of the pieces were already in place that made it possible for them to dominate the regular season in the final three years of the AFL. Lining up against Nance was a good front unit of Ike Lassiter, Dan Birdwell, Ben Davidson, and Tom Keating. All had long, productive careers and made it to at least one Pro Bowl each, but they would be assaulted and battered on many occasions on this afternoon.

After the Raiders had to punt away their first possession, the Pats took over at their own 26. The first give was to Nance, who went straight up the gut and broke into the clear for 16 yards. On the next play, the handoff went to Garron, who picked up 5 yards. Nance added 11 yards on his next three carries. The big play of the first Boston drive was a 33-yard toss from Parilli to tight end Jim Whalen. This one pass would account for half of the Patriots' air yardage on the day and brought them to the Oakland 3. Two plays later, Nance went off left tackle and into the end zone.

The Raiders went three and out on their next series but lost their starting quarterback, Tom Flores, in the process. From that point on, Cotton Davidson, a 35-year-old with a very spotty career, would be running the Raider offense. After Nance had gained another 16 yards on three carries, Howie Williams picked off a Parilli pass, but the Davidson-led Raiders could manage only one first down before having to boot the ball away again. Mike Eischeid, their punter and kicker, would punt six times in the first half.

The Pats took over on their own 8, and Nance was crashing back into the line again, picking up 14 yards on two carries. On first and 10 from the 22, Parilli handed off to Garron, who went around the left end. What he found there was acres of smooth driving. He was finally knocked out of bounds at the Raiders' 24 by safety Warren Powers. Mostly on the strength of that run, Garron would rush for 73 yards himself that day.

Larry Garron: We'd [Nance and I] always laugh at each other. I'd say, "Hey, I'm going to beat you today." He'd say, "No way. I'm going to beat you." We had a little game going. And he'd say, "Remember one thing when you throw your block for me: Get out of the way or I'm going to run over you." And that was motivation enough. He was like a tractor coming through there, but a fast one.

While the Raiders were still settling after Garron's gallop, Parilli went right for the throat, hitting Gino Cappelletti for the touchdown on the next play. Cappelletti's second extra point put the Patriots up 14–0 at the end of the first quarter.

Neither team did much on its first possession of the second quarter. Nance gained just six yards on three carries before Jim Fraser punted to the Oakland 49. After four consecutive futile series, the Raiders put themselves right back in the game in an instant. Cotton Davidson connected with Clem Daniels for a 51-yard scoring strike and, just like that, it was 14–7. On the Patriots' next possession, they found themselves with a third and 4 on their own 17. In the huddle, Parilli called Nance's number again.

Babe Parilli: I would call his running play to the right, and he said to me, "Babe, my right shoulder's hurting me; you mind running me to the left?" So I did, and I just kept giving him the ball because he was dragging those Raiders right with him.

This time, he got through the line and broke into the clear. For the second time in the half, the Raiders had surrendered a 54-yard gain. On the next play, Nance punched it up the middle for another 20 yards, giving the Patriots a first and goal at the 9. The drive stalled there, however, and they had to settle for a 14-yard field goal from Cappelletti. Davidson couldn't get the Raiders going on their next possession, but Oakland got the ball right back when Parilli aired it out on first down, only to be picked off by safety Warren Powers. At this point, Parilli was just 2-for-7 with three interceptions. Mike Holovak pretty much abandoned the passing game from there on out, leaving the offense on Nance's shoulders for the duration.

It was a burden Nance was only too happy to carry. His work in this game was extraordinary and was emblematic of the effort he put forth in 1966 and 1967. (See "The Hardest-Working Running Backs of the 1960s," on page 75.)

Both teams went three and out again. A short, 32-yard punt by Fraser gave the Raiders excellent field position at their own 49. Time was running out. An 11-yard completion to Fred Biletnikoff afforded Oakland a field goal opportunity, but it was beyond the outer reaches of Mike Eischeid's range. He would go just one for nine from beyond the 40 in 1966, and this one, from 45 out, was one of the misses.

The half ended with the Patriots leading 17–7 and Nance having run for 159 yards on 19 carries. The Pats had a 220–4 advantage in ground gains, while the Raiders had been better in the air, 102–57. Oakland had run only a handful of what could be considered successful plays to the halfway point but, thanks to a couple of interceptions, was still very much in striking distance.

Very soon in the second half, the Raiders were given an excellent opportunity to make the Patriots sweat. On Boston's first play from scrimmage, Larry Garron was hit as he entered the line and coughed up the ball. Linebacker Gus Otto recovered, and the Raiders were in business on the Boston 27. Davidson failed to connect with Biletnikoff and Art Powell, and it was up to Eischeid again to get them some points. This time, from 28 yards out, he hit the upright, and the score remained 17–7.

The Patriots managed just one first down on their next possession, but after punting the ball away, they got it right back when Tom Hennessey, who had once taught phys ed at a Jesuit college in Baghdad, intercepted Davidson on the Oakland 43 and ran it back to the 19. With a chance to really put some distance between themselves and the Raiders, Boston went nowhere but backwards. Garron rushed for no gain, then they were called for illegal procedure, giving them a second and 15. In the days when it cost 15 yards, nothing broke the back of a drive like getting flagged for holding, which was just what happened to the Patriots on the next play. With the passing game malfunctioning, the give was to Nance on second and 30, and there resulted a collision that is still reverberating in Boston when big Ben Davidson brought him down after a three-yard gain. Finally, Cappelletti lined up for a 44-yard field goal attempt, only to have it fall short. The ball was downed on the 1, a rare good break for the Patriots in a rotten half to that point.

When Davidson couldn't get anything going again, Eischeid now had to punt from the back of his own end zone. He got the ball out to Joe Bellino at the Oakland 38. Bellino had gotten as far as the 25 when he was hit and fumbled, but the Patriots managed to recover. It was another short trip to the end zone for the Patriots, who were good to go with a first and 10 at the 22. Nance got them 10 yards closer on his next two rushes. After Davidson got in Nance's way again on his next carry, Parilli hit Garron for 9 to give the Pats first and goal at the one.

On the next two plays, both Parilli and Nance were jammed up at the line trying to find their way across the goal. Just when it looked like the Raiders might hold Boston to a field goal attempt, Nance went off left tackle and found pay dirt. The third quarter ended with the Raiders moving the ball, trailing 24–7.

No sooner did Oakland begin to get some traction than the drive stalled with two missed connections between Davidson and Biletnikoff. It was then that Eischeid was called on to try the only 50-yard-plus field goal of his career. (After 1966, the Raiders and then the Vikings would limit his kicking duties to punting.) What may have looked like a risky decision to modern eyes was in fact a hedge—the ball fell 10 yards short and was returned by Jay Cunningham, who brought it back to the 28. The 52-yard attempt was really no gamble at all, but an elaborate punt with an outside chance of scoring a few points.

The Pats gave the ball back and, for the first time all day, the Oakland offense really got rolling. Davidson hit Daniels for 38 yards and Hewritt Dixon for 11. On first and 10 from the 22, Daniels went off right tackle and scampered in for the touchdown. It was next that Nance had his one bad moment on the day. After getting banged down by Ike Lassiter and Dan Birdwell after a four-yard gain on first down, he took the handoff on second and lost the ball. Dan Conners, Oakland's middle linebacker, pounced on it, and the Raiders had the ball on the Patriots' 24-yard line with plenty of time on the clock. Davidson hit Dixon for 10- and 12-yard completions, and Daniels finished off the trip with a one-yard end zone penetration, making the score 24–21. It was suddenly looking very dicey for Boston.

Cunningham made a nice 31-yard return on the ensuing kickoff. Nance's three rushes in this series left the team with a fourth and 2 on their own 48. Counting on Nance to bull his way for two yards might have been a reasonable gamble, but Holovak wasn't going for it. Instead, Fraser punted to the 12, where Rodger Bird made a fair catch.

There was more than enough time left for the Raiders to cover the length of the field, either to score a touchdown or get into Eischeid's limited kicking range so that they could at least go home with a tie. On first down, though, Larry Eisenhauer and Bob Dee sacked Davidson for a five-yard loss. He compensated with a 19-yard strike to Powell, and Oakland's hopes revived. On second and 10, though, Chuck Shonta stepped in front of Davidson's last pass, intercepting it. The Patriots ground out the clock and came away with the 24–21 victory and the lead in the Eastern Division.

THE REST OF THE WAY

The 1966 season would end in yet another second-place finish for the Patriots (see "Two Games That Changed the World for the 1966 Patriots," on page 73). In the final week of the season, they fell behind the Jets 31–13 and never caught up, sealing their fate and, in many ways, ending the happy time in the Patriots' AFL era. Nance would reel off five consecutive 100-yard games later in the season and lead the league in rushing. He was named the Most Valuable Player of the AFL. It couldn't—and didn't—get any better than that.

Nance shouldered another heavy workload in 1967 and had a second consecutive outstanding season, but the Patriots fell to 3–10–1 and last place. Things got worse from there. In a preseason game on Labor Day prior to the 1968 season, Nance's foot found an irregularity in the turf at Harvard Stadium and he twisted his ankle. He missed the first game of the year, but suited up for the contest against the Jets in the second week and reaggravated the sprain, making it worse. He somehow managed to play in all but two games, although his workload was greatly reduced from the previous season and his yards per carry was the lowest of his career, save for his rookie season. There were some suspicions that he was doing a bit of acting, but the physician who examined him at the conclusion of the season was astounded by what he found.

"I really don't know how he ever ran on that ankle. It certainly had to kill him on every step," the doctor opined. It turned out that the ligament had been completely torn loose. The cartilage was missing in some spots, so that whenever he moved, the bone was moving against other bone. What had started as a simple sprain caused by stepping in a hole in a game that didn't count ended in three hours of surgery.

Nance rebounded in 1969, leading the AFL in rushing attempts while catching a career-high 29 passes. The team's fortunes continued to wane over the next two seasons, and Nance gave way to Carl Garrett as the team's featured back in 1971.

A PATRIOT NO MORE

The Pats traded Nance to Philadelphia on July 25, 1972. The Eagles released him in early September, just prior to the start of the regular season. In a testament to how far Nance's star had fallen, this Eagles team, which didn't need Nance, would go on to finish 24th out of 26 teams in rushing and end the year with a 2–11–1 record.

By spring, Nance had ballooned up to 262 pounds, and it appeared he would never play football again. Instead, he made up his mind that things were going to change and set about getting back into playing shape. In the New York Jets he found a team willing to give him his comeback shot. He had an ally there in the person of the new Jets backfield coach: Mike Holovak.

"There was no way I was going to go out of football the way I did last year," he told the *New York Times* prior to the start of training camp in 1973. "I want to prove something to some people, and I'm glad it's with the Jets. New York is the only place to play."

Nance was one of nine running backs in the Jets camp. He showed up to work having lost 24 pounds. Meanwhile, the team's most valuable player of 1972, John Riggins, desired a significant raise from his previous salary of $25,000 and did not report to camp. Things were certainly looking up for Nance when he led the AFC in rushing during the pre-season, rolling up 311 yards on 72 carries for a 4.3 average.

"You tack a few more carries on that and it could project into a thousand yards a year, couldn't it?" said an optimistic Nance at the dawn of the 1973 season.

Unfortunately, his NFL resurrection was about to take a different turn. Riggins reported for duty just in time to get the start against Green Bay in the opener, and Nance got only one carry in that game. Furthermore, he missed a block in the red zone and Joe Namath was dumped for a 10-yard loss. The Jets were very nearly shut out, and Nance wound up in coach Weeb Ewbank's doghouse. For many Jets games, he wasn't even dressed. He did not play when the Jets visited New England on

October 14, although he did get four carries against the Patriots at Shea Stadium on November 11. Ironically, these would prove to be his last carries in the NFL.

Nance's ill-fated turn with the Jets had at least proven one thing: He was back in playing shape. An opportunity to prove that arose in 1974 with the birth of the World Football League. Nance signed with the Houston Texans and began tearing it up like it was 1966 all over again. He carried the ball 300 times, much like he had at his peak with the Patriots. But the redemption was ultimately incomplete. The Texans were forced to move to Shreveport, Louisiana, in midseason and once played a road game in Philadelphia attended by 750 people in a stadium designed to hold 100 times that number. When the WFL folded in the middle of the 1975 season, Nance was second all-time in rushing yards to Tommy Reamon.

In his post-playing career, Nance's weight began to take a serious toll. In 1983, he suffered a heart attack and then, 24 hours later, a stroke. He recovered but was never quite the same. He passed away at the age of 49 in 1992.

Larry Eisenhauer: Jim Nance was special. When I say special, I am looking at him beyond Jim Nance the football player to Jim Nance as a man. He was quiet, introspective. He always had a ready smile. He was a gentleman, a guy that you would just look at him and give him all the respect in the world. He was a kind, respectful person to everyone. I loved Jim Nance as a man. I was so proud to see him get into the Patriot Hall of Fame. He belongs in the NFL Hall of Fame.

APPENDICES

Two Games That Changed the World for the 1966 Patriots

For what would prove to be the last time as the Boston Patriots, the team found itself in a close race for the Eastern Division title in 1966. One thing that worked against them was a quirk in the schedule that allowed the Bills to play the expansion Miami Dolphins two times, while the Patriots saw them only once. The Bills murdered them, 58–24 in Buffalo and 29–0 in Miami, while the Patriots defeated them 20–14, on the road. Since the Dolphins' only wins came against the last-place Oilers and Broncos, the Patriots likely would have beaten them a second time as well, especially since that second game would have taken place in Boston.

Given that they finished a half-game out of first place, any of the four losses or two ties the Patriots endured could be blamed for torpedoing their season. There were two outcomes that were especially tough to swallow, however. A couple of different breaks in either of these games and the Pats would have, at the very least, forced a tie with the Bills for the division title.

Jets at Patriots, October 2

The Jets were 3–0 and favored by more than a touchdown against the 1–2 Patriots, in spite of the fact that the game was being played at Fenway Park. For the first three quarters, Boston made a mockery of the betting line. Larry Garron rushed for two touchdowns, while Gino Cappelletti was scoring one and adding a field goal, leading the Pats to a 24–7 advantage at the sound of the third gun.

To that point, Mike Holovak's defensive game plan had included plenty of blitzes designed to harass Joe Namath, who was still not up to full strength after missing the preseason with the knee problems that would plague most of his career. Through three quarters he was just 14 of 33 for 133 yards. (Had things continued in this vein, it would have easily been the worst performance of Namath's young career; a quarterback rating under 20.0.) Furthermore, the Patriots had intercepted him three times and jammed up the running game to such an extent that the Jets nearly abandoned it altogether in the second half. Adding to New York's frustrations were missed field goals from Jim Turner, who was short on a 48-yard attempt and dented the upright with a 38-yard try.

The worm turned in the fourth quarter. Suddenly, Namath was hitting receivers with frequency and precision. In the space of five and a half minutes, he took the Jets on scoring drives of 62 and 56 yards and brought them to within three. When the Patriots went three and out for the third time in the period, another Jets drive ensued, but it stalled on the Boston 23. Turner missed his third kick of the day, and the Pats got a respite from the onslaught.

Once again, though, the Boston offense stalled and the Jets got the ball right back. This time they were on their own 40, and there were just two minutes to go. Once again, Namath drove the Jets right through the Patriots with two long gainers to Bill Mathis. (Namath rolled up 205 yards in the air in the fourth quarter, completing 14 of 23 passes.) New York was in an excellent position to win, but on third and 1 at the Patriots' 9-yard line, Namath fumbled the snap. The Jets recovered, but their chance for victory had passed. With 30 seconds on the clock, Turner finally put one through the uprights from 17 yards out, securing the 24–24 tie. Had the Patriots been able to hold their lead, they would have finished at 9–4–1, identical to the Bills.

Broncos at Patriots, November 6

Conditions at Fenway Park were miserable on this sopping autumn day. The stadium was half full, and those in attendance witnessed a messy affair played in a driving rainstorm that left man and ball alike soaked to the skin. To this point, the Broncos were just 1–7 and had been outscored by an outrageous 264 to 108, but the weather proved an equalizing force. Each club fumbled six times, losing five apiece. One of these resulted in a touchdown for the Patriots in the second period when defensive tackle Jim Hunt fell on a loose ball in the Broncos' end zone for the game's first score.

Nobody had any way of knowing it at the time, but there occurred a play in the third quarter upon which the entire season hinged. With a fourth and 1 at their own 21-yard line, Holovak chose to defy convention by going for it in this obvious punting situation. With his fingers numbed by the cold, Babe Parilli fumbled the snap from center and fell on it just short of the first down. The Broncos made the short trip to the end zone in seven plays, giving them a 10–7 lead.

With the score tied 10–10, the Patriots mounted a late-game drive that started on their own 19. The drive succeeded in the twin functions of eating up most of the remaining game time and also getting the Pats well within Gino Cappelletti's kicking range. When they called time-out with 20 seconds on the clock, the ball sat at the Denver 14, making it a 21-yard attempt for Cappelletti. But his kick sailed wide and the Broncos took over with a long way to go and a short time to get there.

The Denver quarterback was Max Choboian, a rookie playing in just the third game of what would prove to be a seven-game pro career. On first down, he completed a pass out to the Denver 36-yard line. With the clock winding down, Choboian heaved his next throw 44 yards downfield, where defensive back Chuck Shonta got his hands on it. The ball slipped past him, though, and found the waiting embrace of the Broncos' Al Denson, who took it the rest of the way into the end zone for the game winner. In a matter of seconds, the Patriots had gone from a seemingly sure 5–2–1 record to 4–3–1.

The Hardest-Working Running Backs of the 1960s

Why could Jim Brown still walk upright 40 years after his career ended? Probably because he quit when he did. While Jim Nance was the workhorse of the AFL, only Brown registered more rushing attempts in a single season during the 1960s. Nance had the two highest totals in AFL history, while Brown had the four highest in the NFL during the same period.

Most Rushing Attempts Per Season, 1960–69

Rank	Att	Player	Year	Team
1	305	Jim Brown	1961	Cleveland Browns
2	**299**	**Jim Nance**	**1966**	**Boston Patriots**
3	291	Jim Brown	1963	Cleveland Browns
4	289	Jim Brown	1965	Cleveland Browns
5	280	Jim Brown	1964	Cleveland Browns
6	272	Jim Taylor	1962	Green Bay Packers
7	**269**	**Jim Nance**	**1967**	**Boston Patriots**
8	258	J.D. Smith	1962	San Francisco 49ers
9	252	Cookie Gilchrist	1965	Denver Broncos
10	251	John Henry Johnson	1962	Pittsburgh Steelers
10	251	Bill Brown	1966	Minnesota Vikings
12	248	Jim Taylor	1963	Green Bay Packers
12	248	Dick Bass	1966	Los Angeles Rams
12	248	Leroy Kelly	1968	Cleveland Browns
15	244	Charley Tolar	1962	Houston Oilers

Nance's heavy usage combined with his talents resulted in the two highest rushing seasons in the course of the AFL.

Most Yards Gained in a Single AFL Season, 1960–1969

Rank	Yards	Player	Year	Att	Team
1	**1,458**	**Jim Nance**	**1966**	**299**	**Boston Patriots**
2	**1,216**	**Jim Nance**	**1967**	**269**	**Boston Patriots**
3	1,194	Hoyle Granger	1967	236	Houston Oilers
4	1,121	Paul Lowe	1965	222	San Diego Chargers
5	1,099	Clem Daniels	1963	215	Oakland Raiders
6	1,096	Cookie Gilchrist	1962	214	Buffalo Bills
7	1,087	Mike Garrett	1967	236	Kansas City Chiefs
8	1,049	Abner Haynes	1962	221	Dallas Texans
9	1,023	Paul Robinson	1968	238	Cincinnati Bengals
10	1,012	Charley Tolar	1962	244	Houston Oilers
11	1,010	Paul Lowe	1963	177	San Diego Chargers
12	981	Cookie Gilchrist	1964	230	Buffalo Bills

Rank	Yards	Player	Year	Att	Team
13	979	Cookie Gilchrist	1963	232	Buffalo Bills
14	954	Cookie Gilchrist	1965	252	Denver Broncos
15	948	Matt Snell	1964	215	New York Jets
16	948	Billy Cannon	1961	200	Houston Oilers

The Greatest Rushing Games in Patriots History

Jim Nance's single-game team rushing record lasted 17 seasons. At one time, he had the three highest game totals in franchise history. Those three games are all still in the top 10, while Curtis Martin now appears four times on the list.

Imagine having a running back gain nearly 200 yards on the ground and still losing by two touchdowns. It happened to the Pats and Robert Edwards against St. Louis in 1998. It makes more sense when you know that their other running backs combined for just four yards, Drew Bledsoe and Scott Zolak completed just 11 passes in 37 tries, and New England had to settle for four field goals on stalled drives.

212—Tony Collins, September 18, 1983, vs. New York Jets
    Won 23–13, 23 carries
208—Jim Nance, October 30, 1966, vs. Denver Broncos
    Won 24–21, 38 carries
199—Curtis Martin, September 14, 1997, vs. New York Jets
    Won 27–24, 40 carries
198—Robert Edwards, December 13, 1998, vs. St. Louis Rams
    Lost 32–18, 24 carries
185—Jim Nance, September 24, 1967, vs. Buffalo Bills
    Won 23–0, 34 carries
177—Don Calhoun, November 28, 1976, vs. Denver Broncos
    Won 38–14, 25 carries
166—Curtis Martin, January 5, 1996, vs. Pittsburgh Steelers
    Won Divisional Playoff, 28–3, 19 carries
166—Curtis Martin, November 5, 1995, vs. New York Jets
    Won, 20–7, 35 carries

164—Jim Nance, December 17, 1967, vs. Miami Dolphins
Lost 41–32, 24 carries
164—Curtis Martin, October 13, 1996, vs. Washington Redskins
Lost 27–22, 17 carries

On a yards-per-carry basis with a minimum of 10 carries, Larry Garron rushed for 116 yards in 10 tries (11.6 YPC) against the Buffalo Bills on October 22, 1961. The Patriots won 52–21. If the minimum is raised to 20 carries, Curtis Martin's 1996 game against Washington listed above is the best at 9.6 YPC.

The Top Running Back Selections of the 1965 NFL Draft

Jim Nance was the 45th player taken overall in the 1965 NFL draft (held on November 28, 1964) when he was chosen by the Chicago Bears in the fourth round. These are the nine running backs who were picked ahead of him:

**Tucker Frederickson (Auburn), New York Giants,
1st round, 1st overall**
It is generally agreed that had Frederickson not destroyed his knee, he would have lived up to the promise accorded the first overall pick in the NFL draft. There were occasionally glimpses of brilliance, but mostly trips to the doctor.

**Ken Willard (North Carolina), San Francisco 49ers,
1st round, 2nd overall**
It would be easy to dun the 49ers for not taking Gale Sayers with the number-two pick, but Willard did not disappoint. While nobody in their right minds would call him a better back than Sayers, he did prove to be the most durable in the draft class of '65. He played the most games and led the class's running backs in rushing attempts, yards, receptions, and scoring, as the chart on page 81 indicates.

Gale Sayers (Kansas), Chicago Bears,
1st round, 4th overall

For sheer watchablility, Sayers might be the greatest back ever. The Bears had three first-round picks in 1965. Right after they took Sayers, they grabbed another future Hall of Famer in the person of Dick Butkus. With the sixth pick, they chose defensive lineman Steve DeLong, who opted to play for the Chargers instead. DeLong finally reached the Bears for a few games in 1972. The best lineman of the 65ers turned out to be Jethro Pugh, whom the Cowboys took in the 11th round out of tiny Elizabeth City State.

Donny Anderson (Texas Tech), Green Bay Packers,
1st round, 7th overall

The heir apparent to the Paul Hornung/Jim Taylor backfield might never have reached those levels, but his career was a productive one nonetheless. He made the Pro Bowl once and got to play in the first two Super Bowls, in the first of which he famously knocked out Fred "The Hammer" Williamson, who collided headfirst with Anderson's knee.

Tom Nowatzke (Indiana), Detroit Lions,
1st round, 11th overall

Nowatzke was chosen higher than any other running back in the AFL draft. The Jets took him with the fourth pick, three spots after their famous selection of Joe Namath. While Nowatzke was in New York to appear on *The Ed Sullivan Show* with all the other All-Americans, Jets owner Sonny Werblin schmoozed him with limo rides. Then, in one of the more outlandish escapades from the AFL–NFL signing wars, Nowatzke, Butkus, and Craig Morton were sort of held hostage in a hotel room by the NFL so that they wouldn't attend the Army–Navy game, where they could be exposed to the representatives from the AFL teams that had drafted them—although it should be stated that they had already stated a preference to play in the senior league. Nowatzke muddled through a few years in Detroit before hurting his neck. He then caught on with the Baltimore Colts, where he famously bulled in for the game-tying touchdown in the waning moments of Super Bowl V. The only other running back selected in the first round of the AFL draft was taken right after Nowatzke when the Chiefs selected Gale Sayers, hoping—to no avail, as events would prove—that he'd choose to go pro a few miles to the east of his college home in Lawrence, Kansas.

Chuck Mercein (Yale), New York Giants, 3rd round, 31st overall

No running backs were taken in the second round of either the NFL or AFL draft in 1965. Released by the Giants midway through the 1967 season, Mercein ended up on the Packers, where the moment for which he is best remembered occurred. In their famous game-winning drive in the Ice Bowl, he accounted for half of the team's 68 yards.

Bo Scott (Ohio State), Cleveland Browns, 3rd round, 32nd overall

It's interesting that the Browns passed on an opportunity to have another bruising running back out of Syracuse when they chose Scott while Nance was still available and ready to follow in the footsteps of Jim Brown and Ernie Davis. Of course, the NFL had its secret draft, too, and Nance was a Chicago pick in that covert operation. Scott was no shrinking violet himself, going six foot three, 215 pounds. He had played well for Ohio State in 1962, but had to sit out the following year due to academic ineligibility. The Ottawa Rough Riders didn't care about his G.P.A. and signed him for the last game of the 1964 season, in which he gained 71 yards on two carries. The Browns drafted him later that year (as did the Raiders, but in the 20th round), but he stayed in the Canadian Football League for another four seasons, accumulating 3,057 rushing yards. He finally made his Cleveland debut in 1969 and was a big contributor in the 1970 and 1971 seasons.

Larry Todd (Arizona State), San Francisco 49ers, 4th round, 44th overall

Todd spent his career with the Oakland Raiders, and while he didn't get very many rushing opportunities, he did finish second only to Sayers in yards per carry among running backs in the 1965 draft.

Career Rushing Leaders from the Class of 1965

Round	Pick	NFL Draft Team	Running Back	Att	Yds	Y/A	TD	Rec	Yds	TD
1	2	49ers	Ken Willard	1622	6105	3.76	45	277	2184	17
4	45	Bears	Jim Nance	1341	5401	4.03	45	133	870	1
1	4	Bears	Gale Sayers	991	4956	5.00	39	112	1307	9
1	7	Packers	Donny Anderson	1197	4696	3.92	41	209	2548	14
13	176	Vikings	Dave Osborn (North Dakota)	1179	4336	3.68	29	173	1412	7
4	54	Cardinals	Johnny Roland (Missouri)	1015	3750	3.69	28	153	1430	6
14	186	Steelers	Cannonball Butler (Edward Waters)	797	2768	3.47	9	89	959	7
1	1	Giants	Tucker Frederickson	651	2209	3.39	9	128	1011	8
3	32	Browns	Bo Scott	554	2124	3.83	18	112	826	6
7	94	Packers	Junior Coffey (Washington)	535	2037	3.81	10	64	487	5

Oakland Raiders at New England Patriots

September 19, 1971

	1	2	3	4	F
Oakland Raiders	0	6	0	0	**6**
New England Patriots	0	0	14	6	**20**

As the character Emily Webb discovered to her dismay in another New England institution, Thornton Wilder's play *Our Town*, the past can be a tricky place to visit. As much as we might like to enjoy it, we arrive with the burden of knowing what comes next. When looking back at these four quarters of 1971 football, it is important to live in the moment and bask in that very specific glow. Everything was new: the quarterback, the stadium, the general manager—even what the team called itself. The future was bright; the dimness of the recent past was gone.

In the hours and days after this game, nobody knew there were still dark times ahead. Everything and anything seemed possible. It would have been nice if there had been an immediate and complete turnaround in the team's fortunes to go with the new stadium, the new geographic designation, the new general manager, and the new quarterback, but the pit of despair into which the club's on-field fortunes had sunk was simply too deep. While the 1971 Patriots were never playoff contenders, they were a vast improvement over the 1970 team. But then, that 1970 team had set the bar pretty low.

THE RUSH ERA
When the Patriots lost 10 games in both 1967 and 1968, many felt it was time to bring the Holovak era to an end.

Jon Morris: Billy Sullivan used Mike Holovak as a scapegoat for the team's failures. Of course, the head coach gets blamed, that's the way things work in pro football. Mike Holovak never had any help from the front office. The drafts were a disaster. None of the top draft choices made the team. Sooner or later you run out of players. If you don't have strong drafts, you fall apart—and fall apart we did.

Leigh Montville: Billy Sullivan had gone to see the Super Bowl between the Jets and the Colts. He was going to hire the offensive coordinator from the winning team. That was his plan. He went there and the Jets won. Their offensive coordinator was Clive Rush, so he hired Clive Rush. The offensive coordinator for the Colts was Chuck Noll. It was a twist of fate right there.

Jon Morris: The mistake Billy made was he should have brought in the Jets' *defensive* coordinator: Buddy Ryan. Chuck Noll was also available, but Pittsburgh got him. We got the worst of the three. It was an absolute and total disaster.

Leigh Montville: It all went downhill, because Clive was just crazy.

Len St. Jean: Clive was sort of destined to fail from the time he got here. When they went to do the press conference introducing George Sauer Sr. as our new GM, Clive electrocuted himself with the microphone wires doing the introduction. It was all downhill for Clive after that. He was a nice person, a personable guy; but he was off the wall.

Jon Morris: Clive Rush had some serious problems. He suffered from depression. He was an alcoholic. He had this idea in his mind that because he worked for Paul Brown in Ohio, he was the next great coach coming down the line. He didn't have a clue. He couldn't deal with his demons, and we as players and fans suffered for it.

One of Rush's first acts was to trade the best defensive player in team history to that point, Nick Buoniconti, to the Dolphins. He was still only 28 and, as it turned out, had many good years ahead of him, but his self-appointed role as the players' spokesman made him just the sort of person Rush didn't want to have around. This mistake was compounded by the mediocre talent Rush received in return. The Patriots got John Bramlett, a linebacker who had had some success early in his career but whose best days were behind him. He spent two mostly unremarkable years with the team. They also received Kim Hammond, a Dolphins backup quarterback who would throw six passes for the Patriots and never appear again. The final return was a fifth-round pick in the 1970 draft, which they used to take Bob Olson, a linebacker from Notre Dame who had been the defensive MVP in the Cotton Bowl. He never played a single down as a pro.

In spite of this, the Patriots actually improved their point differential by 127 points in 1969, although they still lost 10 games for the third year in a row. Also mitigating any sense of improvement was that they lost their first seven games, and the four games they did win were against teams that went 17–35–4. Whatever improvements there were proved fleeting, and in 1970 they stumbled to a 1–6 start.

Upton Bell: Clive Rush was fired in the middle of the 1970 season. John Mazur took over for him. There were all sorts of rumors about Clive, drinking and psychiatric problems and things like that. The team really slipped down.

Leigh Montville: Mazur was a guy that was built to be an assistant coach. I don't think he was ever meant to be a head coach. He stumbled into it when the wheels came off for Clive, and he took it upon himself as his great break. He was a solid guy, but he had no imagination.

The Pats had an identical 1–6 record under Mazur, but gained 30 fewer yards per game and surrendered 60 more on defense. Still, when Upton Bell took over as general manager after the season, he was not allowed to bring in his own man.

Upton Bell: The team was in a state of chaos. John Mazur, the coach, was on a one-year contract. That's never good. There was no scouting combine. There weren't a lot of draft choices there. Their first choice from the year before, Phil Olsen, was coming off a knee injury. In retrospect, I probably shouldn't have come. I should've gone into a situation that was clean and where I could hire my own coach. Or, at least, I should have been allowed to judge the situation and make my own decision as far as what I wanted with the coach at the end. I did agree to come in and look at the situation for a year.

THE WANDERERS

There was, too, the question of the team's homelessness. When the franchise was still relatively young, owner Billy Sullivan had tried to find a permanent home in Boston.

Patrick Sullivan: My father was trying to get a stadium built. When my folks moved out of their house in Wellesley, we moved thirteen models of proposed stadiums out of their attic. Their wished-for locales ranged from Neponset to South Station to Norwood to Weston to the Rockingham Park area, in New Hampshire, and, of course, in Foxborough. There was absolutely no appetite whatsoever to build a stadium with public money. The closest we ever came was 1964. Everything fell into place to build a stadium at what would now be the end of the Mass. Pike. It was going to be a fifty-five-thousand-seat stadium with a retractable roof. The Red Sox had agreed to play there. Most people don't know that [Red Sox owner] Tom Yawkey had agreed to move out of Fenway Park in 1964. In those days Fenway was thought of as an old dump. They had horrible attendance in those days. What sank the deal was, the legislature said they would only float the necessary bonds if they had to get all four sports teams agreeing to long-term leases. All four teams—the Patriots, Red Sox, Bruins, and Celtics—did. At the last minute, though, the Bruins pulled out because their owner, Weston Adams, had wanted a bigger piece of the Celtics' concession revenue.

And so, the Patriots remained as guests and tenants in the homes of others. (See "The Many Homes of the Boston Patriots," on page 104.)

Houston Antwine: Oh man, we were like gypsies. We went from Boston College to Harvard—all over the place.

Gil Santos: They played at Boston University, they played at Fenway Park, they played at Harvard Stadium, and they played at Boston College. They even played a home game in Birmingham, Alabama!

Len St. Jean: Every year we'd come back and it was like, "Where are we going to be playing this year?" There was always a cloud that hung over us. But the camaraderie of the players was great—everybody hung together. It wasn't easy, but we were resolved that someday things would get better.

Gino Cappelletti: The league demanded they find a stadium or else they had to move.

As part of the deal between the AFL and the NFL, no team was going to be allowed to play in a stadium that held fewer than 50,000 fans. That meant Fenway Park was not an adequate facility for the post-merger Patriots. An attempt to get a football-only stadium built in Boston had been rejected by the city, and it appeared that the Patriots were going to have to move somewhere else entirely. The Birmingham game, played in the second week of the 1968 season, was an attempt by promoters there to showcase the town for future consideration as the Patriots' new home. The attendance was a disappointing 29,192, many of whom were on hand because the Crimson Tide's favorite son, Joe Namath, was leading the opposition Jets.

In addition to Birmingham, Seattle, Memphis, and even Montreal were being bandied about as destinations. The Patriots stayed put, though, at least relatively. Instead of lighting out for territories unknown, Sullivan found a place some 20 miles to Boston's south.

Patrick Sullivan: The deal in Foxborough revolved around one thing: free land. E.M. Loew, who also owned the Loew's theater chain, owned Bay State Raceway, and he had agreed that if he could keep the parking revenue from the games, he'd give up the acreage to build the stadium. That's why it ended up down there.

So Loew gave the land to the Patriots for the formal fee of $1.00, and Billy Sullivan set about raising all the necessary capital for construction. Unfortunately, he came up just a little short.

Patrick Sullivan: It was a real journey for my dad. He really spent a lot of time on the deal. He had to have commitments to sell 7.1 million dollars in stock in the stadium before a certain date. On the last day possible, he was still three hundred thousand dollars short to getting the deal done. Running out of ideas, he called a guy he knew named George Doran.

In his capacity as an executive with Narragansett Beer, Doran was the man who had helped get the Boston Braves and Red Sox on radio and television. He had since moved on to the F. & M. Schaefer Brewing Company. Schaefer had been the best-selling beer in the world, but its market share was receding by the 1970s. Still, they were a major player in the industry.

Patrick Sullivan: Dad called George and said, "We're three hundred thousand short, and I have an idea: If you give me the three hundred, I'll give you the right to name the stadium and you guys will also be the exclusive beer in the stadium." It was the first naming rights deal in the history of pro sports—and that's how that deal got over the top.

Given the state of stadium building in modern times, the numbers that accompany the construction of Schaefer Stadium are fairly astounding.

Patrick Sullivan: It was originally budgeted at 6.9 million dollars, and it was two hundred thousand over budget, so it cost 7.1 million. Another amazing stat is it was built in 327 days.

Even adjusting for inflation, $7.1 million is not a lot of money. That is equivalent to around $40 million in today's market—and nobody builds stadiums for that little these days. Schaefer (and, as it was later called, Sullivan and then Foxboro) Stadium was certainly short on amenities, but how many amenities do football fans really need? Football supporters—especially those in harsher climates like New England—are a hardy breed. The bells and whistles of modern ballparks are seemingly superfluous in that fans take up residence in a stadium only 50 hours a year, at most.

Based on aesthetics and accessibility, Schaefer Stadium was not utopia, but it was home.

Patrick Sullivan: My father said that if he couldn't get the deal done for the new stadium, he'd have to move the team. I'll tell you, there were a lot of suitors, but as far as my father was concerned, moving the team out of the area wasn't going to happen on his watch.

Len St. Jean: It felt pretty good to have that sense of stability and security. Schaefer Stadium wasn't the Taj Mahal, but that is the cornerstone of the Patriots. If it hadn't have come about, I sincerely believe there would be no New England Patriots today.

Patrick Sullivan: I always say that Foxboro had its limitations, but I totaled it up, and something in excess of thirty million people went through that stadium in its time. I don't think it owed anybody anything.

THE NEW NAME

For decades, sports teams had gone by the name of a single city, with very few exceptions. In 1950, the Regina Roughriders officially became known as the Saskatchewan Roughriders, a name they would take into the Canadian Football League. Being named for a whole province or state was a new concept in sports-team designations and one that was slow to catch on. Not including roller derby's Jersey Jolters of 1949 or the wartime hybrid teams in the NFL, the first examples of this sort in American sports came in 1961 when baseball's Washington Senators became the Minnesota Twins and the NFL created the expansion Vikings. Using the state name in these cases was a natural choice and a good workaround for the old problem of favoring one twin city,

Minneapolis or St. Paul, over the other. In 1965, the Los Angeles Angels moved to Anaheim and chose the designation California. Later in the decade, a number of teams in the American Basketball Association chose state names rather than cities, and the practice was especially common in the minor Continental Football League, which even had a team named after a whole country: the Mexico Golden Aztecs.

The distinction of being the first team identified by something beyond a single state probably belongs to the Carolina Cougars of the American Basketball Association. It was something of a misnomer in that when they moved from Houston to North Carolina in 1969, they played their home games in four different cities in that state, but not in South Carolina. The next step in the evolution would be a name that suggested an entire region, but before that could happen, the Patriots came up with a different twist: they would have as their place designation not the name of their state, but their state's *nickname*. In February of 1971, they announced they would no longer be known as the Boston Patriots.

Upton Bell: When I got there, they were called the Bay State Patriots.

Bay State was also the name of the racetrack that had donated the land for the new stadium. This sort of name was unprecedented in major league sports. Soon after arriving, Bell reported that the first newspaper headline he read about the team referred to them as the "BS Patriots." Bell was alarmed. "Oh, no. The BS Patriots? Like the *Bull Shit* Patriots?" he said at the time.

Before the ink could dry on the revised stationery, Bell wanted to do away with the new designation.

Upton Bell: I thought since we were moving to Foxborough and we would be sort of in the middle—closer to Providence than Boston—that the name should be changed to the New England Patriots. The board of directors agreed to it.

So, on March 23, 1971, before they'd even played a game under their new moniker, an announcement was issued that the Bay State né Boston Patriots would henceforth be known as the New England Patriots.

THE DRESS REHEARSAL

It was a tumultuous summer for the new New England Patriots. One of their first moves was to part ways with Joe Kapp, who had fallen from grace faster than any former MVP the NFL has ever known. He had thrown for a record-tying seven touchdowns in one game while with the Vikings in 1969, but managed just three TD passes in 10 games for the Patriots a year later—and those three touchdowns were accompanied by 17 interceptions. Whoever was to blame for the Kapp debacle—and there was blame aplenty to go around for everyone, from the league office to the teams to Kapp himself—the Patriots felt they needed to start their new era without him. So, with the first pick in the draft—which Kapp certainly had an unwitting hand in securing—the Patriots took Heisman Trophy–winning quarterback Jim Plunkett of Stanford.

With their second pick they chose defensive end Julius Adams from Texas Southern, and he would spend 16 years with the team. Aside from those two, only Josh Ashton, who played 40 NFL games in his career, and Alfred Sykes, who played four, ever made a dent in the big league.

Upton Bell: That first training camp was kind of chaotic. It was prophetic of what would happen coming down to the first game. I traded Carl Garrett to Dallas for Duane Thomas, who I thought was the best running back around; the heir to Jimmy Brown. He had played against my old team, the Colts, in the Super Bowl, and was named Rookie of the Year. But I didn't know at the time that he was pretty heavy into drugs. Therefore, his stay here was less than a week.

Thomas, aside from a number of other quirks, did not use the three-point stance.

Upton Bell: The coach threw him off the field. I don't think Mazur ever wanted him. I thought he would be great. I didn't think that

Garrett, who was a good running back, was in the same league as Thomas. And they both had problems and I figured, why not trade one problem for another? But the real reason he was no longer here is he couldn't pass the physical. What happened was I called the league office, and we were able to restructure the deal. We sent Thomas back to Dallas and got Garrett back. Essentially, when someone can't pass the physical you can't keep him. I negated the trade, the commissioner got involved, and we were able to work it out with Tex Schramm. Ironically, he went back to Dallas and they went to the Super Bowl and he was named the MVP of Super Bowl VI. They were a more established team that could control the problems that he had. Then, as we know, after the Super Bowl he went off the deep end and didn't play for Dallas again, either.

Before the newly rechristened Patriots could take the field, everyone felt it was essential to have a few dry runs at using their new stadium. It was a good thing they did.

The first preseason game at Schaefer Stadium was scheduled for August 15 against the New York Giants. Before it happened, though, the team famously orchestrated what came to be known as the Great Super Flush, prompted when a couple of building inspectors showed up two days before the Giants game and asked the ultimate hypothetical question: "What if the fans just happened to flush every single toilet at the same time?"

With a sellout crowd anticipated, the last thing the Patriots wanted was to be shut down by public servants, so they got all hands on deck and pulled the handle on every john in the place.

Patrick Sullivan: I was on the Super Flush team, assigned to the east side of the stadium. They had put in this temporary tank system, and thank God they did or we wouldn't have been allowed to play it.

Along with Sullivan, the Super Flush team consisted of every able-bodied person the Patriots could round up, including his father, Billy, his brother Chuck, sportswriters, stadium hands, and team and racetrack personnel. They lined up at the team offices and, on command, raced off to the restrooms to flush the toilets simultaneously. When Armageddon did not ensue, the inspectors gave the building an approval rating and the show went on. There were other problems, of course, as there always must be with new ventures.

Upton Bell: I was worried we wouldn't have the goalposts installed in time. I believe the last one had to be flown in by helicopter. We got it in three or four hours before the game. I was talking to [Giants owner] Wellington Mara before the game and he said, "I'm glad we got the goalposts in"—you know, making a joke! He had no idea!

The major hassle with the first game, though, should have been easier to foresee than a mass malfunction of the commodes.

Gino Cappelletti: I had a hard time getting to that game because the traffic on Route 1 was just delayed to the point of being ridiculous. It was a huge event—a happening here in New England with a new stadium like that.

Gil Santos: I was sitting in the radio booth, looking to my left up Route One facing north, and commenting early on about the never-ending line of headlights coming down to get to the stadium.

Upton Bell: The problem, too, was that Route One coming down there, once you got off of Interstate 95, there weren't enough lanes for all the traffic that was going to flood in there—and no one planned for any of this.

Patrick Sullivan: Everything was so poorly organized. The raceway guys controlled the parking lot. They hadn't seen more than ten thousand people at the raceway in twenty-five years. It was a real mishmash.

Len St. Jean: After the game, they had a function for us at the stadium. It went on for a long time. I left there at five A.M., and I still had to wait in line to get out of the parking lot! I had friends who I had given tickets to, and they never even made it to the game. They turned around and went home and still didn't get home until two or three in the morning. It was one of the biggest fiascos I've ever been involved with. It was a nightmare.

Only about half the 60,000 ticket holders ever got inside the stadium. *Sports Illustrated* reported that traffic was backed up to the Rhode Island state line. Cars were still stuck heading south when the game ended, and those who had made it began exiting northward, further snarling the situation.

Upton Bell: Since Nero watched Rome burn, there was nothing like that. I stood at the top of the stadium and looked out on something that looked like the Blitz of London. The next day, after this disaster, it was on the front pages of every newspaper in the area and on television. Imagine what it would be like today with the Internet and the feeding frenzy and everything else. It would be on YouTube. Just add music and there would be fifty million hits to see the greatest traffic jam ever. It was like Woodstock without the mud and the drugs.

Gino Cappelletti: So we got to the game, suited up, and went out against the Giants. Once again, on our first possession we moved downfield. It started off with an attempt for a field goal, and I said, "Déjà vu." Just like the first game with the Patriots at BU. So I went in to kick the field goal, then went out and played some.

As he had 11 years before, Cappelletti put the Pats up 3–0. In the second half, those who had managed to make it into the stadium got a real thrill. *Sports Illustrated* reported that "When Jim Plunkett, Heisman Trophy winner and Rose Bowl hero, came in to quarterback the Patriots in the second half of their exhibition against the Giants, he received an ovation usually accorded only to Kennedys in New England."

Jon Morris: When they drafted Plunkett, there was a huge amount of enthusiasm. Veteran players can tell right away when a rookie comes into camp if a guy has it or not. I remember when John Hannah came into camp for the first time. We were all checking him out because he was a number-one pick. In an hour, we knew that the bar had been raised for offensive-line players. This was a new way to play offensive line. It was almost the same with Plunkett when he came into camp. He had a cannon for an arm. We looked at that and thought, This guy can throw the ball. When we signed his college teammate Randy Vataha, the two of them looked great together.

That Plunkett had no impact on the final score—a 20–14 victory for the Patriots—was beside the point.

Upton Bell: There was so much controversy the next day. The state transportation people demanded that we change the night games we had set up as exhibition games to day games. I had to call all the teams and get them to change from night to day, which would change the gate. You're not going to get as many people to come to your game on a Sunday afternoon in a blistering summer to come off the Cape and watch it as you would a night game. The Rams said the only way they'd do that is if we gave them a draft choice!

Apparently undeterred by the hassles, 53,271 showed up for the preseason game against the Rams two weeks later, which New England lost 31–21. The upside of that game was that Deacon Jones, the Rams' all-world pass rusher, was convinced enough of Jim Plunkett's greatness that afterward he predicted the rookie would be a superstar.

In all, the Patriots lost five of their six preseason games. Their victory over the Giants was not only the sole exhibition they won that summer; it also marked the first time they had beaten a pre-merger NFL team in any game, regular season or otherwise. Their record against NFL and pre-merger NFL teams (Baltimore, Cleveland, and Pittsburgh, who had jumped to the AFC in 1970) in the first two seasons of the merger—1970 and 1971—was 1–11. Oddly, they won all three of their interconference games in 1972, their only victories that year.

Upton Bell: One day during practice, I got a call from the board of health. They were closing the place down until we could get enough water pressure. The team couldn't practice at the stadium. They could get dressed there, but we had to bus them somewhere else to practice. There were many things that made me think, Why am I here?

Gino Cappelletti: It was becoming questionable to the organization and to me as to whether I was going to continue playing or not. There's no question the Patriots really hit bottom during those last few years of the decade. There was some disorganization, some mismanagement, some decisions that had to be made that turned out badly. The team was in the doldrums; the morale was down. It was a tough time. I made the decision to announce my retirement. I did that before the season started.

On one hand, the tumult continued, but on the other, the team had turned a corner. The new stadium and the new quarterback and all the other attendant newness sent a message to the fans that things were changing.

Patrick Sullivan: We had sold out on a season-ticket basis. I think it was [future Boston mayor] Ray Flynn who tried to file legislation to prevent us from selling more than fifty-five thousand season tickets. What a strange business it is where somebody actually tries to file legislation to prevent you from selling your product!

THE OPPONENTS

From 1967 through '69, the Oakland Raiders had run up a 37–4–1 record. This remains the second-best three-year record in NFL/AFL history, second only to the 1941–1943 Bears, who went 29–2–1. John Madden had taken over the team in 1969 and, at 12–1–1, had one of the best records ever for a first-year coach, although he was simply maintaining the greatness that John Rauch had left behind. The Raiders fell to 8–4–2 in 1970 but still won their division and first-round playoff game before falling to the eventual winners of Super Bowl V, the Baltimore Colts, in the inaugural AFC Championship Game. In terms of eventual career win-loss records, the head-to-head pairing of Madden versus Patriots head coach John Mazur is one of the great mismatches of the era. (See "Madden NFL 71," on page 105.) Oakland would go on to post another 8–4–2 record in 1971 and miss out on the wild-card spot, although they had the most dynamic offense in the conference and would score more points and surrender fewer than the 1970 team had (and against a tougher schedule).

The '70 team was famous for the numerous comebacks and last-second heroics of veteran quarterback/kicker George Blanda. At 44, he was back for more in 1971, ready to spell Daryle Lamonica if things got dicey. Kenny Stabler was hanging around the bench, too, giving the Raiders three interesting choices to handle the quarterbacking. Lamonica's favorite target was Fred Biletnikoff. The future Hall of Famer would lead the league with 61 catches that year. Tight end Raymond Chester was a Pro Bowl selection in 1971, as was fullback Marv Hubbard, who averaged 4.8 yards per carry and caught 22 passes. Pete Banaszak had eight rushing touchdowns and the third-most yards from scrimmage on the team.

It was Oakland's starting offensive line that day that still resonates today, boasting some of the most famous names of the era. Four of the five have been enshrined in Canton: left tackle Art Shell, left guard Gene Upshaw, center Jim Otto, and right tackle Bob Brown. Right guard George Buehler is the odd man out in that group, but he played nearly as well as the rest in 1971 and had a very productive 10-year career.

The Raiders defense was somewhat improved over its down year of 1970, but it was still two years away from the killer unit it would become in 1973. Its star was left cornerback Willie Brown, at the peak of his Hall of Fame powers. Nobody was throwing near him by this point. Safety Jack Tatum was a rookie making his NFL debut that day, as was linebacker Phil Villapiano. Big Ben Davidson was slowing down, and playing in his last opener.

THE GAME

It was the beginning of a new era, but there was some business to take care of from the era just passed. The Patriots decided to have the Schaefer Stadium regular-season inaugural also be the occasion of

Gino Cappelletti Day, in honor of the only original Patriot who lasted the entire run of the American Football League and who was now calling it a career.

Gino Cappelletti: My mother was there, came from Minnesota, my dad was ill at the time. My family, two of my daughters, they presented me with a station wagon, and it was a very nice thing to have happen to you. As much as they may have appreciated some of my play during the decade, I appreciated the fact that there was a Lamar Hunt and a Billy Sullivan to bring the AFL into being and to provide opportunities for many players like me to experience playing professional football.

Houston Antwine: It was a day of a lot of excitement. Spirits were running high. When we got out on the field I said, "You have to do what you have to do. Give your best of everything." That's what I always tried to do. I'd put everything out there. That day made you put more—you pulled it from your gut . . . Sometimes I astounded me!

Patrick Sullivan: It was a typical New England fall day. The crowd was huge, and everybody was having a blast.

Phil Villapiano: None of the toilets worked. By game time, guys were flushing them and it was putrid. They were all backed up. Our locker room stunk. There was water coming out of the bathroom. No one wanted to go in there.

The first person to touch the ball was the Patriots' kicker, Charlie Gogolak, whose brother Pete had been the first player to reverse the trend and jump from the AFL to the NFL. Gogolak's kick went to Clarence Davis at the Raiders' 1-yard line, and he brought it out to the 23. The first play from scrimmage was a 13-yard run by Marv Hubbard, who was finally brought down by cornerback John Outlaw.

The next eight plays were runs as Hubbard and Banaszak ground the ball forward to the New England 28. It wasn't until the 10th play of the drive that Lamonica tried a pass, missing Chester with Clarence Scott on the coverage. On third and 10, he hit Biletnikoff for 16 yards down to the 12 and things were looking grim for the Patriots.

This drive typifies two things about football at the time, things that make modern fans scratch their heads because of what has come since. Because the rules favored pass defenses, teams threw the ball only about 45 percent of the time. Today the ratio of passes to runs is reversed. In 2011, NFL teams passed a bit under 55 percent of their plays and ran 45 percent. The second thing was that holding penalties were worth a 15-yard setback. A hold with a 10-yard penalty is costly enough, but imagine how devastating 15 yards was at a time when it was harder to make up ground through the air.

This is relevant here because on Biletnikoff's 16-yard reception, future head of the NFL Players Association Gene Upshaw was flagged for holding, which sent the ball back to the Patriots' 43, a swing of 31 yards in New England's favor. The next pass failed, and Mike Eischeid punted the ball to Hubie Bryant, who called for a fair catch at the 11. On the first series in their new stadium, the Patriots didn't even try to go to the air. In spite of the gift of a first and 5 situation when George Atkinson jumped offside, they ran into the line every time and came up empty.

Things took a turn for the better for New England when Lamonica was flushed from the pocket and lost the ball. Linebacker Eddie Philpott pounced on it, and the Patriots were in business at the Oakland 41. Plunkett opened the possession by trying his first NFL pass, only to have it knocked away by Tatum. On third down, he notched his first completion, a 14-yard hookup with tight end Roland Moss.

Mike Garrett got the call on first and 10 from the 30, went left, and burst into the clear. He was all the way down to the 14 when he was hit and lost the ball. Tatum, who had to be having one of the busiest debut quarters of any rookie defensive back, scooped up the fumble at the 10 and began wending his way up the field. He'd gotten 20 yards before he was hit and coughed it up himself. Tom Neville fell on it for New England. As the first quarter ended, the Patriots were back where the play had started: at the Raiders' 30.

The next series was stalled by two plays: a holding penalty that took the Pats out of field goal range and a non-pass-interference call on

Nemiah Wilson, who had appeared to trip Ron Sellers, much to the displeasure of the screaming crowd. Neither team could generate much traction on their next two possessions. With 4:50 left in the quarter, though, the Raiders started on their own 40 and mounted a drive that proved sustainable. Halfback Don Highsmith got the call on four consecutive plays and moved Oakland 26 yards closer to pay dirt. Passes to Chester and Banaszak got the ball to the 4 before Banaszak swept left and got the ball across the line just inside the flag.

Dating back four full years to the opening game of the 1967 season, George Blanda had kicked 190 consecutive conversions. He never got a chance on this one. The snap literally never left the ground. In what had to be one of the worst hike jobs of Jim Otto's career, he rolled a grounder right past holder Kenny Stabler with such force that it would be corralled by the Snake some 25 yards from the line of scrimmage, leaving the Raiders to kick off without their extra point.

The Pats' Bob Gladieux took the kick at the 20 and was on his way to a very nice runback when he lost the ball. Once again, Tatum was there to recover. Oakland had the ball on the New England 44 with 49 seconds on the clock, but plenty of time-outs. Banaszak got them to within field goal range by catching a Lamonica dump at the 36 and juking his way to the 24. The Pats jumped offside. Lamonica overthrew Rod Sherman in the end zone and then, after Hubbard gained six on a draw, also overthrew an open Eldridge Dickey, missing a scoring opportunity. The Raiders could have very easily gone into the locker room with a 13–0 lead. Instead, they figured on settling for 9–0 . . . but didn't even get that as Blanda's field goal attempt went wide right.

Plunkett had thrown the ball only four times in his first half of NFL football, completing one of them for 14 yards. The way the Pats were moving the ball (24 total yards on offense), they were fortunate to be in the game.

New England received to open the second half but punted the ball away after getting one first down. The Raiders' next series featured three separate gains of 13 yards, but thanks mostly to another holding call, they were forced to punt from the Patriots' 43. Eischeid was left out to dry by a bad snap, however, and when he tried to run with it, Tom Beer dropped him at midfield.

And then, suddenly, it all started to click for the Patriots. Plunkett hit a quick one to Sellers for eight yards, and then Gladieux sliced through the line for a 9-yard gain before being put down by Atkinson. On first and 10 from the 33, Plunkett found Sellers running in stride at the 2 and the Patriots were on the board with their first points in the new stadium.

Phil Villapiano: Jim Plunkett kept deking it and deking it. We were both rookies, so I was kind of rooting for him to succeed because he was such a nice guy—but I didn't want him to beat us.

The next Oakland series displayed Daryle Lamonica's day in microcosm. On first down, Marv Hubbard dropped an easy catch. On second down, Ike Lassiter hurried Lamonica and he missed his target high. On third down, he tried to hit Chester and was very nearly picked off by linebacker Jim Cheyunski.

The Pats got the ball back at their own 30 and, on second and 6, Plunkett had his first successful hookup with a familiar face.

Upton Bell: One of the gems that we found was Randy Vataha, who at that time was working as one of the Seven Dwarfs at Disneyland. He had been Plunkett's battery mate at Stanford. We found him and signed him as a free agent. There were a lot of people that we brought in to try change the tempo of the team around.

Vataha's first career reception covered 39 yards. He barely missed one on the next play, leaping in a futile attempt to haul in a high pass. On the next play, Plunkett looked downfield for another newcomer, Roland Moss.

Phil Villapiano: Moss was a running back from the University of Toledo that had been switched to tight end. In college, he was a big shot. I got a chance to grab him and throw him around a little bit that afternoon, which I enjoyed.

Upton Bell: I had seen Roland Moss as a running back at Toledo, so we drafted him when I was with Baltimore. His second year there, they cut him and I picked him up on waivers for the Patriots. Plunkett faked and hit Moss for a touchdown, and that was one of the key plays in the game.

Plunkett had found Moss wide open at the 10-yard line, and he brought it home from there for the 14–6 lead. The third quarter ended with the Patriots holding the ball again, Dennis Wirgowski having recovered a Pete Banaszak fumble at the Oakland 42. The drive stalled soon enough, but Gogolak nailed a 46-yard field goal to make it 17–6. Lamonica floundered again, and Madden called on Stabler to try to get something going. When his series went nowhere, the miracle man of 1970 was called on to get the Raiders back in the game. By the time George Blanda took over at quarterback, however, there was only 4:16 on the clock and the Patriots had built their lead to 14 points on another Gogolak field goal. Given what Blanda had accomplished the year before, though—winning the MVP based almost solely on his late-game heroics in five contests—this did not seem like an impossible task. Could the Patriots hold on?

The Raiders were able to move from their own 16 to midfield, but their slim hopes ended when Larry Carwell picked off Blanda's long heave intended for Chester at the New England six. As the Patriots ran out the clock, the sellout crowd went crazy. For now, at least, all was right with the world.

Len St. Jean: I don't know if we played above our heads or what, but it was a tremendous feeling to knock the Raiders off.

Phil Villapiano: I would have to say we were just flat. It was one of those games where everything we did, we did wrong. We looked like shit.

Upton Bell: The people in the press box? Their heads were spinning. They couldn't believe it.

"We just keep wheeling and dealing," Ike Lassiter said at the time. "We kept the pressure on them and we kept our poise. We played four quarters instead of two."

What made the win even more impressive was that the Raiders turned around and shut out the Chargers 34–0 the next week and went on to lead the conference in scoring. Their six points in this game was their lowest total of the year.

"We did what we said we would do—we're going to be winners. Now we stand tall," said Mazur, flush with the glow of victory.

"Now we're winners and we want to keep it that way," added Plunkett. And who could blame them? What team *hasn't* been overly optimistic after a big opening day? Put it out of your mind that it didn't quite work out that way. Live in the moment as they were.

Upton Bell: That really started people with high hopes for this team. We beat the Raiders, and later on we knocked the Colts and then the Dolphins out of first place. Three of the biggest upsets of the season. Then there was the downside; the games where we really looked terrible. At the end of the season I felt the coach should be replaced. I felt we needed to go in a different direction. That's when I found out Billy never promised me the authority to hire and fire the head coach. I would not have come here if I didn't have that. I felt like we had to be good enough to fill the stadium. I knew the best I could do was do as much as I could get done before the end came for me, which could be quick.

Patrick Sullivan: It was a great part of the history, but it was very short-lived, because we had what I'd call epic dysfunction between Upton Bell and John Mazur, the head coach.

Upton Bell: The negatives were the ownership, which was in constant flux. There was also a board of directors besides the owners, totally twenty or thirty people. On top of that, you were really dealing with a coach that—I'm not sure, I won't say didn't want me here—but knew the pressure would be on him. At the end of the year, I thought I had the authority to hire and fire the head coach. That'll come later on. As a result, we went to training camp with a lot of new people.

Beyond the final score, though, the Patriots were finally in a home of their own.

Gil Santos: It was a great feeling to know that this team had arrived to the point that they finally had their own field.

Upton Bell: A guy by the name of Dan Marcotte, the stadiums operations guy at Fenway Park, said the day Schaefer Stadium was built it was already obsolete, but it served its purpose, and the sight lines were great. Sure, there were problems with the plumbing, and the parking lots weren't paved, but I can't rap that because there was no place else to go.

Gil Santos: It only cost seven million dollars to build. It was spartan; certainly nothing fancy with aluminum benches to sit on and no regular back chairs. A lot of people ridiculed it as the years went by. The fact of the matter is this: If that stadium was not there, the team would not have been in New England; not in the state of Massachusetts. There were people who wanted to move to all kinds of different places, but Billy Sullivan held fast, got the stadium, and it was a godsend because it kept the team here.

APPENDICES

The Many Homes of the Boston Patriots

Not only did the Patriots of the AFL not have a real, permanent home; they were the second tenants wherever they went. They played second banana to the Boston University Terriers, the Boston Red Sox, the Boston College Eagles, the Harvard Crimson, and even the Alabama Crimson Tide. During the Red Sox' "Impossible Dream" season of 1967, the Patriots were forced to play on the road for their first five games. This included two trips to San Diego to play the Chargers. When they finally did return to Boston, it wasn't to Fenway Park but to Alumni Stadium, in Newton, where they would play all their home games in 1969. They didn't play their first game at Fenway until week seven and ended up one home game short, going 1–6–1 on the road.

YEAR	Nickerson Field			Fenway Park			Legion Field			Alumni Stadium			Harvard Stadium		
	W	L	T	W	L	T	W	L	T	W	L	T	W	L	T
1960	3	4	0												
1961	4	2	1												
1962	6	1	0												
1963				5	1	1									
1964				4	2	1									
1965				1	4	2									
1966				4	2	1									
1967				1	4	0				1	0	0			
1968				2	4	0	0	1	0						
1969										2	5	0			
1970													1	6	0
Total	13	7	1	17	17	5	0	1	0	3	5	0	1	6	0

Madden NFL 71

Sometimes forgotten in view of his more recent incarnations as video-game magnate and oft-caricatured TV commentator is the fact that John Madden has the greatest regular-season record of any coach in the modern era. Discounting one- and two-game wonders and co-coaches, only Hall of Famer Guy Chamberlin has a better winning percentage, going all the back to day one in 1920.

This, of course, makes the Patriots' victory on opening day 1971 that much more of an upset in that their head coach, John Mazur, had a record quite the opposite of Madden's. He won just 30 percent of the games he coached (9–21), whereas Madden won three quarters of his regular-season contests (103–32–7). In fact, Mazur was the losingest coach to beat Madden during his 10 years in charge of the Raiders. Paul Wiggin of the Chiefs had a career record similar to Mazur's, but he had five cracks at Madden to come away with his win, while Mazur just had the one.

Including the postseason, Madden lost 39 games to 21 different coaches. Of those 39 losses, 15 came against a core group of Hall of Fame legends: Hank Stram, Chuck Noll, Don Shula, and Paul Brown. The man against whom he had the most trouble was one of the Patriots' original assistant coaches: Red Miller.

Even against the coaches who beat him, though, Madden had the upper hand, going 60–39–3 against them overall for a winning percentage of .607. That alone would be good enough to rank him among the top 50 all-time, but then consider that he went 52–0–4 against everyone else. This includes Hall of Famers Sid Gillman, Weeb Ewbank (3–0 each), Marv Levy (2–0), and wins in his only encounters against Tom Landry, George Allen, Blanton Collier, and Dick Vermeil, a group that had a career .579 winning percentage.

Mazur truly slew a giant that day in 1971.

Those Who Beat Madden

Coach	Team	Career Record					Head to Head Vs. Madden				Beat Madden
		W	L	T	PCT.	W	L	T	PCT.	
Don Shula*	Dolphins	328	156	6	.676	3	4	0	.429	1970, 1973, 1978
Paul Brown*	Bengals	213	104	9	.667	3	4	0	.429	1969, 1970, 1975
Red Miller	Broncos	40	22	0	.645	4	1	0	.800	1977, *1977*, 1978 (2x)
Bud Grant*	Vikings	158	96	5	.620	1	3	0	.250	1973
Don McCafferty	Colts	28	17	2	.617	2	0	0	1.000	*1970*, 1971
Don Coryell	Chargers	111	83	1	.572	1	1	0	.500	1978
Hank Stram*	Chiefs	131	97	10	.571	4	7	2	.385	*1969*, 1971, 1972, 1973
Chuck Noll*	Steelers	193	148	1	.566	5	6	0	.455	1972, *1972*, 1973, *1974*, 1975
Chuck Knox	Rams	186	147	1	.558	1	0	0	1.000	1977
Joe Schmidt	Lions	43	34	7	.554	1	0	0	1.000	1970
Chuck Fairbanks	Patriots	46	39	0	.541	2	2	0	.500	1976, 1977
Bum Phillips	Oilers	82	77	0	.516	1	3	0	.250	1975
John Ralston	Broncos	34	33	3	.507	2	7	1	.250	1972, 1974
Lou Saban	Bills	95	99	7	.490	1	6	0	.143	1974
Nick Skorich	Browns	45	48	2	.484	1	2	0	.333	1973
Dick Nolan	49ers	69	82	5	.458	1	1	0	.500	1970
Tommy Prothro	Chargers	35	51	2	.409	1	8	0	.111	1977
Norm Van Brocklin	Falcons	66	100	7	.402	1	0	0	1.000	1971
Jack Patera	Seahawks	35	59	0	.372	2	1	0	.667	1978 (2x)
Paul Wiggin	Chiefs	11	24	0	.314	1	4	0	.200	1975
John Mazur	Patriots	9	21	0	.300	1	0	0	1.000	1971
Total		1949	1516	68	.561	39	60	3	.393	

*= Hall of Fame. *Italics indicate playoff game.*

New England Patriots at Oakland Raiders

DIVISIONAL PLAYOFFS
December 18, 1976

	1	2	3	4	F
New England Patriots	7	0	14	0	**21**
Oakland Raiders	3	7	0	14	**24**

Losing always hurts, but perhaps never more so than when the refs are involved. It's easy enough to say, "Get over it," but when you know you made the play, and you never get credit for it—it's hard to let go.

What makes this one even harder to get over was that this team was the real goods. The 1976 Patriots were easily the best team the franchise had put together to that point, and arguably the best before the Bill Belichick era. And after almost 20 years of futility, it was the franchise's best shot at glory.

Steve Grogan: Seventy-six was a fun year. We had a lot of young players. We picked up a lot of first- and second-round draft picks in the trade for Jim Plunkett. Then we had some veteran leadership that really set an example for us. We got on a roll, had a lot of fun. It was a close-knit team. We catapulted ourselves into the playoffs for the first time since 1963.

THE '76 PATRIOTS
After the disastrous 1972 season, during which head coach John Mazur was replaced after nine games by Phil Bengston, the Patriots looked to

the highest echelons of the college football coaching ranks for a new sideline leader.

Pat Sullivan: Dad had been out and about. He talked to Tom Osborne [the offensive coordinator] at Nebraska; he talked to Joe Paterno and Bo Schembechler.

He also talked to Chuck Fairbanks, who had run up a career record of 52–15–1 as the head coach at the University of Oklahoma. He was coming off consecutive number-two finishes in the AP poll.

Pat Sullivan: Fairbanks was actually the second or third choice. The first choice was Joe Paterno. I was sitting in Dad's office when Paterno accepted the job. He called the next morning and said he'd thought it over and had to respectfully decline.

So the job fell to Fairbanks, who left Oklahoma just in time to miss sanctions leveled against his former program for improprieties he maintained he knew nothing about. The improvement to the Patriots' fortunes was immediate (see "The Largest Year-to-Year Improvements in Patriots History," on page 128), although it's hard to imagine how the team could have gotten any worse than they were in 1972. The Patriots got better still in 1974.

Pat Sullivan: Chuck was remarkable because he was completely confident in his own ability, so he surrounded himself with the best assistant coaches you could find.

Steve Nelson: He surrounded himself with a great coaching staff. A number of the coaches later became head coaches in the league. When you look back, he was never afraid to have people around him who knew more about a position than he did, or knew more about defense than he did. I think he had a lot of confidence in his ability as a coach but more as a player-personnel guy. That's a great combination when you're a head coach, and he had control of the franchise and did a great job.

John Hannah: All but one or two of [the coaches] had professional experience. Not only professional experience, but were considered great coaches in the NFL. You had Red Miller, Hank Bullough [often credited with bringing the 3-4 defense to the pros], Charlie Sumner, Ray Perkins, and Larry Weaver. You had some great, great coaches coaching the positions. You could see within the coaching staff, there's a chance there.

Patrick Sullivan: Fairbanks loved to stir the guys on his staff. He knew they all had big egos. He'd sit with the defensive coaches and tell them the offensive coaches didn't think they were doing their job, and vice versa. Then he'd go to his office, drink a bottle of Scotch, and listen to the rumblings next door. He was a very interesting guy who knew how to motivate players.

Leigh Montville: He was an X's-and-O's guy. He was steely. That's the word for him. He had the look. He had a wandering eye or something. It was like a dead eye. You'd ask him what you think the weather is going to be on Sunday and he'd just stare at you.

Gil Santos: Not only was Fairbanks a terrific coach, and terrific organizer but, he had a great eye for talent. They became very good very fast.

Steve Nelson: I think one of Coach Fairbanks's strongest traits was talent recognition. The year before I was drafted [1974], they picked John Hannah, Sam Cunningham, and Darryl Stingley. In my year, they also picked Sam Hunt and Prentice McCray, who was a good player for us. The next year, it was Russ Francis and Steve Grogan. In '76 it was Mike Haynes, Pete Brock, and Tim Fox in the first round. He got a lot of really good players.

John Hannah: We had the players that were coming, the first-rounders. Then there were guys like Steve King, and Leon Gray the next year, we got Steve Nelson and Andy Johnson. And I saw this and said to myself, "Gosh, Fairbanks is going to turn this booger around." I got excited then.

Even in a year when NFL teams were throwing only 41 percent of the time, the Pats were extreme, attempting the second-fewest passes in the league. They also had the third-most rushing attempts in the NFL. They very nearly rushed twice as much as they threw. Sam Cunningham and Andy Johnson got the most carries, but third back Don Calhoun led the NFL in yards per attempt with 5.6.

John Hannah: Our line coach, Red Miller, was one of the best of all time. He was with the Cardinals in the late sixties, and in 1969, four of his five offensive-line starters made the Pro Bowl on a team that only won four games. When he came to us, he really did a great job. The first year, he brought in an old-timer by the name of Bob Reynolds that played left tackle and had me play next to him and he had Leon Gray kind of playing right tackle next to Lenny St. Jean so that we were being schooled by the two veterans. The next year, he put Leon and I together. Contrary to that book that was written about L.T. [Lawrence Taylor] being the guy who initiated the rush from the quarterback's blind side, that's been going on since time immemorial. Red put Leon and I over there and basically put us up against the pass-rushing side, and we attacked it hard. I bet you we ran three or four running plays—maybe as many as six—and featured them during a game. Fairbanks and the coaching staff had a theory: Let's be good at what we do. We had fewer plays so we could have more repetitions with them.

New England was not the place to be a wideout. Their two leading receivers were running backs: Sam Cunningham, with 29 catches, and Andy Johnson, with 27. Tight end Russ Francis had 26 catches, while Darryl Stingley led the wide receivers with 17. Marlin Briscoe and Randy Vataha combined for 27 catches. When the Pats got anywhere near the goal line, Steve Grogan was just as likely to keep the ball himself as he was to hand it off or throw it. Grogan had been tabbed in the fifth round of the 1975 draft and had taken over in the middle of that season, putting an end to Jim Plunkett's Patriots career. His 12 rushing touchdowns broke the record for quarterbacks held by Johnny Lujack and Tobin Rote, and remained the all-time scoring record for that position until it was broken by Cam Newton in 2011. It also equaled all the other rushing touchdowns on the team combined.

John Hannah: I think Chuck Fairbanks did a really good job with matching our offense with the skills that he brought in, but Jim Plunkett didn't match up with the offense we were riding. He had an unbelievable arm, but he was really, really slow. We ran four- and five-man patterns, and our offense was designed to have the ball gone in 2.8 to 3 seconds. Unfortunately, he got traded over to San Francisco and they ran the same offense, so he didn't do very well there. When he got to the Raiders, they ran three- and four-man patterns, which got him that extra second. That allowed him to go out and do what he did best, which was throw that football, and he won a couple of Super Bowls that way.

In the first round of the 1976 draft, the Patriots made one of their greatest picks ever, tabbing defensive back Mike Haynes from Arizona State. Haynes hit the ground running on his Hall of Fame career, picking off eight passes and returning two punts for touchdowns. Teams threw more passes against the Patriots than against anyone else in the NFL and they responded well, allowing just 4.5 net yards per pass attempt, good for fifth-lowest in the league. Teams averaged 4.0 yards per carry against New England, just a bit below league average. The Patriots arguably had the best return men in the NFL that year: Haynes on punts and Jess Phillips and a host of others on kickoffs gave New England a combined average return yardage that was the best of any team.

The Patriots' 1976 season schedule opened with four games against the who's who of AFC football in the mid-seventies: Baltimore, Miami, Pittsburgh, and Oakland. If the Pats were not better than they'd been in 1975, it would become very apparent very soon.

In the opener, Grogan was intercepted four times, while Bert Jones was a very efficient 17 for 23 with two touchdown passes. (Baltimore and New England would end the season as the number-one and number-two scoring teams in the NFL, but their two meetings were fairly subdued. The Colts won the opening-day affair 27–13, and the Patriots took the return match in week 10, 21–14.) In week two, the Patriots swiped three Bob Griese passes, while Grogan threw three touchdowns without a pick and the Dolphins fell, 30–14. The next week, the Patriots showed they were for real with a hard-fought win over the defending Super Bowl champion Steelers.

In week four, the Raiders came in sporting a 3–0 record, and the Patriots ran them silly, rushing for 292 yards on 52 carries while Grogan threw just 17 times (three for touchdowns).

Mark van Eeghen: We got absolutely destroyed in Foxborough. It was the first time I was home, close to Rhode Island, playing a game. The combination of the fact that we were never good on artificial turf, that it was a three-time-zone trip—we didn't do well on those—and, to top it off, in my estimation we were playing the best team in the league. We got killed.

Phil Villapiano: I think if we played them ten times, they'd beat us eight. I really believe the Patriots had our number. They had a Super Bowl championship–caliber team.

Gil Santos: It was one of Steve Grogan's greatest games as a Patriots quarterback. He ran a bootleg play for a touchdown in that game that fooled everybody in the stadium, including his teammates. The only person he told he was going to run the naked bootleg was the running back he was going to hand the ball off to. He called the play, and he told him as they broke the huddle, "I'm going to fake to you and run the bootleg to the other side." So he was the only guy that knew it. Therefore, all of the assignments by the offensive linemen and the receivers were carried out as if it was going to be a running play to the other side of the field. Everybody went in that direction, and Grogan went in the other direction and walked into the end zone standing up. They just buried that Oakland team that day.

It would be the Raiders' only loss, making the '76 Patriots one of those very few teams who managed to destroy a perfect season. (See

"Perfection Denied," on page 342.) Furthermore, the 48–17 beating is one of the very worst ever endured by an eventual Super Bowl champion (see "The Worst Defeats Inflicted on Championship Teams," on page 132). Obviously, these two distinctions are possible only because of what eventually happened in the playoffs; had things gone differently there, footnotes about perfect seasons and greatest losses by champions would be moot.

The Pats fell flat on their visit to Detroit, losing 30–10 as the Lions took an early lead and repeatedly stole Grogan's passes as he tried to engineer a comeback. A thrashing of the hapless Jets was followed by a 26–22 defeat of the Bills in which Sam Cunningham outgained O.J. Simpson, 118–110. In week eight, the Patriots made the pilgrimage to Miami for their annual road loss to the Dolphins. From that game forward, they brushed aside all comers. They built a 7-point halftime lead on the Colts and made it stick by pitching a shutout in the second half. They built big leads on the Bills, Jets (intercepting a fading Joe Namath five times and Richard Todd twice), Broncos, and Saints, and won going away in each game.

Heading into the last weekend of the season, the 10–3 Patriots had already guaranteed themselves a playoff appearance, but would need to win their own game and have Baltimore lose to Buffalo in order to take their first division title since 1963. Winning the division would mean a home showdown with the rampaging Steelers in the first round of the playoffs, whereas the wild card would bring with it a visit to Oakland. A Pats victory seemed assured, as New England was traveling to Tampa to try to finish off the winless inaugural season of the expansion Buccaneers. Instead of a romp, though, they found themselves in their first real dogfight in more than a month.

The Patriots allowed the 0–13 Buccaneers something they had never had before: a 7-point lead—two of them, in fact. (The Bucs had held a number of 2- and 3-point leads, and only once been ahead by as much as 6). Against New England, though, they went up 7–0 and 14–7. After three quarters, the game was tied 14–14, but it had become apparent there would be no division title for the Patriots. A glance at the scoreboard showed that Baltimore had a five-touchdown lead on the Bills and was cruising to a 58–20 win. Now all that was left to play for was avoiding the humiliation of becoming the first-ever victim of the Tampa Bay franchise. With more than half the fourth quarter gone, though, the game was still tied and the Bucs were driving. In a flash, any hope of an upset vanished when Sam Hunt picked off a Steve Spurrier pass and ran it the other way for a 68-yard touchdown. The Pats added 10 more points to close out the regular season with the 31–14 win.

THE RAIDERS

Despite posting one of the best records in history, the 1976 Oakland Raiders did not destroy many of their opponents. It wasn't until their 11th game that they beat somebody by more than two touchdowns. When they showed up undefeated in Foxborough in week four, they had barely gotten past their first three opponents, winning by a total of 7 points. Among the teams with the greatest win-loss records of all time the '76 Raiders have the worst point differential. After playing mostly difficult and close games through the early part of the season, their last five games had margins of victory more befitting an eventual champion, outscoring their opponents 155–53. But only one of those games was against a team (Cincinnati) with a winning record.

This doesn't mean they weren't an excellent team; it's just that they weren't (or shouldn't have been) intimidating to the Patriots—especially given what had happened in their regular-season meeting. The Raiders had a decent enough run defense, ranking 10th in yards allowed in the NFL. Their pass defense was quite suspect, ranking only 20th (out of 28 teams) in yards allowed per passing attempt. Of course, that was not a shortcoming a dedicated running team like the Patriots was in good position to exploit. Phil Villapiano and Ted Hendricks were the standouts on a defense that always seemed to know when to stop giving up points.

George Blanda was enjoying the first year of his retirement and, 49 years old or not, he would have been preferable to what the Raiders were using to do their target kicking in his place. Apart from the expansion Buccaneers, the Raiders had arguably the worst kicking game in the league, with Fred Steinfort and Errol Mann booting just four field goals apiece while registering the second-lowest success percentage. Fortunately for Oakland, they were scoring so many touchdowns that it rarely mattered.

The Raiders' greatest strength was their passing game. Kenny Stabler threw 27 touchdown passes in 1976. Along with the six added by backup Mike Rae, it was by far the most tossed by any team in the league. Stabler averaged 9.4 yards per passing attempt, an excellent figure. His 66.7 completion percentage was, at the time, the second-highest ever. The Snake's favorite targets were Pro Bowlers Cliff Branch, who led the league in touchdown catches, and Dave Casper, the tight end, with the veteran Fred Biletnikoff still getting a nice share of balls thrown his way. Rushing leader Mark van Eeghen totaled 1,012 yards. John Madden was still counting on Art Shell and Gene Upshaw to anchor his O-line, and both turned in Pro Bowl–worthy performances.

As good a run as the Raiders were on—they had missed the playoffs just once in the previous eight seasons—they had yet to win the Super Bowl. Lately, they hadn't even been getting *to* the Super Bowl, bowing out in the first or second round in their last seven playoff appearances. If they didn't beat the Patriots, their reputation as bridesmaids would be cemented.

THE GAME

Nobody believed the Oakland–New England playoff meeting was going to be an exact repeat of their regular-season contest, least of all the linemakers, who had the Raiders installed as the favorite. Chuck Fairbanks told the *New York Times,* "We had no reputation then, and perhaps they didn't take us seriously as they might have. But now they know how good we are, from their own experience and from what else we've done. And this is a playoff. Everybody will be bearing down on both sides."

Steve Grogan: We thought we were playing some good football. We felt like we were matched up pretty well against the Raiders in the first round. We had beaten them fairly easily early in the season. We were not intimidated at all going into the Oakland Coliseum. We felt pretty good about our chances going into that game.

Mark van Eeghen: We had a lot of respect for the Patriots, but we did not think that we were the inferior team to the point of 48–17. You could argue that position for position they were as good a team in the league as there was in the NFL—as good as us, as good as Pittsburgh, as good as anybody. That group of guys were solid, and that about says it all. We knew we might be playing our Super Bowl in Oakland in that game. That was the team we had to beat. Thankfully, we were in our own place. Going back to Foxborough would not have been good. I'm not making excuses; forget about the time-zone trip. We were a horrible, horrible team on turf. We weren't used to it. We didn't play on it much. With Denver and San Diego, even most of our divisional away games were on grass. It was good that that game was at home.

Phil Villapiano: We knew we had a battle on our hands. I'm glad we had them at home in Oakland. My job was to take Russ Francis off his game plan. I was prepared. I studied hard and knew what the Patriots were going to do. I knew if Francis and Sam Cunningham handled me we would lose. I had to stop them. I'm sure every player feels the same way. I took it personally: If we lost, it would be on me.

Ray Guy, one of the most famous punters in NFL history, was also handling the kickoff chores for the Raiders. He started things off by hitting the ball to the 1, where Jess Phillips, who had spent the previous season in Oakland, caught it and brought it back to the 15. Grogan's first pass of the day was to Cunningham, good for 7 yards. After a quarterback keeper netted a first down, the drive stalled. On third and 12, Grogan threw over the middle for Vataha, but the pass went high and fell incomplete.

As Vataha was slowing up with both arms at his sides and clearly not in possession of the ball, Jack Tatum launched himself forearm first into Vataha's face mask and drove all the way through, knocking the receiver over backwards. The NFL players of 1976 didn't celebrate after every play with the enthusiasm that they do today, but Tatum was demonstrably very proud of the lick he laid on Vataha—one that would draw a penalty and perhaps a sizable fine in today's game. Receivers were fair game for this sort of treatment in that era, and it would be disingenuous to suggest that Jack Tatum—"the Assassin"—was the sole practitioner of this deadly art. He was the hardest-hitting of the league's defensive backs, though, and he'd knocked cold larger men than Vataha, who popped right up after the blow, seemingly none the worse for wear. Knowing that two years later Darryl Stingley was paralyzed by a Tatum hit makes this gratuitous blow seem that much more appalling.

The Raiders had a nice 30-yard punt return halved by a personal-foul penalty, but drove the ball into New England territory on the ensuing drive. On third and from the Patriots' 43, though, Sam Adams broke the back of the charge, sacking Stabler and forcing another punt.

The Patriots started from their own 14 and began to grind the ball forward, as was their wont. On third and 7 from the 33, though, Grogan switched things up and dropped back to pass. The Raiders made only a token rush, and Grogan had plenty of time to throw. The two Sams, Cunningham and Adams, were left with nobody to block. Russ Francis got open as he crossed from left to right, angling deep. Although he was overthrown, he put up one arm and came down with the ball at the Raider 40. He ran another 13 yards before he was dragged down by George Atkinson. On third down, the Raiders again failed to apply any pressure and Grogan did a bit of play action with Andy Johnson and then found Stingley cutting across the middle at the 13. He took it from there to the 1, where Tatum made a touchdown-saving tackle. It merely delayed the inevitable, though, as Johnson rammed it home on the next play for the 7–0 lead.

Stabler got things moving on the Raiders' next possession with long gainers to Biletnikoff and Branch. On third and 8 from the 23, he tried to find Biletnikoff in the end zone, but threw short. Prentice McCray made an acrobatic leap and appeared to have the ball snared, but he couldn't hang on to it. Madden sent in his kicking team. Between his time with Detroit and Oakland in 1976, Mann was just 2 for 11 from the 40 and beyond, so this was no guaranteed delivery. The kick was true, though, and the Raiders were on the scoreboard. (Mann would kick a 40-yarder in the AFC Championship and a 39-yarder in the Super Bowl. He then bounced back to have one of the better seasons of his career in 1977.)

Early in the second quarter, the Patriots embarked on a 10-play drive from their own 17 that saw them move forward a net of 4 yards. They were twice called for holding penalties, which cost them 20 yards (the penalty having been reduced from 15 to 10 prior to the 1974 season).

John Hannah: It sounds like sour grapes, but I think it was a lot of the officiating was one-sided. I love [Raiders middle guard] Dave Rowe to death, but the last thing an offensive lineman had to do was hold Dave Rowe. Dave is a good guy, but he was an average defensive lineman. If you count the number of holding calls that they called on [Patriots center] Bill Lenkaitis—like third-and-one situations, third-and-three situations—it wasn't just those big calls, it was all through the game. There wasn't a holding call against the Raiders the whole game.

During this possession, Stingley made a nice diving catch for a 12-yard gain and, while he was lying on the ground, Tatum dove into him helmet first when a simple pat on the shoulder would have sufficed to down him. The possession ended badly when Cunningham fumbled at the 21 and it was pounced on by Willie Hall, giving Oakland the ball right on the threshold. It was a partial atonement for Hall, who had dropped an easy pick-six two plays earlier. The Raiders gave it right back, though, as Sam Hunt stripped Clarence Davis on second down and Mel Lundsford came up with the fumble.

The Pats' ensuing drive was marked by two nice runs from Grogan and a face-mask penalty on the Raiders, their second of the game, although this one was of the 15-yard variety.

Phil Villapiano: In those days you had Bert Jones in Baltimore, Bob Griese in Miami, Grogan, and Terry Bradshaw. Just when you thought you had the coverage they would fucking run. I hit Grogan one time as hard as I have ever hit a quarterback. I knew he wasn't going out of bounds. That was a big plus to their offense. When you take care of everyone else, you had to deal with him.

Fairbanks went for a first down on fourth and inches at the Raider 42 and was vindicated when Don Calhoun burst through for 6 yards.

It all came to naught, though, thanks to an ill-fated trick play. On an end-around, Francis streaked through the backfield to the right and took the ball from Grogan. With Raiders bearing down on him, he stopped short and began backing up. He threw off his back foot, letting fly down to the 6, where Stingley was drawing double coverage from Skip Thomas and Tatum. Thomas came down with the underthrown pass and ran it back to the 24.

Three completions, the longest of which was an 18-yard gainer by Dave Casper, brought the Raiders to the New England 31 with under a minute left to play in the half. On first down, Stabler went for the gold, putting the ball up for Biletnikoff as he crossed the goal line. He leapt and made the catch in spite of coverage from Bob Howard that was so tight, an interference flag resulted. The half ended with the Raiders up by 3.

The third quarter belonged to New England. Their first drive appeared over when they were forced to punt on fourth and 3 at their own 27, but a penalty against the Raiders let the Patriots keep the ball, and they made the most of it. Cunningham broke loose for 22, and Grogan hit Francis for another 20. Another holding penalty against the Patriots pushed them back to the Raiders' 35, but it proved a minor inconvenience when Grogan found Francis streaking from right to left and led him perfectly for the score.

The Raiders went three and out on their next possession, greatly hindered by Julius Adams's sack of Stabler. Another Raider special-teams penalty, this time on the kicking team for an illegal man downfield, forced a re-kick. The second punt netted the Pats 29 yards' worth of field position and they started their next go-round well situated on their own 45. The Raiders held firm, though, and New England had to punt on fourth and 4. And then, for the third consecutive series, the Raiders shot themselves in the foot with an infraction on a punt. This time, they were offside (they later insisted they had been drawn by New England movement on the line), giving the Patriots the yardage they needed for a first down. Seven plays later, Jess Phillips went up the gut from the 3 to put New England up by 11. En route, the Patriots got a 15-yard boost from yet another personal-foul call on the Raiders.

The Patriots got seven first downs via penalties in this game. That number blew the doors off the previous playoff record (three) and was two shy of the all-time record of nine. Ironically, it would be penalties, either real or imagined, that would ultimately dismantle the Patriots in the fourth quarter.

THE CALL

The Raiders had just pushed into New England territory when the fourth quarter began. Lost as they looked in the previous quarter, they now had their passing attack properly synced. Stabler hit on all five of his throws on this drive, bringing them to the doorstep, where van Eeghen banged over from the 1. There were nearly 11 minutes left to play.

Now with a four-point lead, the Patriots stayed on the ground on their next possession and took nearly three and a half minutes off the clock, before kicking it away to Neil Colzie at the Oakland 16. He brought it out to the 27, but an Oakland clipping penalty moved the starting line for the drive back to the 14. The back of the ensuing drive was broken by another Julius Adams sack; he downed Stabler at the 10. Ray Guy took the long snap in his own end zone. When his punt rolled out of bounds at the Oakland 48 with 6:24 remaining, the Patriots were looking very, very good.

Once more, New England kept on the ground. Grogan picked up 10 yards himself, leaping over two defenders on his way to the Oakland 37. On second and 8, Cunningham rumbled left, making for the sidelines and the first-down marker.

John Hannah: They had about three guys chasing him, so Sam went out of bounds. The guy with the yard marker leapt backward to get out of the way. When Sam went out of bounds, he didn't make the first down because the guy holding the yard marker was a few yards from the line. It was unbelievable, it really was.

The officials actually gave Cunningham a somewhat generous spot, but the measurement came up an inch short. With two plays to pick up the first down, this did not seem crucial at the moment.

Steve Grogan: But we jumped offsides on a third down, which moved the ball back.

Now, with third and 5, Grogan threw his first pass of the quarter, trying to hit Francis going to the right at the 29. Raider linebacker Phil Villapiano was right there with him.

Steve Nelson: When Villapiano mugged Russ on a third down, it was probably the most critical play. You keep telling yourself one play doesn't determine the outcome of a football game, but when you look at that game . . . it really did.

Phil Villapiano: The refs would come up to us and say, "Cut the shit. You guys are out of control." They kept saying stuff like that to Russ and me, but we couldn't. I knew he wouldn't stop. He knew I wouldn't stop. So we kept it up. That was one of the most favorite games of my whole life.

Steve Grogan: There was a lot of grabbing and pushing and shoving. Russ wasn't getting the calls, which makes you wonder what the officials were thinking. I think Villapiano broke Russ's nose at one point; threw a forearm through his mask and broke his nose. He had to leave the game for a little bit and get that all patched up. He was just mugging him all the way down the field on most pass patterns. That hurt us. Russ was a big part of our offense, and for him to not get the calls or get open was detrimental, of course.

Phil Villapiano: He came down the field and shoved me, and I grabbed his arm and the ball bounced off his chest. I think the referees had had enough of us by then and basically said, "Hey fuck you, guys." They got tired of calling penalties on me or Russ. It was too brutal. He was coming off the line of scrimmage and he just blasted me. I ripped his arms down. It was a beautiful football game for a linebacker and tight end. If you could ever see what went on between us, [I think you'd agree] it was probably the greatest tight end–linebacker battle of all time. Russ and I have been together many times since then and we laugh about it.

Replays showed that Villapiano did interfere on the play, which would have given the Patriots a first down. If Francis had made the catch and been tackled on the spot—which is what the game footage suggests was the likely outcome—the Patriots might not have had the first down anyway. They would have been looking at 1 to 3 yards needed on fourth down, which might have been close enough to go for. On the actual fourth and 5, though, Fairbanks went the other route.

Steven Grogan: We ended up having to try for a field goal when we probably should have been driving in for the score.

Kicker John Smith, who was in his third year in 1976, had tried one field goal from 50 yards out and missed it, although he had made a 49-yarder against the Broncos in week 12. Smith had made only three of his last nine attempts down the stretch, though. This kick fell short, giving Oakland the ball at their own 32 with 4:12 left to play. The Raiders could feel Stabler's confidence as he called the first play in the huddle.

Mark van Eeghen: There's a quarterback up in Foxborough right now that's the same way Stabler was. I talk to people about the value of your quarterback being a cool, calm, and collected gunslinger. My son-in-law, Patriots center Dan Koppen, has firsthand knowledge of this. The role that Kenny played and the role that Tom Brady plays is leading not by yelling but by being cool and calm and showing confidence. No matter what the odds are against you, just showing a steely-eyed look. If Kenny looked at you a certain way, you knew what that said. You could read his eyes. If you missed a block or if your guy got through and Kenny was on the ground, he would never say anything. He'd get up and just give you a look and that would never happen again. He was ice water in the veins, as they say. That sums him up. He was our leader. Very similar to how Tom Brady must be to the guys up the street.

Stabler went to the air and found just about everybody he was looking for, hitting on four of his first five passes of the drive. The big one was a 21-yarder to Dave Casper on the first play after the two-minute warning, giving Oakland the ball at the New England 19. Oddly, Casper did not try to get out of bounds, although he very easily could have.

Instead, the next snap didn't come until 1:38, when Lunsford sacked Stabler for an 8-yard loss back to the 27. Then Stabler tried to connect with Casper at the Patriots' 5 and missed. There was now under a minute to play, Oakland staring at a desperate third and 18.

The Snake dropped back to throw while Carl Garrett streaked down the left sideline. Ray Hamilton broke through and was right in Stabler's face when he got off a high, arcing pass that was well defended by Dick Conn and Willie Germany. It appeared as though the Raiders were down to one last desperate throw into the end zone. But there was a flag in the backfield. Referee Ben Dreith had called Hamilton for roughing the passer.

Steve Grogan: In today's game, that would have been the call. Back in those days, they weren't calling it that tightly, so we thought it was a very questionable decision by the referee to throw the flag on that play.

Phil Villapiano: We were all being warned about hitting in the face. I've seen the film, and that elbow went right up in Kenny's face. It was very callable. It wasn't a phantom, like the tuck rule.

It does appear that Hamilton's hand hit Stabler in the head— especially from the NBC replay. This would be an automatic penalty in the more quarterback-friendly rules of today's game, but was not a given in the NFL of the 1970s. He certainly didn't arrive late, though. In fact, he was already so close that Stabler had to change his throw. The pass was barely away and Hamilton had already started on his launch before Stabler had let go of the ball.

With the ball moved half the distance to the goal, the Raiders had 52 seconds to score from the 13. Stabler hit Casper for 5, and he stepped out of bounds. Clarence Davis went up the middle for 4, and then Pete Banaszak was stopped by Lunsford after a gain of 1, which was probably enough, but the Raiders, it seemed, wanted to make sure.

Tim Fox: We thought we stopped him short of a first down, and as he was getting up he pushed the ball forward and pushed right in between

Prentice McCray's feet, and McCray took it and kicked it back to him and we got flagged for the penalty for being unsportsmanlike.

Instead of fourth and inches, the Raiders now had a first and goal and less than a yard to go. After jamming up Banaszak at the line on first and goal, the Patriots dug in for second down with 14 seconds left to go. Stabler took the snap and rolled to his left. Gene Upshaw pulled out in front of him and sealed off Mike Haynes to the outside. Stabler cut in and fell across the goal line with just 10 seconds on the clock.

Steve Nelson: There he was, kind of falling into the end zone, and there I was, a half-step behind him. I said to myself, "Why couldn't I have been there two steps quicker?" I would have had a great angle to hit him.

Tim Fox: Every couple of years I see the highlight from that game of Stabler scoring that touchdown and I'm coming up as he's diving in the end zone. I basically jumped over the top of him. For a long time I regretted not drilling him. I had an open shot as he was crossing the goal line. I was in cover on the play, so I wasn't going to get to him in time to keep him from scoring, but I probably could've put my shoulder into his back and ended the Raiders' Super Bowl run, but I decided not to do it for, I don't know, maybe the first time in my life. I've come to know Kenny over the years, and now I'm glad I didn't do it—but for a long time I wondered about that.

Steve Nelson: After a game like this, you try and find how you can do better, because it was so crushing.

John Hannah: We may not have beaten them on the score, but we didn't lose. When I look at that team and the way that we played that day, everyone played as hard and as well as they could have. Even though we didn't finish on top on the scoreboard, that team fought like everything to win that game.

Phil Villapiano: The funny thing about Madden and Raider teams is that if you won, you don't say a word. I'm so glad we had this rule that we don't talk about it, because there were times I played like shit and we won. On the other hand, there were times I'd make twenty-five tackles and we'd win and nobody would say, "Good job." We got in the locker room after the game, and the only thing we talked about was the Pittsburgh Steelers the next weekend. We knew we got away with murder. Our mentality was, "Fuck 'em, we're better than they are anyway." I don't remember Madden saying anything. We were moving on. That was the Raider mentality.

Patrick Sullivan: We went out to Oakland and there was a severe drought in California. There was a water ban. We arrived the day before the game, and we were walking around the field at Oakland Coliseum in mud and four inches of grass. Al Davis was a creative guy and wasn't above playing games. The Raiders had a reputation for speed, but we were a much faster team. The grass was two inches longer than it should have been and the field was soaked. It was a fix job from the get-go. I don't know of a worse job of officiating in an NFL game.

Tim Fox: It's pretty easy to cover guys when you're allowed to hold 'em. And it's pretty easy to protect a guy when you're allowed to hold as well. Again, I was a young player at the time and I remember coming out of that game thinking they weren't gonna let us win that game. I just really felt that the referees took that game from us. I played 11 more years in the league and never felt that way again.

Leigh Montville: I took it upon myself to call Ben Dreith three different times in five years. He would never answer my calls—he never answered any calls on that game. I really felt that game was stolen away from the Patriots. A bad day at Black Rock for sure.

Darryl Stingley weighed in on the Raider style of football: "If they're going to go all the way, they'd better clean up their act and start playing some football. That's why they can't win the big game. Their method catches up with them. If they continue taking cheap shots and stuff, they're going to have a lot more penalties called on them than they did today."

Two days after the game, Billy Sullivan had a letter delivered to Commissioner Pete Rozelle. "I protested about the total of things that happened to us rather than the judgment of officials. I did it my way so that I am still in the good graces of the league, because I am not objecting about individual plays, but rather what happened to our team in the game. Some of the things that happened just defy logic."

Gil Santos: The Patriots, in my opinion, were a better team than the Raiders in 1976, and only the phantom roughing-the-passer call against Ray Hamilton prevented them from what I believe would have been a Super Bowl appearance. That was a great team, had all kinds of weapons. Sam Cunningham, they had Don Calhoun as a backup running back. They had Russ Francis. They had Darryl Stingley. They had a lot of great players; John Hannah holding together the offensive line; an outstanding defense. It was really a terrific football team. I think they would have won the Super Bowl had they gotten their. But that's the way it went. They didn't get there because of that particular play.

Steve Nelson: We had that good, young football team. Pittsburgh was all banged up. The team from the NFC was Minnesota that year. We knew we could beat both of them. It was one of those chances that a young player thinks there will be a lot of. Well, there *aren't* a lot of them. When you have these opportunities, you have to make the most of them and we just didn't do it.

The Patriots' only consolation was that a thousand fans met them when they landed at Logan Airport long after the game.

Phil Villapiano: Some years after that game, I was in Hawaii with my wife, and Russ, who's a pilot and flies around the Islands, offered to take us on a flight to see whales. So we got out over the ocean right above these whales, and Russ flung open the door and said, "I want to know: Did you hold me in that playoff game?" My wife was screaming, "You're out of your mind!" I finally yelled back at him and said, "Yes! Yes! I held you!" Then he closed the door. That story has grown over the years, but it's true.

Ray Clayborn: Ironically, I was at the AFC Championship Game the week after the Raiders had beaten the Patriots. I was in Palo Alto getting ready for the East-West Shrine Game and saw the Raiders beat the Steelers, not knowing the backstory with New England. Then I got drafted by the Patriots right after that. When I came to camp that summer, I wasn't really a big Patriots fan at the time, and being from Fort Worth and having gone to the University of Texas, I really was a Dallas Cowboys fan. I really got caught by surprise because of the uproar over how they felt they had been cheated out of an opportunity to go to the Super Bowl. In camp one day, they brought in some league officials to talk about what was going to be expected of us during games. When the officials got up there in the auditorium, those guys went crazy. The profanity and the language that they were using! They acted like they really wanted to go up there and get those officials. The coaches had a projector set up, and they showed where Sugar Bear [Ray Hamilton] hit Stabler on the shoulder and not in the head, which is what they called the penalty for. It was wild. Right then I knew the desire and the hunger to get to the playoffs and the Super Bowl my new teammates had.

APPENDICES

The Largest Year-to-Year Improvements in Patriots History

Every franchise has its ups and downs, and the Patriots are no exception. Even in the Bill Belichick era and its seeming parade of wins, there are ebbs and flows in the team's fortunes, albeit not as extreme as in previous eras in Patriots history. Fortunately for Pats fans, those ebbs still look like high tide for most teams. The list below focuses more on point differential and strength of schedule than it does on win-loss record, although the first transition listed does represent the biggest improvement in wins ever registered by a Patriots team from one season to the next: eight.

1975 to 1976 (plus 240 points over previous season)
The steady progress that was being made under the auspices of head coach Chuck Fairbanks came crashing to a halt in 1975. There was a complete breakdown in the relationship between Fairbanks and Jim Plunkett. The Pats' season also got off to an unorthodox start when they voted 39–2 in favor of not playing their last exhibition game of the preseason, to protest the lack of progress between the NFL Players Association and the NFL Management Council in their negotiations regarding pensions, free agency, medical insurance, and other matters. They expected their opponents, the Jets, to join in, but they didn't; nor did any of the other teams around the league. The game, scheduled for the Yale Bowl in New Haven, was canceled, but a larger work action never materialized. Plunkett was injured to start the season and was mostly ineffective when he did return in week three. The Pats lost their first four games and their last six to finish 3–11.

In 1976, they stepped over the body and outscored their opponents by 140 points. How does this 240-point swing measure up to the best turnarounds of all time? It's top-ten material. Here are the best swings since 1960:

377: 1998–99 St. Louis Rams (-93 to 284)
274: 2000–01 Chicago Bears (-139 to 135)

265: 1974–75 Baltimore Colts (-139 to 126)
265: 1997–98 Minnesota Vikings (-5 to 260)
261: 2003–04 San Diego Chargers (-128 to 133)
254: 2005–06 New Orleans Saints (-163 to 91)
253: 1963–64 Chicago Bears (-119 to 134)
250: 2007–08 Baltimore Ravens (-109 to 141)
240: 1975–76 New England Patriots (-140 to 100)
238: 1962–63 Oakland Raiders (-157 to 81)

The 1999 Rams are so far off the chart that their 377-point improvement looks like a typo. The '76 Patriots are the third-best among teams with 14-game schedules.

1972 to 1973 (plus 212)

There was really nowhere to go but up for the Patriots in their first year under Fairbanks, fresh from the campus of the University of Oklahoma. The team had an excellent draft in 1973, getting Hall of Famer John Hannah in the first round and all-time team rushing leader Sam Cunningham in the second. Talented wide receiver Darryl Stingley came in the third round, and longtime defensive lineman Ray Hamilton was found in the 14th. All were able to contribute as rookies, although their best seasons lay ahead. It was a year of some frustrations, like low-scoring losses to the Jets and Chiefs and a blown 17-point lead to the Eagles. There were high points in the 5–9 record, too, like their game against the Packers, in which they trailed 24–9 and responded with 24 unanswered points, and a 32–0 blanking of the hapless Oilers. The improvement is dampened somewhat by the quality of the teams they beat. Their victims—the Oilers, Chargers, Bears, Colts, and Packers—were a combined 15–52–3.

1995 to 1996 (plus 183)

Bill Parcells did what was expected when he took over as head coach: he moved the team from a 2–14 record in 1992 to a 10–6 mark by 1994. What was not expected was the dropoff in 1995, when the team was outscored by 83 points. The turnaround from this down season was very nearly absolute as the Pats scored the second-most points in the

NFL, registering a 183-point swing in their differential and making a trip to the Super Bowl. Only two Patriots teams improved by more than the five games achieved by the '96 Pats: the '76 and '01 teams. The '91, '94, and '03 Pats also improved by five wins. The '61, '66, and '71 teams got better by four in the 14-game era.

2006 to 2007 (plus 167)

It's not that the 2006 team was bad; it's just the 2007 team was *so good*. They scored 204 more points than their predecessors while allowing 37 fewer on the way to registering the best point differential of all time: 19.7 points per game. The 2006 squad had been seventh in the NFL in scoring, yet the 2007 team passed them in the second quarter of only their 11th game.

1960 to 1961 (plus 163)

After a disappointing inaugural campaign in which the team went 5–9 and was outscored by 63 points, head coach Lou Saban was fired five games into the 1961 season. The Pats were 2–3 when he was let go and would go on to a 7–1–1 finish under new coach Mike Holovak, so it's hard to argue with the results. It *can* be argued, however, that they were already playing better under Saban, outscoring their opponents 145 to 134 in his five games in 1961. Of course, that includes a 45–17 whipping of the hapless Denver Broncos,

1970 to 1971 (plus 125)

Were the 1970 Patriots the worst entry in franchise history? Perhaps not, but they're in the police lineup. The '81 team was only 2-14, but they were barely outscored over the course of the season, and weren't really blown out in any of their losses. The 1–15 team from 1990 is certainly going to get a lot of votes, but they had two extra games to amass their 265-point gap. The '70 team was outscored by 212 points in 14 games, which isn't quite as bad as the '90 team; plus, they won an extra game. They scored only 149 points, though, which would be a team worst if it weren't for the strike of 1982. And even with that, the asterisk is barely needed, as the '82 Pats put 143 points on the scoreboard in five fewer games.

The real claimant to worst ever, though, might be the 1972 team, in spite of their comparatively sterling 3–11 record. Two of their wins were by 1 point, and the other was by 7. Only two of their losses were close. The rest of the time, the '72 Pats' end zone was getting dented early and often. They are also the authors of the worst defeat in team history, a 52–0 drubbing by the undefeatable Dolphins. Playing behind a ragged O-line, sophomore quarterback Jim Plunkett threw 25 interceptions to just eight touchdown passes.

1973 to 1974 (plus 101)

The two-year turnaround perpetrated by Chuck Fairbanks is nothing short of astounding. We're talking about a 313-point swing in point differential between 1972 and 1974. The difference between '73 and '74 represents 101 points of that, although it came with only a two-game improvement in the standings. The '74 team collapsed down the stretch, but there was a point where they could have very easily been 8–0. Their comeback against the Bills in week six came two points short, 30–28. Two weeks later, the Bills beat them again, 29–28. This time, Buffalo rookie Jeff Yeates blocked a John Smith field goal attempt with under a minute to play. Had those two games gone the other way, New England would have been the wild-card team, not Buffalo, even with the Patriots' five losses in their last six games.

The Best Patriots Teams on the Scoreboard

Seven of the best Patriots teams by point differential have come in the Belichick era. It would be natural to assume that all three top positions are from this dynastic era. Yet the 1976 team more than holds its own.

Also included are their largest margins of victory and defeat. The 2003 season should be noted for its remarkable symmetry. The Pats opened with a 31–0 loss to the Bills and closed with a victory over them by the exact same score. Both games qualified as the most extreme on either end of the spectrum.

Year	Diff	Positive	Negative
2007	19.7	56–10, Bills	none (three 3-point wins)
2010	12.8	45–3, Jets	14–34, Browns
2004	11.1	42–15, Browns	20–34, Steelers
2011	10.7	34–3, Cheifs	17–25, Steelers
1976	10.0	41–7, Jets	10–30, Lions
2006	9.2	35–0, Packers	0–21, Dolphins
2009	8.9	59–0, Titans	17–38, Saints
1962	7.1	41–0, Chargers	15–27, Oilers
2003	6.9	31–0, Bills	0–31, Bills
1996	6.6	45–7, Chargers	8–34, Broncos
1986	6.6	34–0, Steelers	7–31, Bengals

The Worst Defeats Inflicted on Championship Teams

If there was any consolation for the '76 Patriots and their conflicts with the Oakland Raiders, it was that they perpetrated one of the worst beatings ever laid on a team that would eventually go on to win a championship. In fact, they had the record for 18 years, and it's still tied for the second-largest such margin ever.

32: Philadelphia Eagles 40, San Francisco 49ers 8 (October 2, 1994)

The Eagles were nine-point underdogs heading into San Francisco, but the Niners were playing with a makeshift offensive line and Philadelphia made them pay for it. Steve Young was harried from the get-go and dumped for a safety early in the second quarter after the Eagles' Charlie Garner had already rushed for two touchdowns. Soon it was 23–0 and, trying to play comeback, Young threw two picks before finally getting the mercy pull from coach George Seifert in the third quarter. The Eagles were flying high in 1994, eventually pushing their record to 7–2 before commencing on a seven-game losing streak that cost coach Rich Kotite his job. The 49ers rebounded from this loss with 10 straight victories.

31: New England Patriots 48, Oakland Raiders 17 (October 3, 1976)

The Raiders allowed an average of 300 total yards in 1976, excluding this game, in which they gave up a season-high 468.

31: Buffalo Bills 31, New England Patriots 0 (September 7, 2003)

See "Shutout Losses by Championship Teams" on page 298.

31: San Diego Chargers 34, Buffalo Bills 3 (October 10, 1965)

The 3–0–1 Chargers went airborne when they visited the Rockpile and the 3–0 Bills, racking up 369 passing yards. Meanwhile, safety Bud Whitehead had three interceptions, including one for a touchdown as Daryle Lamonica and Jack Kemp were each picked off twice. They would meet twice more, in San Diego: a 20-all tie on November 25 and then a showdown in the AFL title game on the day after Christmas, in which the Bills got their revenge with a 23–0 victory.

28: San Francisco 49ers 56, Cleveland Browns 28 (October 9, 1949; AAFC)

It is a surprise to see the Cleveland Browns of the All-America Football Conference on this list. They lost just four times in the four years the AAFC was in operation (going 47–4–3 from 1946 to 1949), and this game marked their first loss in 30 games. The 49ers made them pay early, jumping out to a 21–0 lead. San Francisco quarterback Frankie Albert threw for five touchdown strikes, and the hometown fans were so thrilled with the victory they tried to tear the goalposts down, only to be stopped by police. How did the Browns respond to this humiliation? By heading down the coast and crushing the Los Angeles Dons, 61–14, five days later. The 49ers met another playoff-bound team—the Buffalo Bills—the following week and beat them 51–7.

28: Pittsburgh Steelers 55, Cleveland Browns 27 (October 17, 1954)

Prior to this contest, Pittsburgh and Cleveland had met eight times, with the Browns taking every decision. In this game, Jim Finks, who would make it to Canton in 1995 as a coach, had four touchdown passes against a Cleveland team that stumbled out of the gate in the '54 season, although they were installed as 7-point road favorites in this game.

The Steelers trailed early but exploded for 21 points in under two minutes in the second period and won going away. Their defense contributed six interceptions, including two pick-sixes. The Steelers got to 4–1 before losing six of their last seven to fall from contention, including their rematch with Cleveland, 42–7. Sixteen championship teams have surrendered 40 or more points in a game. The third-highest after these two Browns beatings was the AFL's '63 Chargers, who were beaten by Denver, 50–34. The 2011 Giants lost to the Saints, 49–24.

28: San Francisco 49ers 28, Detroit Lions 0 (October 12, 1952)

It seemed like the Niners were the team of destiny early in the '52 season. They went into Detroit and held the Lions to just 65 total yards, improving to 3–0. It was San Francisco's second win over Detroit, who were playing without injured running backs Doak Walker and Pat Harder in this game. Y.A. Tittle was brought in to relieve Frankie Albert and engineered two scoring drives in the second quarter. San Francisco would move to 5–0 before falling to 7–5 and irrelevance. Meanwhile, the Lions won 10 of 11 in the wake of this game and took the National Division, their tiebreaker with Los Angeles, and the championship against Cleveland.

28: San Diego Chargers 35, Pittsburgh Steelers 7 (November 18, 1979)

Terry Bradshaw had a game to forget in this one, throwing five interceptions, including a 77-yard-return-for-touchdown by Woodrow Lowe in the third quarter. The visiting Steelers were also stunted on the ground as both Franco Harris and Rocky Bleier averaged just over two yards a carry. It was the first time in seven tries the Chargers beat the Steelers. Both teams would end up 12–4, but San Diego would bow out in the first round of the playoffs, while the Steelers would roll to their fourth Super Bowl victory of the decade.

27: San Francisco 49ers 44, Los Angeles Rams 17 (October 28, 1951)

27: Jacksonville Jaguars 44, Indianapolis Colts 17 (December 10, 2006)

27: Chicago Bears 30, Green Bay Packers 3 (September 20, 1936)

Win One for the Quitter

Heading into the last week of the 1978 season, the decision to bring Chuck Fairbanks out of the college coaching ranks was looking like a good one. The Patriots had risen from the depths into a solid on-field performer. They had made the playoffs two years before and were headed there again, and he had four more years to run on his contract. Then the marriage crashed on the rocks.

Mosi Tatupu: Being a rookie, all I wanted to do was play, and I didn't know what the business situation was. Come to find out Coach Fairbanks had already made a deal with the University of Colorado. It was supposed to be a hush-hush deal, and when the old man found out about it, the old man being Mr. Sullivan, he actually kicked him out of the locker room when we were having our pregame speech. He told him to get out of the locker room because he lied and everything—right there and then. I couldn't believe it.

Ray Clayborn: It was very bizarre. We were sitting there in the locker room, and the next thing I know I see Billy Sullivan and Chuck Fairbanks coming out of his little office there. And Chuck had his bag and he was walking out. Billy Sullivan stepped up and said, "I just fired Chuck Fairbanks."

The Patriots then went into the last game of the 1978 season with a unique coaching arrangement.

Mosi Tatupu: We had co-coaches, the offensive [Ron Erhardt] and defensive [Hank Bullough] coordinator taking over the helm and making two pregame speeches, and it was crazy because right there and then we just saw how divided our team became. We never recovered after that game, even though we already won the division—not needing that game, it was always a big game down in Miami, and we hadn't won there in a long time.

Ray Clayborn: Ron Erhardt—we called him Fargo at the time because he was from up there—jumped up and started giving the speech and then Hank Bullough got up and gave a speech. It was comical. We were like, "What?! What is going on?!"

Steve Grogan: I don't think anyone had ever had to go through that before. It was extremely difficult.

As was custom at the time, the Patriots lost to the Dolphins in what was, for them, a meaningless tune-up for the postseason.

Steve Grogan: Then Chuck came back for the playoffs. There were a lot of things in the papers and on the radio about what was going to happen. There were a lot of things on our minds that we didn't need to be dealing with at that particular time.

Mosi Tatupu: We tried to regroup for the playoffs, but it wasn't the same. Fairbanks was reinstated for that game against the Houston Oilers. They were the wild-card team coming into our home and they just played together as a team and we were somewhat in disillusion and divided.

It was the first-ever Patriots home playoff game, and it was a disaster. New England was trailing 24–0 in the third quarter before getting on the scoreboard on an Andy Johnson option pass and a TD strike from backup quarterback Tom Owen. The comeback was snuffed when Owen was intercepted by Gregg Bingham, and the Oilers went on to win 31–14.

Why would a man breach his contract like that? (And, moreover, why would an institution of higher learning engage in negotiations with a man who was contractually obligated elsewhere?)

John Hannah: Everybody kind of knew Fairbanks was going to leave, I think. At least *I* did. Basically, regardless of what other people might think, Fairbanks was always a man of integrity to me. He always walked the talk. When he came to the Patriots, he was supposed to be in charge. I've talked to him since, and there were basically two things that happened. The first was Leon Gray and I held out in '77. Leon and I found out that our base salary was a third of what the other players were getting per year. Coach Fairbanks had called us at two o'clock in the morning and we got a deal worked out, but the owners wouldn't let him sign the agreement. The second thing was that in the preseason of 1978, Darryl Stingley didn't have a contract. Fairbanks said, "Look, we've reached a verbal agreement. We need you. We're going to have a great year. Come on out here, play with us, and we're going to get ready for a Super Bowl season." So Darryl did, and he got hurt. After a couple of weeks, when we found out Darryl was going to survive, the attorney went to the owners and said "I'd like to finalize our agreement." Well, they reneged. All that benevolence we read about was, in actuality, a settlement reached on the courtroom steps. I knew right then that Fairbanks wasn't going to stay around. We'd just lose that one year. But the owners felt betrayed and went crazy and pulled a boner. (Then, the following season when they traded Leon away, that had to be one of the most bone-head moves in NFL history. I couldn't believe it. Here Leon and I were considered the best left-side tandem in football and they want to separate us? It made no sense.)

Ray Clayborn: I guess some of those guys knew it had been building up over the past. A lot of people speculated, I listened to guys, but nobody really knew what was going on. It had a lot to do with the Sullivans' lack of compassion for the injury that occurred to Darryl Stingley. I understood that Darryl had agreed in principle to a contract to make him one of the highest-paid wide receivers at that particular time, and when he got hurt I heard Chuck Sullivan reneged on the deal, and that was part of it. There were a lot of other things that had been promised to Chuck Fairbanks as coach and general manager, that he had all of those decisions because he was the head coach and GM or whatever at that time, and those were his decisions and I think that was part of it. Those were the rumors that were going around in the locker room.

Patriots fans were angrier at Fairbanks than the Patriots themselves, hurling insults and concession-stand fare at him as he left the field under police protection at the end of the loss to the Oilers. The Sullivans would not let Fairbanks out of his contract, but a group of Colorado boosters threw money at the situation and bought him out. For their trouble, Colorado got three years out of Fairbanks before he bolted Boulder for the new USFL. He compiled a 7–26 record with the Buffaloes before going to 6–12 with the upstart New Jersey Generals and then leaving coaching forever. Given that the University of Oklahoma program was slammed with sanctions immediately after his departure, it can be said that Fairbanks left all four of his career head-coaching gigs under a dark cloud.

Gil Santos: It was a circus. It was just another in a long line of bad karma and bad things happening to the Patriots. It seemed like the franchise was stuck under this cloud. Whenever things were going good, something would happen for things to go badly. That was another example. It was a crazy time and not one conducive to helping the franchise out in any way.

Miami Dolphins at New England Patriots

December 12, 1982

	1	2	3	4	F
Miami Dolphins	0	0	0	0	**0**
New England Patriots	0	0	0	3	**3**

"Mark Henderson, serving 15 years for burglary, stole one yesterday from Don Shula and the Dolphins."—*Boston Globe*, December 13, 1982

It wasn't the best game in Patriots history, and it certainly wasn't the highest-scoring. In fact, by proper football standards, what the players accomplished on the field on December 12, 1982, was . . . very little. But it was, without a doubt, one of the oddest, most fascinating games ever played.

Actually, its now familiar moniker—the "Snowplow Game"—is a misnomer: There was no snowplow present at Schaefer Stadium on December 12, 1982. It was a John Deere 314 Tractor with a brush attachment. Somehow, "the John Deere 314 Tractor with a Brush Attachment Game" doesn't have quite the same ring.

THE TEAMS

The Patriots were in one of their all-too-familiar transitional periods, coming off a disappointing 1981 season that saw them drop from 10–6 to 2–14—albeit a hard-luck 2–14. They were outscored by only 48 points. Eight of the losses were by a touchdown or less. It's the sort of record that almost guarantees a much better follow-up year, but head coach Ron Erhardt would not be around to enjoy the bounce-back. He was replaced by Ron Meyer, one step ahead of the NCAA recruiting violations that would come to claim the Southern Methodist University football program a few years later.

Leigh Montville: Ron Meyer was a rah-rah kind of guy. I don't think he knew much about football. He did know how to cheat.

John Smith: He didn't seem to like me or most of the players. He told Stanley Morgan he was finished. He told Steve Grogan he was done. I was on injured reserve. He came to me the Monday before the game and said he was bringing me off injured reserve and that he brought in two kickers. "You're going to kick against each other Monday through Thursday. Whoever wins plays against the Dolphins on Sunday." I beat the crap out of both of them. Their minds were so messed up by Thursday, they didn't know where they were. Meyer called me in and he was absolutely pissed. He wanted one of those young kickers. He wanted me out of there. He said, "You played with their minds, didn't you?" I said, "I sure did, Coach. Nobody comes in and takes my job!"

The season itself was shortened from 16 games to 9 by a 57-day players' strike. In lieu of the usual divisions, it was decided that the top eight teams from each conference would make it into an expanded postseason tourney. Going into the game, the Patriots were 2–3, but still had a lot to play for: They were very much in the hunt for a playoff spot, but they pretty much had to win to keep pace in the playoff hunt.

As for the Dolphins, this was the season after the great divisional playoff matchup against San Diego (the "Game No One Should Have Lost") and the year before the arrival of Dan Marino. At this point, they were known primarily for their Killer B's defense (Bill Barnett, Bob Baumhower, Doug Betters, Glenn Blackwood, Lyle Blackwood, Kim Bokamper, Charles Bowser and Bob Brudzinski), their Pro Bowl–bound fullback Andra Franklin, and their coach, the legendary Don Shula. They were one of several 4–1 teams going into the game and among the favorites to represent the AFC in the Super Bowl.

THE FIRST HALF

Some great football players took the field that day in Foxborough, Massachusetts, but the day will always belong to a prison work-release Patriots employee named Mark Henderson.

Mark Henderson: I was on pre-release, and my stepfather worked for the staff in the concession stands. He got me the job at the stadium. The job began while the Patriots were on strike. We got an early start that day. There was a lot of snow, and it was supposed to snow all day. We had a meeting in the morning and they asked for a volunteer to ride the tractor during the game. Nobody wanted to ride the tractor—that meant you couldn't watch the game as much. I knew I was low man on the totem pole, so I sheepishly raised my arm and said I'd do it. By the end of the game, all the guys wished they had volunteered.

John Smith: The day before the game, there was a torrential rain. The night before, it froze, and then, in the middle of the night, a nor'easter came in. By six o'clock in the morning there was six inches of snow on the field.

This combination created a thick layer of ice across the AstroTurf. By kickoff, the playing field resembled something people would use for a primitive game of pond hockey, only in this case there were no skates. The footing was dreadful, and the players slipped and slid across a white, snow-covered surface. Normal cuts simply weren't possible.

The announced crowd was 25,761—less than half the stadium's capacity of 60,000—but watching the tape of the game today, it sure looks like even less. Game-time temperature was 22 degrees, with winds that included gusts up to 30 miles per hour and constant snow that went on for much of the game itself. The Patriots cheerleaders get extra credit for their professionalism, doing their routines in their red jumpsuits on the sidelines despite steady blasts of snow in their faces.

The bulk of the Pats' carries on the first few drives went to Mark van Eeghen.

Mark van Eeghen: I thought the weather conditions were awesome. I played at Colgate. We were plowing practice fields in late October. I was kind of juiced up by it. It wasn't good for the fans or the game. But, as far as I was concerned, I embraced the fact that it was cool and different.

Ray Clayborn: It was tougher for them than for us. They were coming from eighty-five, ninety-degree weather, while we had practiced in the cold weather. We were used to it. But it was a difficult situation for anyone to be out there trying to play football on frozen AstroTurf.

Tony Collins: It was one of those games, where because of the cold, even if you loved football, you don't want to play in it. But, we always loved playing Miami late in the season because it was usually very cold and they didn't like playing in cold weather.

Mosi Tatupu: It was really cold. Nobody could throw the ball, so we pretty much had the same game plan as the Dolphins. We both ended up just running the ball.

Leigh Montville: It was just a disastrous day. No one could move anywhere.

The first few drives for both teams were characterized by north–south rushing attempts and stalled drives. Franklin was successful on his first few carries for the Dolphins, but he didn't seem to understand the utter futility of trying to bust his runs outside—every time he tried, he lost yardage.

Early in the second quarter, the Patriots drove down to the Dolphin 1-yard line. A key play in the march was when John Hannah leveled A.J. Duhe to spring van Eeghen. After that, Mosi Tatupu took over, delivering several nice runs, including a spin-o-rama on the ice that would have made Cam Neely proud.

Steve Grogan: The guy who had the most success was Mosi Tatupu. A guy who was born in Samoa, raised in Hawaii, and who went to school in Southern California. He was running on the snow better than anybody else. That was odd to me.

John Smith: Nobody could knock him over. He was so wide.

Mosi Tatupu: I have flat feet, so I just plugged along, slid here and there, and got my yardage.

Tony Collins: Those types of games were fit for Mosi. He was a straight-ahead runner and he just ran over people. I needed a dry field. He had a great game.

Dante Scarnecchia: After the game, they asked Mosi why he ran the ball so well in the snow. He pointed to his feet, which were big and wide. Those feet worked really well in the snow.

But the drive did not have a happy ending for the Patriots. After getting stuffed on third and goal, Meyer elected to send in John Smith to attempt a kick that was shorter than an extra point. He'd been injured since camp, and it was his first attempt of the year.

John Smith: When fourth down came, Ron Meyer couldn't make a decision whether to run the ball—which he'd done every single play—or kick the field goal. There was something like ten seconds left on the clock when he finally shouted, "Field goal." I went running out there, and I didn't even get to the holder by the time he called for the snap. I kicked it, and as I did, my feet went up in the air. The ball hit John Hannah in the butt and I landed on my back.

Ray Clayborn: We missed a field goal. John Smith just slipped.

John Smith: When I went to the sideline I ran up to Steve Grogan and said, "Son of a gun, Steve; I've had to compete all week for my job and I've just missed a field goal. I'll be gone on Monday." He said, "Don't worry, Smitty: I'll get you in range."

The Dolphins answered with a drive of their own. They got into Patriots territory, once again eschewing the innovations of modern NFL offense in favor of straight-ahead running. Play-by-play man Jay Randolph joked to his broadcast colleague Bob Griese, "It might as well be the Carlisle Indians and the Akron Eskimos out there, right?"

A Clayton Weishuhn sack assured that the Dolphins wouldn't even be able to attempt a field goal, and brought punter Tom Orosz onto the field. For the third time that day, he kicked the ball into the Pats' end zone for a touchback. This drew the ire of Don Shula, who was upset that Orosz was hurting the team's ability to control field position. It was nothing compared with how angry Shula would get about an hour later.

The first half ended in a scoreless tie and, notably, took less than 55 minutes of real time to play. The pace was heightened because there were so few incompletions or other stoppages in play. New England and Miami had combined to throw just six passes, although five of them were completions. The Snowplow Game was the NFL version of a pitchers' duel.

THE SECOND HALF

At the start of the third quarter, the teams traded nondescript possessions before the Dolphins moved the ball back into Pats territory on a long drive that featured both a big run and a key completion—of all things—by Tommy Vigorito. But quarterback David Woodley missed on a few throws, and on came Uwe von Schamann to attempt to break the tie with a 44-yard field goal attempt. It never had a chance. Kicking into the wind, Von Schamann slipped, and the kick was blocked by Ken Sims and Luther Henson.

Up in the NBC broadcast booth, announcers Jay Randolph and Bob Griese had taken notice of some non-football activity down on the field.

As the [third] quarter drew to a close, the unlikely—and as yet unknown—hero in the day's drama got the attention of the broadcast team as he cleared off the yard markers. "I hope nobody decides to throw long while that guy's on the field down there," said Griese.

"It's really remarkable to me, Bob, that they're working on the sidelines while they're playing," answered Randolph.

"In between plays, he's rushing across with his little tractor and brushing off the lines," observed Griese.

Mark Henderson: I was on the field the whole day. I was right at the sidelines the whole time. When they were playing the game, I couldn't clear the field. During the TV time-outs and so forth I'd make a pass. My main concerns were the major markers and the sidelines. It was difficult to find out if you had the first down or not. I guess I felt I should be mostly on the Patriots side when they were playing. I didn't want to lend any support to the Dolphins. But wherever I was when they blew the whistle to go back to play, I'd just get out of the way and try and see the best I could.

Grogan threw a pick to Gerald Small on the first play of the fourth quarter. Shortly thereafter, the strangely prescient TV feed was filled with the image of Mark Henderson and his John Deere 314, brush attachment and all. The Dolphins' offense stalled, and Orosz was called on to punt. The ball was downed on the Pats' 7-yard line, and for a short time, Don Shula was a happy man. The drive that was about to happen would certainly change that.

Van Eeghen started with four nice runs to get the Pats out from the shadow of the goalposts and out past the 30-yard line. Then Mosi Tatupu took over, going for runs of 15, 26, 3, and 9, getting the Pats back in field goal territory.

Patrick Sullivan: Mosi Tatupu allowed us to control the ball. He was a key part of our offense that day.

Ray Clayborn: Being low to the ground and a good running back, Mosi Tatupu was able to maneuver through the snow.

Mark van Eeghen: I think Mosi and I were the type of runners that the weather didn't affect us too much. I remember looking in the faces of Peter Brock and John Hannah. They loved it when we ran the ball, and I think we appreciated each other in our intensity and our desire to fire off and run. There was a lot of that. I had a ball playing the game.

Mosi Tatupu: Me and Mark van Eeghen kept rotating carries and got almost a hundred yards. It was good; we just got behind those big tackles in front and they did their jobs and we just saw where the creases were and plowed our way along. That's what we did all day, just tried to hang on to the ball and get as much yardage as we could.

The drive consumed 11 plays and ate seven minutes off the clock. To put this game in perspective, an average NFL contest in 1982 would have 130 plays from scrimmage. In this case, the Dolphins and Patriots combined for just over 100 plays. Jay Anderson's early NFL analogy was quite apt: This was a game of running and field position, much like football had been in the 1920s.

New England had driven to the Miami 13. On third and 7, Grogan handed off to Tony Collins, but he lost the ball. For a moment, it appeared as though their long march was about to end in a turnover, but Collins recovered his own fumble, bringing up fourth and 10 from the 16. It was time for Smith to come out and battle the elements again.

Steve Grogan: We finally got down into field goal range. I remember running to the sidelines and asking John Smith, our kicker, how close I needed to get him.

John Smith: Steve came to me and said, "Smitty, how close I gotta get ya?" I said, "You gotta get me inside forty, but what you really gotta get me is a time-out. There's six inches of snow and then there's an inch of ice, and I need time to clear it."

Dante Scarnecchia: I made the suggestion to Ron to take a timeout so our linemen could kick out an area, so that John could get his plant foot down. I was a first-year special teams coach and I felt really proud because Matt Cavanaugh looked over at me and said, "That's a really good idea." I said to myself, "Well damn, I must be doing something right here." Ron, who always thought beyond the box, said, "Let's get the snowplow guy to do that." He actually said, "Go get the snowplow guy to carve out a spot."

Steve Grogan: We got down in there and called a time-out to line up to kick the field goal. I was walking to the bench, and Meyer told me to run down there and tell the guy to sweep the line. We were hoping our blockers would have good footing. We didn't want to get the kick blocked. John was clearing out his spot at his normal seven and a half yards [behind the line of scrimmage].

Mark Henderson: Ron Meyer called a time-out; there was 4:45 left. I guess he spent most of the whole time-out looking for me. I had this idea he was going to get me on the field to clear it. He couldn't spot me on the field. At the end of the time-out, he spotted me. That's when you see him on the film running out there. I was off the tractor, although it was still running. As you can imagine, I was freezing my butt off, sitting in the snow all day. I was soaked from top to bottom. I was actually standing beside the tractor dancing, jumping up and down, trying to generate some heat. I was freezing. Meyer was waving his arms. He was looking at me and pointing to the field. He said, "Get out there and do something." I knew exactly what he was talking about. I had already been thinking about it. My dad was a Marine, so I was always in ready mode.

Mark van Eeghen: You know how when you are playing golf and you see someone do something and you think, I don't know if there's a rule against that, but it doesn't seem right?

Mark Henderson: I jumped on the tractor, which was parked at the 20-yard line. I drove out on the 20. Matt Cavanaugh saw me, started clapping his hands and said, "Follow me." I followed him out there, and he pointed to this one-foot-square patch that the linemen and kicker were trying to clear. I came down the line and veered over, and put my brush down. I cleared a patch and there was this beautiful green carpet. And the rest is history.

John Smith: So when the guy was going across the field, which he was doing every five yards, all he was doing was producing the ice. We get out there. I had Matt Cavanaugh, the offensive lineman, digging out the ice for two feet where I can make my run up. The offensive linemen were digging around the area. The snowplow came across and swept snow all over Matt Cavanaugh where he had already made a spot. Matt was swearing at the snowplow guy, saying, "Get the hell out of here." So am I. We had to move the spot a foot. So we were digging out another area because he just swept snow on the area we had cleared.

Steve Grogan: The guy on the snowplow, Mark Henderson, cleared a spot for John which turned out to be at six and a half yards instead of seven and a half yards. That would have bothered some kickers tremendously. John was very tough mentally about that kind of thing, though. He lined up and kicked it from the spot Henderson had cleared.

John Hannah: Trouble was, he [Henderson] hit the wrong damn spot and we had to dust it off where the ball was going to go. He missed the spot and buried it and we had to clean off again. All that stuff, it's kind of a joke, as a player. He hurt us more than helped us.

Many viewers, particularly Dolphins fans, would beg to differ.

Mark Henderson: John Smith said the tractor didn't help him at all, which was total bullshit, because you can see his feet on the green right where I cleared it off.

Patrick Sullivan: John Smith later said Mark didn't get the right spot. I think John is a little annoyed that people think this guy helped him out. John was a good kicker. He was a clutch kicker.

Steve Nelson: I was on the field goal team. I didn't really have a clue what was happening until I saw him. He put down his brush and made a perfect spot seven yards behind the ball. Smitty says to this day he could've made it without that. It had to help. It was a miserable field.

Mark van Eeghen: He [Henderson] did it perfectly. I didn't think too much of it other than that was kind of weird. Was that a hometown edge? You're damn right. I had a nice chuckle about Don Shula getting pissed off for so long.

Tony Collins: The expression on Don Shula's face was incredible. I remember that. He was very upset. He turned red.

Steve Nelson: Shula will never forget that one. In fact, I was at an event with him. He brought up the Snowplow Game. It was probably the lowlight of his career. A Hall of Fame coach basically being railroaded by a guy out on work release. That was nuts.

Shula was quoted years later in an NFL Films documentary about the game, calling it an "unfair act" and joking, "I should have gone out and thrown myself in front of the snowplow."

The Dolphins weren't done quite done yet. They started a drive and faced a fourth and 1 as the two-minute warning arrived. Henderson wasn't quite done having fun at the Dolphins' expense.

Mark Henderson: At the two-minute warning, I jumped on the tractor again; I was going to go around the field to do the outside lines. I went down in front of the Dolphins bench. The wind was blowing just perfectly. Every bit of the snow that I picked off the sideline blew right in the Dolphins' faces. Somebody yelled—maybe even Shula—"What the F is going on?" A couple of the players came out at that point. These guys had fire coming out from underneath their helmets! There was so much steam, I couldn't see their faces! One of the Blackwood brothers and somebody else, and they came up to me and said, "Asshole! What are you doing? Get out of here!" I was going really slow.

The Dolphins converted the fourth and 1 and made it all the way down to the Patriots' 9-yard line, begging the question, would Henderson reprise his role for the visitors?

Mark Henderson: One of the Dolphins coaches came over and grabbed me. He gave me an armlock that I couldn't get away from. He asked me, "If we get another chance to get a field goal, are you going to clear it for us?" I wanted him to think I was being fair. "Absolutely," I lied through my teeth. If that had happened, I think the tractor might have had a problem with the starter.

In the end, it didn't come to that. David Woodley threw an interception to Don Blackmon and the game was all but over.

Patrick Sullivan: I went to Mark and I told him I wanted him to go underground. I didn't want him talking to anybody. Just go in the utility room and stay there.

Mark Henderson: At some point, Patrick Sullivan came up to me and said, "Whatever you do, don't talk to the media." He didn't want to upset Don Shula any more than he already was; we all knew he was on the rules committee. He thought the best way to handle it was for me to keep my mouth shut. I was trying to get the tractor up the ramp to get off the field. When I got five feet up the ramp, the damn tires started spinning and that's when the reporters converged on me. I didn't have any choice but to give the interview.

Patrick Sullivan: They had no clue about Mark's background. He didn't disclose it. One of the writers kept badgering him, saying, "Shula is a member of the competition committee and this is going to result in fines." Mark looked at him and said, "It's a football game. What are they going to do, throw me in jail?"

Leigh Montville: Everybody went to see the guy, who turned out to be Mark Henderson. He's nice, but there was something strange about him when he was talking. He was not filling in a lot of details. We got through talking with him and someone found out that he was on work release from the prison. Then we went back and found him and got the whole story. It was bizarre.

Mark Henderson: I was due back at the prison by five o'clock. Around four-thirty, I used the phone and called and said I was going to be late, that I'd be back at six. That didn't happen, either. I was giving all these interviews and I said to the reporters, "Guys, can you give me a break, I have to call in." I called in again and they didn't even know what was going on at the pre-release. The game was blacked out in our area because it wasn't a sellout. Fortunately, because I was one of the better inmates, they extended me that courtesy. Otherwise they would have said, "Get your ass back here."

Dante Scarnecchia: Ron Meyer was asked after the game if he was the one who told that guy to do that. To Ron's credit, he said, "Yeah, I did." He didn't deny it.

The game prompted a turnaround of sorts for the Pats. They won two out of their last three to snare the seventh seed in the expanded playoffs, setting up a rematch with the number-two-seeded Dolphins in the first round of the playoffs at the Orange Bowl. The Dolphins won that one 28–13. As for Mark Henderson, he remains a legendary figure among Patriots fans.

Mark Henderson: I went back to the last game at Foxboro Stadium, against Miami. Bob Kraft called me into his office. I went down there with my son, who was about thirteen at the time. Bob Kraft gave us both a big hug.

And the tractor? It currently hangs from the ceiling as part of an exhibit in the Hall at Patriot Place in Gillette Stadium, forever secure in its prominence in New England sports history.

APPENDICES

Single-Score Games Since 1943

Since the last 0–0 game in 1943, 22 NFL games have ended with just one score. (Two AAFC games ended at 7–0. No AFL game ever ended with just one tally.) In those games, the touchdown or field goal came in the first quarter six times and in the second and third quarters four times each. These are the eight games in which the only score didn't take place until the fourth quarter:

Date	Away	Pts	Home	Pts
December 19, 1948	Chicago Cardinals	0	Philadelphia Eagles	7
December 16, 1962	Detroit Lions	0	Chicago Bears	3
November 14, 1971	Green Bay Packers	0	Minnesota Vikings	3
December 1, 1974	San Francisco 49ers	0	Cleveland Browns	7
October 7, 1979	Chicago Bears	7	Buffalo Bills	0
December 16, 1979	Kansas City Chiefs	0	Tampa Bay Buccaneers	3
December 12, 1982	Miami Dolphins	0	New England Patriots	3
November 26, 2007	Miami Dolphins	0	Pittsburgh Steelers	3

The 1948 game was the NFL Championship, played in a horrific snowstorm, much like the Dolphins–Patriots contest of 1982. The Browns' win in 1974 was played in conditions so bad that more than half of the paying customers stayed home. The game that came the closest to finishing at 0–0 was the most recent game on the list, a *Monday Night Football* telecast played on a field in Pittsburgh that looked more like a rain-soaked meadow than a professional football grounds.

Last Ties by Franchise

At the time of the Snowplow Game, it had been 15 years since the Patriots last registered a tie. With that fateful field goal, New England preserved a streak that persists to this day. They have gone the longest of any team in NFL history without playing a tie game. Their last draw came on October 8, 1967, when they blew a 14-point lead against John Hadl and the Chargers.

Since the overtime rule was instituted in 1974, there have been just 18 ties. Nine franchises played their last draw in the pre-overtime era, and 19 have played at least one since. The Seahawks (begun in 1976), Panthers (1995), Jaguars (1995), and Texans (2002)—all born in the overtime era—have yet to play a tie game.

1967: Patriots, 31–31 at San Diego
1969: Cowboys, 24–24 vs. San Francisco
1971: Titans (Oilers), 13–13 vs. New Orleans
1972: Bills, 21–21 vs. Detroit
1972: Bears and Rams, 13–13 at Chicago
1972: Saints, 20–20 at San Francisco
1973: Chargers, 16–16 at Cleveland
1973: Raiders, 23–23 at Denver
1978: Vikings, 10–10 at Green Bay
1980: Buccaneers, 14–14 vs. Green Bay
1981: Dolphins, 28–28 vs. New York Jets
1982: Colts, 20–20 vs. Green Bay
1984: Lions, 23–23 vs. Philadelphia
1986: Cardinals, 10–10 at Philadelphia
1986: 49ers, 10–10 at Atlanta
1987: Broncos and Packers, 17–17 at Milwaukee
1988: Jets, 17–17 vs. Kansas City
1989: Browns and Chiefs, 10–10 at Cleveland
1997: Giants and Redskins, 7–7 at Washington
1997: Ravens, 10–10 vs. Philadelphia
2002: Falcons and Steelers, 34–34 at Pittsburgh
2008: Bengals and Eagles, 13–13 at Cincinnati

The Lowest-Scoring Victories in Patriots History
(Combined Points)

With the last 0–0 game in NFL history having occurred in 1943 and the last 2–0 game coming in 1938, you would be right to assume that the 3–0 victory over Miami in the Snowplow Game is the lowest-scoring game in which the Patriots ever played.

Total	Score	Opponent	Date	Scoring
3	3–0	Miami Dolphins	December 12, 1982	John Smith FG
7	7–0	New Orleans Saints	December 4, 1983	Tony Collins 3-yard rush, Fred Steinfort XP
9	6–3	Miami Dolphins	November 20, 1988	Two Jason Staurovsky FG, one for Tony Franklin
9	6–3	New York Jets	December 15, 1991	Two Charlie Baumann FG, one for Louie Aguiar
9	7–2	Cincinnati Bengals	December 12, 1993	Drew Bledsoe–to–Ben Coates 8-yard TD, Scott Sisson XP; intentional safety
12	9–3	Cleveland Browns	October 26, 2003	Three Adam Vinatieri FG, one by Phil Dawson
12	12–0	Dallas Cowboys	November 16, 2003	Two Vinatieri FG, Antowain Smith 2-yard rush TD
12	12–0	Miami Dolphins	December 7, 2003	Vinatieri FG, Tedy Bruschi INT for TD, safety
13	10–3	at Cincinnati Bengals	October 15, 1978	David Posey FG, XP, Sam Cunningham 3-yard rush; Chris Bahr FG
13	13–0	at Buffalo Bills	December 28, 2008	Two Stephen Gostkowski FG, LaMont Jordan 2-yard rush, one XP

Three of these games came in a two-month period in 2003. That makes sense when you know that 11 teams outscored New England that season, but nobody surrendered fewer points, and that there was a big blizzard in the 12–0 win over the Cowboys in that stretch. All but two of the victories listed above came at home, and most in the cold and snows of December, when the NFL reverts to its lower-scoring roots. (Matt Cassel's 13–0 dismantling of Buffalo came in conditions so windy that the groundskeepers couldn't keep the goalposts straight.) As for low-scoring losses, the Patriots were blanked 6–0 in 1992 and 1993 by the Colts and Jets, respectively. They lost 7–0 to the Houston Oilers in 1975. Their lowest-scoring playoff game was the 7–6 loss to Pittsburgh at the end of the 1997 season. On November 10, 1963, the Patriots were nipped by the San Diego Chargers 7–6. It was the lowest-scoring game in the 10-year run of the American Football League.

From Blighty to Foxborough

In *The Glory of Their Times,* Lawrence Ritter's classic oral history of early 20th-century baseball, a number of old-time ballplayers stated that the first major league game they ever saw was one they were playing in. How many modern NFL veterans can make the same claim in this age of blanket television coverage? Probably just one. Not only had John Smith never seen an NFL game before he took the field in a New England Patriots uniform; he'd never seen *any* kind of American football.

Smith was not the first Englishman in the NFL. Bobby Howfield had played top-level soccer in his home country and also kicked for the Broncos and Jets, and Mike Walker had kicked for the Patriots in 1972. But the man who would go on to end one of the longest 0–0 ties since World War II in the Snowplow Game had one of the quickest journeys from complete novice to professional in the history of the game. It happened like this:

I was a good soccer player. I was playing professional soccer when I was sixteen. I also went to university because I wanted to be a teacher. While I was there, my mother answered an ad in the

London newspaper for students to go over and work in America for the summer. This was 1970. I went and had an interview for a camp in western Massachusetts and I got the job. The soccer team I was playing for didn't want me to go, so my brother went instead.

I finally went in 1972. It was a camp in Pittsfield, Massachusetts, for very wealthy Jewish boys from Shaker Heights, Cleveland, and Long Island. I was teaching soccer. I was always practicing every day and kicking a soccer ball around. One of the kids I was looking after brought a football up to the soccer field. I'd never seen American football before. I didn't know a thing about it. He said, "Can you show me how to kick it? There's a guy called Gogolak playing for the Giants and he's a soccer-style kicker." I said, "Fine, stick it down, I'll kick it over the soccer posts."

So I did. Now it gets very complicated. The head guy at the camp called Jack Rohan, the basketball coach at Columbia. Basketball was the top sport at the camp. He saw me kicking it and he said, "You should have a go at this." I said, "Oh yeah, big deal."

When camp ended, I spent the last week of the summer with my auntie in New Jersey. There were eight weeks of camp and one week at the end of the summer, then I went back with 250 students back to England. Jack Rohan lived in Teaneck, New Jersey. He said, "On the way to the airport in New York, can you stop by the field and kick some footballs for a friend of mine? I'll put you back on the bus afterwards so you could make the plane." I agreed. I kicked some footballs, got on the plane, went back to England. This was September 1972.

In December I graduated from university with an honors degree in education. I was going to teach. It was the middle of the English soccer season, I was playing semi-pro. I couldn't get paid in college. I got a letter from the Jets. They were asking me to come out and try out because this guy had seen me kicking. I wrote back and said, "No, thanks. I'm playing soccer right now and the soccer season goes to the end of April. I have no clue what American football is. I'm going to be playing pro soccer in the summer and teaching." I figured that was the end of it.

It was the first week in May 1973, and the soccer season had just finished. I lived in this little village in the Cotswolds, the middle of the boondocks in England. I got a phone call on a Tuesday night from an American lad named Peter Huthwaite. He said he was an agent and had a four-day tryout lined up for me with the New England Patriots on Thursday. Could I be at the TWA desk at the London airport Thursday?

I was getting married a few weeks from then, June 2, to my wife, Vivian. I called her and said, "There's a Yank on the phone and he wants me to kick footballs." She encouraged me to go over. I came out for the tryout; didn't even remember the name of the team he had told me on the phone. I got to Logan Airport and Huthwaite picked me up and took me to the Holiday Inn in Dedham. It was the first tryout for rookies that Coach Chuck Fairbanks had when he came from Oklahoma.

When I walked into the locker room, the first guy I met was John Hannah. What the hell have I done? John Hannah, Sam Cunningham, Darryl Stingley, the three number-one draft picks that year. It was a free-agent camp. There were about ten kickers there, and obviously I was the most inexperienced. We kicked for the weekend. I got a little better each day. At the end of the weekend, they told me they wanted me to stay around until they brought in the veterans the next week: a guy called "Super Foot"—Mike Walker—and Charlie Gogolak. I kicked with them the following weekend. I figured that was it. That's the end of this job. I'm going back to England, getting married. And they asked me to come out for training camp and sign a contract. I said, "I don't know if I want to do that." I said, "Let me tell you what I'm going to do: I'm going back to England, getting married, and going on honeymoon for ten days to Yugoslavia. After that, I'll call you."

We went on honeymoon. I took a football with me. We'd just left college. We had about a hundred bucks in our pocket, so we said what the heck—we might as well go over. It's one summer—I can always come back and play soccer and teach. We might as well try it. That's how I ended up at training camp in the summer of '73.

The first game of football I ever saw, I was in. I didn't even know what a down was. It was the Hall of Fame game in Canton, Ohio. I didn't play at all in the first half. All I had to do was kick off once in the second half, and it was a bad one. It was the first time I kicked off with live guys in front of me. They were going to hit me! In practice, I'd been sending my kickoffs into the end zone, but this was the first time I lined up with a guy in front of me that was shouting all sorts of abuse at me. I kicked it and it went to about the twenty-yard line on the left side and just barely stayed in bounds. Howard Cosell was on doing the game on TV and my wife was watching back in Pittsfield. Cosell said, "Here's this kid, they brought him over from England, and if he keeps kicking like that, he'll be on the first boat back there."

When I got back to Boston, Pete Huthwaite called me and told to bring my playbook; they were going to cut me the next day. I got there and he said, "We're not actually going to cut you. We think you have lots of talent. You just don't know anything about the game. You need some more experience. We're going to trade you to the Pittsburgh Steelers and you're going to kick against Roy Gerela, the number-one kicker in the league. Then they're going to send you back." At that time, the last team to cut you had the last chance to pick you up. The Steelers were the best team, and the Patriots were the worst, and they wanted to hide me. The Steelers cut me after a week. I kicked against Roy Gerela. I didn't know it was a deal. Roy Gerela's contract was up. So they had me kick against him for a week. I beat him every single day of the week. He signed his contract on Friday and they cut me on Saturday.

When I got back to Boston, they asked me to play for a minor league team called the New England Colonials. The head coach was former Patriot Tommy Yewcic. We played up and down the East Coast. We won the league that year. I was nineteen out of twenty-one on field goals. What happened was this: The patriots had a kicker called Bill Bell for the first three or four games, a straight-on kicker. He was doing badly the first few games. And Coach Fairbanks told Peter Huthwaite to bring John Smith up from the Continental League. Peter said, "We can't do that." Apparently, there was a clause in the league that players that were developing couldn't be brought up to the NFL in the first year. They couldn't bring me up, so that's when they brought in Jeff White. I made it the following year.

New England Patriots at Miami Dolphins

AMERICAN FOOTBALL CONFERENCE CHAMPIONSHIP
January 12, 1986

	1	2	3	4	F
New England Patriots	3	14	7	7	31
Miami Dolphins	0	7	0	7	14

From 1970 through 1985, the Miami Dolphins won 90 percent of their home games against their intradivision rivals, the Colts, Jets, Bills, and Patriots. The Jets fared the best of the lot, at 4–11–1 in the Orange Bowl. The Colts won two games in that period and the Bills just one; the Patriots, none at all.

Patrick Sullivan: Every time you'd go into Miami, whether it was for a game or vacation or whatever, you had to drive by the damn place. The only way you could avoid seeing it was to fly into Fort Lauderdale. For fifteen years, every time I drove by there I'd say, "Until we win there we're not going anywhere."

Of course, the Dolphins of that era were so good, they had a .611 winning percentage on the road, so it only stood to reason that they would be nearly unbeatable at home. Unfortunately for the Patriots in 1985, their road to the Super Bowl went right up to the entrance gate of the Orange Bowl. If they were going to get to the big game for the first time ever, they were going to have to throw off their curious inability to win on the road against the Dolphins. (See "Hell Down in Miami," on page 185.)

When the Patriots walked onto the field at the Orange Bowl for the American Conference Championship on January 12, 1986, it had been 19 years, one month, and 16 days since they had registered their one and only victory there. Apart from overcoming a quality opponent, could they also surmount this depressing streak?

RAYMOND BERRY AT THE HELM

The run to the 1985 championship actually began in week nine of the 1984 season when general manager Patrick Sullivan made a coaching change.

Ray Clayborn: I was surprised at the disdain and the dislike that some of our key players had for Ron Meyer. When he came in '82, he let a lot of people go. I think out of the fifty-man roster we had, there were only ten to fifteen veterans that he kept. So we had around thirty to thirty-five first- and second-year players that he brought in because he felt that's what the team needed—and I think a lot of guys were upset that a lot of their friends weren't kept around. I really felt that Ron was headed in the right direction and that the only mistake I think he made was firing coach Rod Rust.

After the Patriots surrendered 552 yards and fell to the Dolphins 44–24 in Foxborough, Meyer pulled the trigger on Rust, his defensive coordinator.

Ray Clayborn: We had gotten blown out by the Dolphins and just had a bad game. When I came into the meeting Monday, Rust was fired. When I came back on Wednesday, Ron Meyer was walking out the door and I said, "Coach, where are you going?" and he said, "I'm literally out of here." I said "What does that mean?" So I walked in and I saw Coach Rust. He was back and Raymond Berry was leading the meeting. Now that was strange.

Raymond Berry: Coach Fairbanks brought me to New England in 1978, and I had a year with him before he left and then I was on Ron

Erhardt's staff for three years. Then our staff got fired and I was out of coaching, living in Medfield [Massachusetts] for three years. All our children were in school at that point, so I got a job with a friend of mine in Boston. I was working with him when the Patriots fired Ron Meyer and they hired me to be the new head coach. We had eight games left. I didn't know all the players and I didn't know any of the coaches, but in two, three, four games I began to realize the team had everything it took to play with the very best in the NFL, so it was a real exciting time. It was the classic case of the right place at the right time with the right people.

Berry, already in the Hall of Fame for his prowess as a wide receiver with the Baltimore Colts, was bucking an ominous trend in his debut: From the merger to that point in 1984, coaches who took over the reins in midseason had gone 2–16 in their debut games. At halftime of Berry's inaugural, it looked like it was soon going to be 2–17. The result was unexpected. (See "The Largest Comebacks in Patriots History," on page 218.)

Patrick Sullivan: We had a core group of players in 1984 that were getting older—John Hannah and Grogan and the guys we had drafted in the mid- and late seventies. They were getting older and I felt that we didn't have too many more shots at the apple. We had to be pretty good. So, I thought we had assembled a pretty good team in 1984, but things kind of disintegrated midway through the season, and I felt we needed someone to come in and stabilize things. At that stage I didn't have any inclination that Raymond was going to lead us to the promised land. I felt he would stabilize things and give us a chance at being successful. He did that in 1984, and his entire philosophy on how to coach, how to play, how to win came to the front in 1985

The players responded to Berry immediately.

John Hannah: During the Ron Meyer years, there were a lot of guys who had lost their confidence. They didn't have faith that they could win, and they didn't believe they were good athletes. That was because of the coaching staff that we had, the press and all the things that had happened in the past. Coach Berry made everybody start believing again. That was huge. We had the mental outlook of going into a game believing we could win.

Mosi Tatupu: I think him being here as an assistant helped; that and the fact that we had a good nucleus. Back in those days, not too many guys moved around. There weren't too many rookies that made the team; we'd keep two or three a year.

John Hannah: He also stressed the elimination of mistakes and conditioning. He told us we were great athletes and that we just had to do a few things better here and there. He went around to each player and said, "I want you to grade your game. Not on the basis of whether you block your guy or not block your guy, but whether from the time the ball is snapped to when the whistle blows if you're giving it one hundred percent. I want you to think about it all week. Then I want you to play the game that way." When it came to my turn, I tried it. I graded it seventy-six or seventy-seven percent. That's all. When I get off the field I was exhausted. When a pass is twenty-five yards down the field, an offensive lineman will usually seven-eighths it down there. All of a sudden we were sprinting down the field. You don't usually do that. Our conditioning was unbelievable. It showed up in the games. If you look at every game, one or two plays in the game are going to win that game. The problem is you never know when that play is going to happen. That's why you give one hundred percent—a receiver might cut back and drop the ball or you might be there to recover a fumble. He had everyone thinking that way. It was a great job on his part, instilling that mentality.

Raymond Berry: I feel like one of the greatest contributions I made to that football team is that I was experienced enough to recognize their talent level. I had been trained by my dad, who was a Texas high school football coach, who used to say, "When you've got players with talent, tell them about it!" So I kept telling them they could win and they could do it. Then we started having some success and they started seeing what I was talking about and they started believing in themselves.

Tony Collins: It was an honor to be coached by Coach Berry because of his personality, his knowledge of the game, and what he brought to the table. He was the type of coach you loved to play for. He had us thinking we're going to win every game.

Dante Scarnecchia: Raymond was a soft spoken man. He had such credibility. He was prepared. He also had a very calming effect on everyone. When he talked, people listened; he was mesmerizing in that respect. He was very even-keeled, win or lose. Everyone really respected that.

Mosi Tatupu: We became a solid team and went on from there and played ball like we were paid to play.

Patrick Sullivan: He taught me one of the truly great lessons in life: You can achieve anything that you want as long as everyone is moving in the same direction. That included everybody: the cleaning crew, the people who sold tickets, et cetera. There was an overall sense of camaraderie throughout the organization that was spectacular. That was all Raymond Berry. He was a very, very special guy.

Raymond Berry: From what I observed in the years I was there, I think Billy Sullivan was the best owner in the NFL. I think he gave us great, great support, and the players knew he would do anything to help us win, but he did not try to get into the football part of it. He turned that over to me and the coaches. I think our players really responded to the leadership we got from our owner.

THE 1985 SEASON

After brushing aside Green Bay in week one, the Patriots met the Bears and got their first taste of one of the great defenses ever assembled. Tony Eason was harassed and hurried all day, throwing three interceptions and getting sacked six times. In losing 20–7, New England was held to just 206 yards, their lowest total of the regular season. The highlight for the Patriots was an Eason–to–Craig James 90-yard touchdown pass in the fourth quarter, the longest in team history. (The record stood until 2001, when it was broken by David Patten.)

After beating the Bills on the road and losing to the Raiders at home, the Patriots stood at 2–2 as they traveled to Cleveland for week five. Things did not go well there.

Mosi Tatupu: After we lost to the Cleveland Browns, a game we had and then let slip out, it just seemed like were going nowhere as a team. Andre Tippett, who was pretty young at that time, stood up and gave a speech about how we weren't playing as a team. He was pretty upset and he tossed a few chairs around.

Patrick Sullivan: He could rearrange furniture fairly readily, but Tipp was a fairly quiet guy and still is to this day. He let loose, and it had a big impact because he wasn't a screamer and a shouter. He led by example and he challenged everybody and said, "We're better than this; we need to play that way." That was the turning point of the season, no question about it.

Tony Collins: When Tipp spoke people listened. The thing was we got fed up with losing and we weren't playing up to our abilities.

Mosi Tatupu: We all were upset, because we knew we had a better team than what we were showing. From then on, we were like a new team. Week after week we played together; we were excited, there for each other, taking one game at a time.

Steve Grogan: We knew we had a good football team. Raymond Berry and his new staff, they were just a great bunch of coaches. I think a lot of guys had gotten frustrated after the Cleveland game. We weren't playing the way we needed to play. Tony Eason was the starter, and I was on the sidelines. I thought my career was over in New England at that time. The next week, against Buffalo, he got hurt and I came off the bench.

Eason was sacked on three consecutive plays, the third of which resulted in a separated shoulder.

Raymond Berry: One of the great strengths of that team was that we didn't have just one starting quarterback; we had two. The odds are that a quarterback isn't going to last all sixteen games, so we cashed in our talent. We had a young talent and an old talent, and they both did the job whenever they were called on to do it. We could not have had a better situation, and that's one reason why, when I started seeing what this team was all about, I knew we could make a run for it.

Steve Grogan: We came from behind to beat Buffalo, and something clicked offensively for us. The offense was what I had run under Fairbanks and Erhardt. I knew it very well. Raymond decided to let me call my own plays. I started talking to guys in the huddle about what we needed to do, what plays to call when. I think everybody got behind that and felt they were contributors to our offense. We went on a six-game winning streak.

Raymond Berry: We had to put in a new offense, and any time you try to learn a new offense, you sputter around a little bit, and that's what we were doing in the first five to seven games of the season. You just can't get all these sets learned in a first-year offense; plus they really did not have a clue how good they could be.

Patrick Sullivan: When Grogan was on the sidelines, he was calling the plays. Raymond had enormous and justifiable trust in Steve. When Tony got hurt and Steve went in, the good play continued. It was a stretch of games that Steve played that were the best of his career.

The streak that followed allowed New England to insinuate itself into the tight AFC East race with New York and Miami. One of the highlights of the run was how well the Patriot defense stymied Dan Marino in their home meeting with the Dolphins. In his worst performance of the year, Marino threw two interceptions without a touchdown and the Pats overcame 11 penalties and a 14–3 fourth-quarter Miami lead to triumph, 17–14. Grogan also helped erase Seattle's fourth-quarter lead with two touchdown passes in the Pats' 20–13 road win over the Seahawks.

The Patriots entered their week 12 showdown with the Jets tied with them for first place at 8–3. Grogan left the game in the first quarter with what was first reported as a sprained knee, but turned out to be a broken leg. As Nick Cafardo wrote in the *Boston Globe,* this was just one of the many structural setbacks Grogan suffered in his career: "Five knee surgeries; screws in his leg after the tip of his fibula snapped; a cracked fibula that snapped when he tried to practice; two ruptured disks in his neck, which he played with for 1½ seasons; a broken left hand; two separated shoulders on each side; the reattachment of a tendon to his throwing elbow; and three concussions."

Raymond Berry: At that point in his career, Steve Grogan had been in the league eleven years. He was a great leader and set a great example. He was a total team player and one of the toughest competitors I've ever seen on the football field. I told him early in the year we were going to go with Eason as the starter and would be depending on him to come out of the bullpen. I said, "I think this gives us our best chance of winning, for you to take this role." And he did it and never looked back, and he supported Tony and he supported the team. We just had a great situation with two talents that had their heads screwed on right.

Tony Collins: Grogan coming in and replacing Eason was inspirational because of him being where he was in his career and being the leader he was. I think that was our biggest strength that year: the camaraderie that we had. Every Monday we'd go eat chicken wings right down the street and have a couple of beers. Just being together. I tell people all the time that that's what I miss the most: being with the guys.

Grogan was replaced by a healthy-once-more Eason. Again New England trailed by 10 in the fourth quarter and again they rallied, tying the game at 13 and sending it into overtime. The winning streak came to an end, however, when Pat Leahy put one through the uprights with less than five minutes remaining in the extra period. A trip to the play-offs was still a possibility, but with two other strong teams in the hunt, the team figured they might have to win out—which meant winning a road game in Miami.

Victories over lesser lights Indianapolis and Detroit led up to the week 15 trip to play the Dolphins on *Monday Night Football*. All three contenders were 10–4, but the Jets lost to the Bears on Sunday afternoon, which meant the winner of the Monday night showdown would take pole position. If the Patriots could win there, then finish up with a win against Cincinnati, they'd get to skip the first week of the play-offs. If they lost, then they would need the win over the Bengals or hope the Denver Broncos lost their Friday night game against the Seahawks if they were going to make the playoffs at all.

The Patriots gave the Dolphins all they could want, battling back late and nearly winning. Ron Davenport scored with 11 minutes and change left in the game to put Miami up, 27–13, but the Patriots erased the deficit when Mosi Tatupu scored on a 1-yard run and Cedric Jones scooped up Joe Carter's fumble on the ensuing kickoff and took it on a 16-yard trip into the Dolphins' end zone. Miami regained the lead on a 47-yard Fuad Reveiz field goal, but there were more than four minutes left in which the Patriots could tie or take the lead. Instead, Eason threw his third interception of the game and Miami remained a black hole in Patriots lore.

The Seahawks did not indulge New England by beating the Broncos, so it was up to the Patriots to earn their way into the playoffs with a win over Cincinnati. Getting right to work, the Patriots rushed out to a 20–6 halftime lead as Eason hit Stanley Morgan for a 50-yard touchdown pass, Tony Collins scored from 9 yards out, and the offense put barefooted kicker Tony Franklin in chip-shot range twice. The Bengals veered close early in the fourth quarter, however, making the score 20–16 before Eason connected with Morgan for 48 yards to put New England in scoring position at the Cincinnati 17. Craig James got the call on the next three plays, the last of which resulted in an 11-yard touchdown run up the right sideline. James would finish the day with 142 yards on 25 carries, the highest total of his injury-shortened career.

The Bengals would not die, though. In a connection between future announcers, Boomer Esiason hit Cris Collinsworth for an eight-yard score, making it 27–23 with 5:43 to go. The Patriots swallowed the clock on the ensuing possession, consuming four minutes. Facing a fourth and 1 on the Cincinnati 42 with 1:52 remaining, Berry weighed his options.

Raymond Berry: We were having a hard time stopping them; the Bengals had a tremendous offense. Rod Humenuik, our offensive-line coach, told me which play to run, so we went for it on fourth down. Robert Weathers broke it for forty-two yards and a touchdown, and that helped seal the game and put us in the playoffs. You get good people on the field, good people on the staff, and a good owner and then you have a chance to go for all the marbles.

THE PATRIOTS

New England allowed the second-fewest points in the conference, sixth in the NFL. They were a half-yard better than league average in both yards per carry and net yards per pass attempt. Overall, they allowed 4.5 yards per play, good for fifth in the NFL. (Surprisingly, it was not the famous Chicago Bears defense that paced the league that year—they finished fourth—but that of the New York Giants, a team the Bears buried in the playoffs, 21–0.)

In short, to that point in New England's history, only the 1963 team had fielded a better defense, and only the '83 defensive unit could argue they were just as good. Left outside linebacker Andre Tippett earned a trip to the Pro Bowl and an All-Pro selection. There were also Pro Bowl honors for left inside linebacker Steve Nelson, right cornerback Ray Clayborn, and safety Fred Marion.

Steven Nelson: I think we had such a good mix. We had young players, we had older players, Julius Adams [at 37] was still playing. I was the oldest linebacker. We had Donnie Blackmon, Andre Tippett, Larry McGrew, and Johnny Rembert all in the prime of their playing careers. Raymond Clayborn was kind of the old man in the secondary, and Ronnie Lippett was a younger player. That match of older and younger players was really beneficial for us.

The Patriots were 10th in the league in scoring. Their passing attack averaged 6.4 yards per attempt, well above the league average of 5.8 and good for sixth in the NFL. The left side of the offensive line was manned by Pro Bowlers John Hannah and Brian Holloway.

Tony Collins: Hannah was the best offensive guard to play the game. A great person as well. He was the anchor of the offensive line. I knew he was going to get his blocks. It was an honor as a running back to see that big butt in front of me—you wanted to run behind someone of that caliber.

New England was a ground-oriented team, however, with pass plays comprising just 44.7 percent of their offense, the fourth-lowest team count. The running plays tallied right at the league average of 4.1 yards per carry. Craig James ran for 1,227 yards on 4.7 per attempt and was named to the Pro Bowl. Tony Collins caught 52 passes out of the backfield to lead the team, while Irving Fryar and Stanley Morgan paced the wideouts with 39 catches each. Fryar added two touchdowns on punt returns. (This was years before Fryar turned his life around, and he would be lost for the AFC Championship Game after an altercation with his wife that resulted in two of his fingers being slashed.)

Grogan, in his limited action, performed better than Eason, who threw 17 interceptions, compared with just 11 touchdown passes, although Eason turned around his TD/interception ratio after coming back from his injury. Berry took a somewhat unique approach in the use of his running backs—almost an emulation of the hockey line model.

Raymond Berry: Bobby Greer, our backfield coach, set me on a way of using our backs early in the year. He said that if we rotated these two sets of backs, he thought they'd all still be healthy in January. He was exactly right. So Mosi Tatupu and Robert Weathers would come in and we'd rest Tony Collins and Craig James and we got four great backs.

Another Patriots strength was the special teams.

Dante Scarnecchia: We had Irving Fryar who was a great punt return guy and made the Pro Bowl as a result of it. We had the ability to return the ball, with Irving, score touchdowns, and create turnovers. What also happened was we had a core bunch of young special teams guys that were led by Tatupu. They took Mosi's lead and thought they could do these things on every play. Obviously it worked out well for us. They were a special group of guys. The day I learned that Mosi died [February 23, 2010] I was going to the combine in Indianapolis. One of the writers on the plane came up and told me the news. I thought how ironic, I'm going to Indianapolis to evaluate and identify great players. Here's a guy like Mosi who couldn't run very fast. He wasn't the niftiest guy in the world, but he was the quintessential football player. He would do everything: He could block, he could catch, and he could make plays. He was the most unselfish person I've ever been around. Those qualities you don't measure with a watch or tape and he had them in droves. The kind of player that he was manifested itself in every game he played in. He was a special guy.

THE DOLPHINS

Now in year 16 of the Don Shula era, the Dolphins had become a fixture in the playoffs. They had made it the past four years, and were coming off a 1984 season that was their best since the perfect run of 1972 (although it ended badly with a 38–16 spanking from the 49ers in Super Bowl XIX).

In their 1985 opener, Miami got off to a 13–0 lead and led until Mike Rozier scored with 25 seconds left in the game to give the Oilers the 26–23 victory. It was a foreshadowing of the season to come: one in which one of the better offenses in the league was paired with one of the most promiscuous defenses. Miami allowed the fifth-most yards per play in the league, yet—and this was what allowed them to go 12–4 instead of 8–8 or 9–7—much of the time they somehow managed to keep their opponents out of the end zone. The loss of nose tackle Bob Baumhower and linebacker A.J. Duhe, their defensive Pro Bowlers from the year before, was telling. Baumhower was especially missed. Had it not been for the injuries that essentially ended his career, he might well be in the Hall of Fame today. In fact, some might say he should be in there anyway.

The Dolphins had scored 513 points in 1984 when Dan Marino had a season for the ages. No one knew it at the time, but at 23, his best year was already in the books; which isn't to say he wasn't formidable for the rest of his career, he would just never hit the inconceivable heights of 1984 again. Miami scored 85 fewer points in 1985, but still had the fourth most in the league. Only the San Diego Chargers, still flying Air Coryell, averaged more yards per passing attempt. Tellingly, no Dolphins defenders were singled out for league honors, while Marino, wide receiver Mark Clayton, left guard Roy Foster, and center Dwight Stephenson were Pro Bowl selections (with Marino and Stephenson also being named All-Pro).

The main running threat was Tony Nathan, who, although he didn't get many carries in their pass-oriented scheme, averaged 4.7 yards per try. More important, he caught 72 passes out of the backfield, more than even Clayton. Mark Duper had previously established himself as one of the league's best receivers, but he was slowed by injuries in 1985, missing seven games. Veteran Nat Moore was in his 12th year with the Dolphins and caught 51 passes, seven for touchdowns.

After their opening loss to the Oilers, the Dolphins won four in a row, including a shutout of a Chiefs team that had scored 83 points in its first two games. The Jets rolled up 476 yards on Miami in week six to end their winning streak, 23–7. Against the 0–6 Tampa Bay Buccaneers in their next game, the Dolphins blew a 17-point fourth-quarter lead and lived to tell about it, winning 41–38 on a late Fuad Reveiz field goal.

Their crowning achievement, of course, was beating the Chicago Bears 38–24 on *Monday Night Football*, a victory that ultimately preserved their ancestral claim as the only undefeated, untied team in NFL history. (See "Perfection Denied," on page 342.) Steve Fuller was starting for the fourth consecutive week for the Bears. They had won his previous starts by allowing just three total points. When the vaunted

46 defense could not stop Dan Marino, the Bears' offense, without Jim McMahon, was not in a position to win a shootout, and they fell 38–24. That game is still the highest-rated *Monday Night Football* telecast of all time.

The Dolphins' defense did register a second shutout in the final week of the season as the 2–14 Bills lost yet again in Miami, this time by the score of 28–0.

THE PLAYOFFS

If the Patriots were going to even get to the Super Bowl, they were going to have to win three road games. Nobody had ever done this before. (See "The Most Successful Bottom-Seeded Teams Since 1978," on page 188.)

Leigh Montville: At that time, the wild-card team was like a poor relation in the playoffs.

The long road started in the Meadowlands, where the fellow wild-card New York Jets awaited.

Steve Nelson: I think both teams kind of welcomed that, being that we knew each other so well. We'd split during the regular season. We knew we could beat the Jets, because we had already beaten them once. Going down there, we put in a total team effort and won.

Raymond Berry: One of the things that happened in that game that was also going to happen during the next two playoff games was how we fared in the turnover situation. We had really been practicing and drilling falling on fumbles, picking up fumbles, and forcing fumbles. Against the Jets we got four turnovers and didn't lose the ball at all. In our first three playoff games we got sixteen turnovers and only lost four.

In the NFL of the early 21st century, it's common practice for defenders to tackle the ball. That was not the case in 1985. Patriots special teams coach Dante Scarnecchia said at the time, "I've been telling them for four years to knock the ball out of people's hands, and I guess they are finally listening."

Raymond Berry: That basic fundamental of learning how to get turnovers I learned in high school in Texas under my dad, who was a head coach. He drilled that into us. My senior year in high school we won our district championship. Our opponents fumbled twenty-nine times that year and we picked up twenty-seven of 'em.

The Patriots defense held Freeman McNeil to just 41 yards on 16 carries, and Andre Tippett concussed quarterback Ken O'Brien at the end of the first half, knocking him out of the game. Tony Franklin was good on four of his five field goal attempts. The key, though, was the turnovers. The Patriots took advantage of three of them to put points on the board, while not giving the ball away once themselves.

John Hannah: It was a hard-fought game. They had a good team. We capitalized on a few errors and busted our humps and were able to survive it. It was a dogfight, as it always was with the Jets.

Steve Nelson: We were really solid, and we took that momentum right to the Raiders.

With the 26–14 win on the books, the Patriots packed up and headed to the coast to play the Raiders. The scene would be different than that of the last New England playoff contest against the Raiders, the ill-fated 1976 game, as Al Davis had battled the league and won the right to move his team to Los Angeles three years earlier.

Patrick Sullivan: My father had testified against Al Davis in his litigation against the NFL. Al had come in and testified against my father in shareholder litigation. So there was a lot of animosity at the ownership level, much more than between the players. A lot of the players that were with us in '85 were not with us when that debacle took place in '76. Some were, though, so there was a lot of animosity among them. There were a lot of negative comments made about the ability of our organization to compete with the Raiders.

Once again, the Patriots shook the turnover tree and points fell out. They recovered three fumbles and picked off Marc Wilson three times. Wilson had an especially rough afternoon beyond the picks, helping the New England cause with erratic passing. All but one of New England's scores were preceded by a Raider turnover.

The biggest play came as the third period was nearing its end. Tony Franklin had just tied it at 20 with a 32-yard field goal, and kicked off to Sam Seale, who reached the 10-yard line, where he was hit by Mosi Tatupu. The ball squirted free and Jim Bowman and Cedric Jones gave chase. It was Bowman who corralled it in the Los Angeles end zone for what proved to be the deciding score in the 27–20 win. Bowman had also made a key recovery in the first quarter when Fulton Walker dropped a punt, setting up the Patriots' first touchdown.

What is often remembered about that day, though, is what transpired after the final gun. Patriots general manager Patrick Sullivan had spent part of the game verbally sparring with Raider Howie Long. In the week leading up to the game, Long, who was from the Boston neighborhood of Charlestown, had said he would not have become as good a player had he been with the Patriots. Sullivan took exception to this and berated him from the sidelines during the game. "So he [Long] said to me, 'I'll see you at the ramp after the game,'" Sullivan recounted afterwards. "At the tunnel, I stopped Howie and we both were yelling at each other; we didn't exactly appreciate what each other was saying . . . Howie didn't do anything, but [Matt] Millen grabbed me by my hair and flung his helmet at me. I never saw him coming."

Steve Nelson: Both teams used the same tunnel, which is never a good thing. John Hannah and I were kind of walking behind the whole thing. He tells me I said this after Matt hit Pat with the helmet. John said, "What should we do?" I said, "Well, Pat got himself into it and Pat will get himself out of it."

Millen claimed not to know who he had hit. "I saw somebody swing at Howie," he recalled. "I didn't know who the moron was, so I swung at him." When told after the fact that it was the son of the Patriots' owner, Millen brightened: "Oh, then it was a good hit."

"I read where Millen said I should have my Ferrari taken away," Sullivan said later, "but I drive a white Pontiac station wagon."

Meanwhile, the Dolphins had earned a bye for the first weekend of the playoffs and hosted the Cleveland Browns the day before the Pats-Raiders game. At 8–8 with a negative point differential, the Browns were nobody's idea of a great team, yet they went to Miami and pushed the Dolphins to the limit. The Browns' stated purpose going into the game was to keep the ball on the ground and out of the hands of Dan Marino. This was not a stretch for them, as they normally rushed more frequently than even the Patriots.

"The thing about Miami's offense is that it puts pressure on your offense," Cleveland's quarterbacks coach, Greg Landry, told the *New York Times* prior to the game. "Teams get impatient against them because they feel they've got to score every time they get the ball."

This helps explain how the Dolphins could give up so many yards per play and not surrender an inordinate number of points. For more than half the game, Cleveland's plan worked. They ran roughshod over the Dolphins with a ground attack that eventually totaled 251 yards, including 161 by Earnest Byner. His 66-yard touchdown romp put Cleveland up 21–3 in the third period. What followed was one of the more substantial comebacks in playoff history. The Orange Bowl crowd cranked up the volume, making it difficult for prodigal son Bernie Kosar to be heard by his Cleveland mates, while Dan Marino eventually filled the air with 45 passes (24 of them successful) as Miami roared back for the 24–21 win.

THE GAME

Mosi Tatupu: Our guys were focused and ready to play. In my eight years, we came close, but kept losing in the end. That day when we played them, we knew them well, they knew us well; it was like old school.

Raymond Berry: There were a couple things that were working for us heading into that game. The first was that I had a veteran coaching staff and we were aware that resting our players would give us an advantage. When we went to Miami to practice for the game, I told the team, "We've already played the Dolphins twice this year; we know them and they know us. All we're going to do is walk around all week. I want you to recover and get your legs back and we're going to go into this game with a full tank of gas." So we rested them well. The second thing that happened to our advantage is that we were on the road, so we were in a good climate to go through our walk-throughs and were able to do all that without worrying about the snow.

Steve Nelson: We were relatively healthy and we were just playing really good, solid football: winning the turnover battle, not getting many penalties, special teams making plays all over the field, running the football and playing really sound defense.

Mosi Tatupu: We couldn't wait. When we found out after the Raiders game that a couple of their guys started jawing about how they just handed the championship to the Dolphins by losing to us, we couldn't wait to get down to Miami to settle the score.

Steve Nelson: When we took the field, we came out of our locker room and the Dolphins were warming up on that end of the field. We had to kind of run around them, but instead, we just ran right through where they were stretching. It was like we're coming to take over their property. I had the feeling that unless we really screwed it up, we were going to beat them—and I think the Dolphins knew it.

This was the era of house touts at CBS and NBC, with oddsmaker Jimmy the Greek filling that role at the former network, and super gambler Pete Axthelm at the latter. The Dolphins were favored by 6, and Axthelm picked them to cover on the NBC pregame show. Bob Costas challenged him by pointing out that the Patriots had covered 13 weeks in a row, but Axthelm held firm. He contended that the Dolphins were the obvious choice; that there was the Patriots' Orange Bowl losing streak to consider and the fact that the Dolphins were 5–0 in AFC Championship Games.

It was an overcast day with temperatures in the mid-sixties. With the weather wet and windy, NBC announcers Dick Enberg and Merlin Olsen pointed out that conditions might be more to the Patriots' liking than the Dolphins'.

John Hannah: In a way, it was probably lucky, us coming from New England, that it was raining and a little cool that day. At the end of the game, their defense was more tired than our offense.

New England's Stephen Starring took Fuad Reveiz's opening kickoff at the goal line and raced up the right sideline nearly untouched before being forced out of bounds at the Patriots' 37. They ran rushing plays only and were eventually forced to punt.

On Miami's first play from scrimmage, Tony Nathan plowed into the line, where he was hit by Steve Nelson, who knocked the ball free. Left end Garin Veris fell on it, putting the Patriots in business on the Miami 20. Eason's first pass of the day was good for 9 yards to Tony Collins in the flat. Then it was back to the ground as Craig James carried twice to bring the ball to the 3-yard line, where Mosi Tatupu hit the middle for a foot or so. Eason then pitched the ball to Robert Weathers as he swept right, but nose tackle Mike Charles punched through the line and hauled him down for a loss. Berry took the conservative approach, settling for a 23-yard field goal by Tony Franklin.

John Hannah: The idea was to keep the ball away from Marino and keep our defense fresh. We were able to do that. Craig James had a great game, as did a couple of the other guys. We just pounded that ball.

Raymond Berry: One of the critical things that happened early in the game was that Rod Humenuik came to me and said that we needed to feature running to the right because Steve Moore, our big right tackle, was a tremendous blocker but he'd gotten overweight. When we ran to the left, he was having a hard time getting his cut-off blocks, but if we ran to the right we were running right behind him. So we started hitting the four hole, and we just kept making yards. We'd come back to the left every once in a while.

The Patriots were repeating the Browns' approach. As Robert Weathers recounted, "Our game plan was to use as much of the clock as we could to keep Marino off the field. Our offensive line was very aggressive. They wanted to go right at those guys."

New England very nearly got a second turnover when Lorenzo Hampton was stripped on the kickoff return but managed to fall on his own miscue. Neither team could move very far on their next possessions, but when Miami got the ball back, they got things going as the first quarter wound down. They drove 80 yards as Marino hit on five of his eight passes, the last of them to tight end Dan Johnson at the back of the end zone, with linebacker Larry McGrew just a step behind and unable to make a play.

Now trailing 7–3, the Patriots stayed on mission, sticking to the ground game with Robert Weathers getting the bulk of the work. On second and 8 from the Patriots' 48, there ensued a play that, with a missed block here or a better tackle there, could have been anything from a 3-yard loss to a touchdown or anything in between. It went as follows:

- Eason handed off to Weathers, who swept to the left side.
- John Hannah helped give him space by flattening Mike Charles at the line of scrimmage.
- Mosi Tatupu led the charge to the outside and sealed off Glenn Blackwood with a nice block near the sideline. When Weathers started to cut to the inside of that block, Hugh Green was on the spot trying to make the play. Tight end Derrick Ramsey got him off the case with a good hit but, in so doing, collided with Weathers and could have easily knocked him down. Weathers stayed up, though, and broke even further outside. Ramsey's block turned out to be so effective, it jammed up three Dolphins as Green collided with line-backers Kim Bokamper and Jackie Shipp after the hit.
- Now free of the block from Tatupu, Blackwood laid himself out trying to catch Weathers from behind, but was hit in midair by teammate

Bud Brown, who just missed ensnaring Weathers. Both went down, leaving a total of five Dolphin defenders in Weathers's wake.

- Now in the clear, Weathers broke down the left sideline. At the 20, he was met by Paul Lankford, who failed to wrap him up and was left in a heap as Weathers, now slowed, continued on his way.
- Trailing the play were wide receiver Stanley Morgan and the Dolphins' William Judson. Morgan was watching Weathers shake free of Lankford and didn't see Judson come up behind him. Had he been turned the other way, Morgan could have easily waylaid Judson and allowed Weathers to go in for the score.
- Instead, Judson got an angle on Weathers and pushed him out of bounds at the 7-yard line.

Since New England was sacrificing big-play offensive opportunities by eschewing the pass, the last thing Miami needed was for the Patriots to get a bomb's worth of yardage on the ground. After the 45-yard run by Weathers, James ran for a couple and Collins picked up 2 on a short pass. On third and goal, Eason rolled right and went into his full throwing motion, only to somehow stop himself in mid-throw and look elsewhere. He had excellent protection and ample time to see Collins turn on a dime in the end zone and head back to the left. Eason nailed him for the score. New England had gone 66 yards on eight plays to retake the lead.

And just like that, the Patriots got the ball back again. On second and 4 from the Miami 37, Marino and Stephenson failed to exchange the snap, and the Patriots' Lester Williams came out of the pile with the ball held high. For their first play, the Patriots tried a flea-flicker and, in spite of unlimited time, Eason overthrew Morgan in the end zone. James churned out a first down and then cut loose for a dozen yards down to the 13. On second down, Eason dropped back to pass and, once again, the Dolphins failed to get any kind of pressure. He found Morgan cutting across the middle on a slant at the 5. Morgan banged hard for a few more yards, giving New England a first and goal at the one. Eason rolled right and targeted Ramsey low as he was fighting off Bob Brudzinski in tight coverage. The pass was perfect, hitting Ramsey as he dove to his knees just inside the goal line.

Nine-plus minutes into the second quarter, New England now had a

10-point lead. This was Miami, though, where Patriots leads had disappeared before. Would this one meet the same fate? One thing was certain: New England was not lacking for crowd support. The amount of cheering after their scores suggests that Patriots rooters either were in the majority at the Orange Bowl or were playing the role of a very vocal minority.

Lorenzo Hampton made a nice return for the Dolphins, taking the kick at the 15 and bringing it out to the 43. Unfortunately for Miami, Alex Moyer had laid out Ernest Gibson on the play with a clip, bringing the ball back to the Dolphins' 17. With Marino at the helm, a 26-yard reversal of fortune was by no means a death sentence. He began snapping off passes with that maddeningly quick release that was always so frustrating to those trying to pressure him. Duper caught one for 11 yards, then Clayton got wide open over the middle for 16. Marino aired one out, trying to hit Duper at the Patriots' 5, but Ray Clayborn got his hand on it and knocked the ball away. A 29-yard gainer to tight end Bruce Hardy gave the Dolphins a first and 10 at the New England 15 at the two-minute warning.

Coming back from the break, Marino zinged a pass to a very open Dan Johnson as he backed into the end zone. It was a guaranteed 6 points, but it went right off Johnson's hands and was very nearly caught by Andre Tippett. Unable to move the ball on the next two plays, Shula sent out Fuad Reveiz to narrow the gap to 7. Instead, the snap was high and the kick sailed wide right. On the way off the field, Don Blackmon turned the knife a bit on Reveiz, who took exception to the comments and slapped him across the face mask.

When the Dolphins got the ball back a minute later, Blackmon had an opportunity to blow the game wide open when Marino rocketed a pass right at him. With 35 yards of open field standing between him and the end zone, he could not hang on; in Blackmon's defense, it had to be surprising to find the ball delivered where it was least expected.

The Patriots would get their shot at another turnover soon enough. On the opening kickoff of the second half, Lorenzo Hampton was on his way to a decent return when he was slowed by Rod McSwain and then blasted by Mosi Tatupu. The ball came free and Greg Hawthorne fell on it at the Miami 25.

From there, James and Collins took turns moving the ball ever closer until it was fourth and 1 at the 2. Berry decided against the chip-shot field goal and went for it. Since New England had run on the five previous plays and needed less than a foot for the first down, the Dolphins queued up in the box, all 11 of them digging deep to hold the line. Berry called the perfect play for the occasion. Eason faked to James while Weathers sprinted out of the backfield wide to the left. The play-action pass floated into his hands as he crossed the goal line.

Now trailing 24–7, Marino tried three passes on the next possession, and two of them were nearly intercepted. Miami got the ball right back, however, when Roland James dropped Reggie Roby's punt and Bud Brown fell on it at the New England 43. Reserve running back Joe Carter broke free for 19 yards. On second and 3 from the 17, Marino fired one over the middle to Clayton, who tripped over Ronnie Lippett and went down. The contact was completely incidental. Regardless, the pass never would have gotten to him, as Fred Marion grabbed it at the 4 and brought it back to the 25. It was his third pick of the playoffs, one in each game.

The Patriots ground forward, draining eight minutes off the clock with run after run. The drive ended with Franklin missing a 41-yard field goal, but it had served its purpose; the third quarter had very nearly been killed.

With 15 minutes left, the result seemed academic, but there was still drama to be had. After Miami stalled at their own 42, Roby punted to Roland James at the 10. He started upfield and was hit by Alex Moyer, who reached in and knocked the ball free. Don McNeal came up with the ball for the Dolphins. The absence of Fryar seemed especially relevant at that moment as Marino and the offense trotted onto the field with new life. He wasted no time. Setting up in the shotgun, Marino hit Nathan at the 2 and he went untouched into the end zone, cutting the lead to 10. When the Patriots went nowhere on their next possession and had to punt it away, that lead seemed especially vulnerable.

Starting from their 37 with over 12 minutes on the clock and the league's most prolific passer at the helm, the Dolphins appeared to be poised for something big. On second and 10, the give was to Carter, who, as he had on his three previous carries, burst through the line headed for good yardage. Lester Williams was not able to make the tackle, but he did get a piece of the ball. Carter tried desperately to control it, but it was soon gone. Miami's Roy Foster fell right on the fumble, but the ball squirted away from him into the gracious grasp of Julius Adams.

There were two key plays in the ensuing drive that culminated in the 1-yard Tatupu touchdown run. On third and 7 from the 31, the Patriots lined up in the shotgun. The Dolphins might have suspected a ruse, as New England had run out of this formation to good effect against Oakland the week before, and Eason had thrown only two passes in the last 18 snaps. The Miami defense appeared to be in chaos, however, with a 12th man barely getting off the field in time to avoid a penalty. Eason gave the ball to Collins and he covered 14 yards. Two plays later, Craig James made a nice move and got free down the left sideline, sprung by a Weathers block on Hugh Green. He was knocked out of bounds just shy of the goal line.

With 7:34 on the clock and the score 31–14, the outcome was no longer in doubt. The Dolphins got close one more time, but were taken aback by a 15-yard unsportsmanlike-conduct penalty on Mark Duper, who flipped out when the refs failed to see that Ray Clayborn had hit him on the arm while he was trying to catch a pass in the end zone.

It didn't matter, though. There just wasn't enough time. It ended with Eason taking a knee and Coach Berry being lofted high by his players.

Leigh Montville: I was on the field in Miami. They were playing the Dire Straits song "Walk of Life," and all the players were dancing to that on the sidelines. It was one of the sweetest things I'd seen in sports.

Clayborn had a great game. He swatted away so many passes that it was a wonder Marino kept throwing into his coverage. Nelson said after the game that he didn't think anybody had caught a ball on Clayborn's side of the field all day. Marino missed on 28 of his 48 passes, with two interceptions. It could have easily been more. Tony Eason was very efficient in the limited use made of his arm. For the third consecutive playoff game, he didn't throw an interception. He missed on only two of his 10 passes. Craig James had his second 100-yard day of the playoffs, and Tony Collins averaged over 5 yards per carry as New England rolled up 255 rushing yards.

"We knew they were going to run and try to control the ball, " said Dolphins linebacker Bob Brudzinski, who'd had a very busy afternoon, "and we did a pretty good job at the point of attack. They just broke some tackles and did a good job of cutting back against the grain."

Ray Clayborn: What struck me about that game was how the younger guys, in particular guys Ron Meyer had brought in, performed. I saw a guy like Lester Williams, who hadn't lived up to the first-round potential up to that time, push Hall of Fame center Dwight Stephenson all over the field that day. I saw Robert Weathers run the ball like he'd never run it before. I saw the young special-teams guys—Johnny Rembert, Jim Bowman, Rod McSwain, Ernest Gibson, and Ben Thomas—just come on and play so well.

Raymond Berry: We ran that ball fifty-something times and threw the ball a dozen, and Tony Eason threw three touchdown passes and we hammered the Dolphins and kept the clock running and only let Dan Marino play nineteen minutes.

Miami's tight end Dan Johnson summed it up this way to the Associated Press: "The missed plays, the dropped balls, the turnovers—that's what lost the game. Everybody's surprised that (all the turnovers) happened. It's something we don't usually do. After we got that second touchdown, we got momentum and thought we had a chance to come back again like last week."

"If you know Coach Berry," tight end Lin Dawson told UPI, "then you know he doesn't believe in long speeches. He didn't have too much to say to us about our eighteen straight losses to Miami in the Orange Bowl, because he doesn't believe in things like jinxes."

Jinx or not, the Miami streak was over. The Patriots were going to the Super Bowl.

Tony Collins: I tell people all the time: That was our Super Bowl, beating Miami.

APPENDICES

Hell Down in Miami

On November 27, 1966, the Patriots made their first-ever trip to the Orange Bowl in Miami to play the expansion Dolphins. Everything ended happily for Boston as they took a 20-point lead and held on for the 20–14 victory while Jim Nance was setting the AFL single-season rushing record, passing Paul Lowe's mark of 1,121. The world would be a very different place by the time the franchise won there again.

The Detroit Lions first traveled to Washington, D.C., to play the Redskins on November 26, 1939. They lost 31–7. Seven decades later, they still haven't won a game in that town. Including three playoff contests, that's a span of 21 games and is the longest such streak in football history. The second-longest visitors' drought belongs to the Patriots at Dolphins. (Technically, the Lions-at-Redskins run stands at 18 regular-season games and the Patriots-at-Dolphins streak was 16 away games, but 18 consecutive in Miami.)

41–32 (December 17, 1967):
A year later, the sophomore Dolphins weren't that much better, but the Patriots were a whole lot worse. They allowed Miami to roll up 28 points on them in the second quarter alone. Rookie and future Hall of Famer Bob Griese had his best game to date, throwing three touchdowns without an interception.

38–7 (December 8, 1968):
Another disastrous second quarter, this one featuring 21 points for the Dolphins, put the game out of hand by halftime. And, just as in the previous year, turnovers were the root cause.

37–20 (December 6, 1970):
The Patriots won a 1969 game held in Tampa to showcase that city's attributes for a future NFL franchise, 38–23. But the curse continued when the teams met back in the Orange Bowl in 1970. The ascendant Dolphins rushed to a 27–6 halftime lead and never looked back.

41–3 (October 17, 1971):
New England won the home half of the series in 1971, 34–13, as part of one of the most difficult schedules in the league.

52–0 (November 12, 1972):
The famous undefeated Dolphins of 1972 didn't usually destroy teams, but they made an exception for the hapless Patriots, handing them what still ranks as their worst loss ever. Up 35–0 in the second half, Don Shula pulled quarterback Earl Morrall, giving rookie Jim Del Gaizo his NFL debut. Novice though he was, he still threw two touchdown passes. Quite simply: one of the greatest mismatches in NFL history.

44–23 (September 30, 1973):
The Dolphins were in the midst of setting the all-time record for most consecutive home games won: 27, between 1971 and 1974. Down 20–0 in the second quarter, the Pats battled back to get within a touchdown, only to be blown out of the water in the fourth.

34–27 (December 15, 1974):
You can count on two hands the number of times a team has held a 24-point lead in professional football history and gone on to lose. This was one of them. The Patriots rushed out to a 24–0 cushion only to see it evaporate. They got the lead again, but lost that one as well.

20–7 (December 1, 1975; *Monday Night Football*):
Not as close as it looks. The Pats didn't score until there were 51 seconds left on the clock. The Dolphins opened the game with 41-year-old Earl Morrall over center, and he completed his first 13 passes.

10–3 (October 31, 1976):
On paper, this was probably the Patriots' best shot to snap the winless streak in Miami, given that the Dolphins were having a down year and the Pats were blowing up the scoreboard. Instead, New England was held to its lowest point total of the season.

17–5 (November 13, 1977):
This game pretty much killed the Patriots' hopes of making the playoffs. The safety was intentional on the Dolphins' part.

23–3 (December 18, 1978; *Monday Night Football*):

As if winning in Miami wasn't hard enough for the Patriots, they were contending with the Chuck Fairbanks situation. (See "Win One for the Quitter," on page 135.) A delegation of 12 players went to ownership and asked that Fairbanks be allowed to coach in this game, but they were denied. Up 20–3 with 30 seconds to go in the game, Don Shula called time-out so that Garo Yepremian could tie the record for most consecutive field goals.

39–24 (November 29, 1979):

The Pats were in this one at halftime, up 17–13. Then the Dolphins hit them with a big scoring stick, putting up 26 straight points.

16–13 (December 8, 1980; *Monday Night Football*):

"This is just a football game, no matter who wins or loses. An unspeakable tragedy . . ." So said Howard Cosell as the clock was winding down at the end of regulation, prefacing his announcement that John Lennon had been shot in New York City and was dead on arrival at the hospital. Overshadowed by that horrific event was this game, in which the Patriots got as close to winning in Miami as they ever would during the streak. They had a 13–7 lead in the fourth quarter and, after Miami tied it at 13, lined up for the game-winning 35-yard field-goal attempt with three seconds to go. It was at that moment that Cosell broke in with the shocking news. Miami nose tackle Bob Baumhower was able to block the kick and send the game into overtime, where Uwe von Schamann won it with a 23-yard field goal 3:23 in.

28–14 (December 6, 1981):

The 2–11 Pats hung tough against the 8–3–1 Dolphins, tying the game at 14 in the third quarter before succumbing to the quarterbacking wiles of David Woodley.

28–13 (January 8, 1982; wild-card playoff round):

Because the strike nearly halved the regular season, the Patriots wiggled out of their yearly hell ride to Miami. Fate hates a loophole, though, and the Patriots nevertheless had to visit the Dolphins right out of the gate in the expanded playoffs. The outcome was no different.

34–24 (September 11, 1983):
It was too little, too late, as the Pats tried to rally after getting behind 27–3 early in the fourth quarter.

28–7 (September 9, 1984):
Moral victory for the Patriots: During one of the best seasons ever registered by a quarterback, they held Dan Marino to his second-lowest passer rating of the season (81.4).

30–27 (December 16, 1985; Monday Night Football):
Coming back from 14 down late, only to be denied in the end: There ought to be a word for that.

The Buffalo Bills were having similar problems in Miami at about the same time the Patriots were, losing 14 in a row from 1969 to 1982. The Dolphins were actually undefeated at home against the Bills going back two more years, having beaten them in 1967 and tied them in 1968. Unlike the Patriots, though, who beat Miami nine times at home during their prolonged woes in Miami (the best game of which was a 34–0 shutout in 1980), the Bills were losing to the Dolphins in Buffalo as well, dropping an NFL record 20 straight games to Miami from 1970 through 1979.

As of this writing (through the 2011 season), there are two similar streaks in progress. The Patriots have beaten the Bills 15 consecutive times going back to 2003 and have an 11-game home winning streak against them as well, dating to 2001.

The Most Successful Bottom-Seeded Teams Since 1978

From 1970 to 1977, only one team in each conference qualified for the wild card. Beginning in 1978, a second wild-card team was added and, in 1990, a third. With the expansion to four divisions in 2002, the number of wild cards reverted to two, but the bottom seed is still a number-six seed. These are the bottom-seeded teams that have fared the best.

2005 Pittsburgh Steelers (4–0, Super Bowl XL victors)
The Steelers were not the first wild-card team to win the Super Bowl, but they were the first bottom seed to do so. They won road games in

Cincinnati (31–17), Indianapolis (21–18), and Denver (34–17) before polishing off the Seahawks for the title, 21–10. Their success does come with an asterisk, though: They were a bottom seed in name only. They had the same record as Cincinnati, but the Bengals won the division based on a superior intradivision record. They were seeded below Jacksonville because the Jaguars won 12 games to their 11. The Steelers had the third-best point differential in the conference, and only one team allowed fewer points.

2010 Green Bay Packers (4–0, Super Bowl XLV victors)

This is not your average bottom-seed team. The Packers had a point differential that was second in the league to only the Patriots. When New England was eliminated in the first round, it left a clear pathway to the top for a superior team such as this. Of their six regular-season losses, four were by 3 points and two were by 4. They snuck up on nobody and were favored in the Super Bowl. In short, a team like this is why wild cards exist: to redress the imbalances that geographical positioning can create in the rewarding of postseason opportunities.

1985 New England Patriots (3–1, American Conference champions)

The overall playoff record of number-six seeds is 40–66 (.377), and 23 of those wins belong to the teams seen here. Since 2005, though, bottom seeds have gone 16–12 in the playoffs. This makes sense when you consider that at least one and oftentimes two of the division winners are usually weaker than the wild-card teams.

2010 New York Jets (2–1)

New York also went 2–1 in the playoffs the year before, but as the fifth seed. With a couple of breaks, the Jets could have beaten Pittsburgh in the AFC Championship Game and we would have had our first all-bottom-seed Super Bowl to cap the 2010 season.

1978 Houston Oilers (2–1)

The Oilers traveled to Miami and beat the Dolphins 17–9 in the wild-card game, then went to New England and trounced the Patriots, 31–14. Then they ran into the Steelers and were taken out 34–5 in Pittsburgh. This is the first of what can be called Losses of Hubris, wherein the bottom-seeded team flies too high and gets a huge comeuppance later in the playoffs. Consider that the largest margins of defeat for the lowest-seeded teams have come not in their first games but in second, third, and fourth playoff contests. The average margin of defeat in the five worst beatings of bottom-seeded teams that won at least one playoff game is 36.6. The average margin in the five worst beatings for teams that lost their only playoff game is 27.7. Makes sense when you think about it.

1987 Minnesota Vikings (2–1)

Minnesota opened the playoffs with the most one-sided victory ever perpetrated by a bottom-seeded team, a 44–10 thumping of the Saints in New Orleans. They then brushed aside the top-seeded 49ers, 36–24, before losing to Washington 17–10. Minnesota was better than its 8–7 record and break-even point differential indicated. In the strike-interrupted 1987 season, their replacement players went 0–3 and were outscored 60–33.

1989 Los Angeles Rams (2–1)

The Rams traveled east and took out the Eagles 21–7 and the Giants 19–13 in overtime before returning to the coast to get spanked by the 49ers, 30–3.

2008 Baltimore Ravens (2–1)

Baltimore ended the Dolphins' turnaround dreams with a 27–9 win in Miami before nipping the top-seeded Tennessee Titans, 13–10. The eventual Super Bowl champion Steelers ended their run with a 23–14 beating in Pittsburgh.

2008 Philadelphia Eagles (2–1)

The Eagles allowed the fewest points in the conference and had the second-best point differential, so their 26–14 victory over the Vikings was not that surprising, although their 23–11 defeat of the number-one-seed Giants was. They were derailed 32–25 by the Cardinals.

Pittsburgh Steelers at New England Patriots

DIVISIONAL PLAYOFFS
January 5, 1997

	1	2	3	4	F
Pittsburgh Steelers	0	0	3	0	3
New England Patriots	14	7	0	7	28

The Patriots owe a lot to Bill Parcells's heart. Had Parcells not required an angioplasty in 1992, he might have remained the Giants' head coach for years to come, perhaps even challenging Steve Owen's team record of 23 years at the helm. Instead, he retired after his second Super Bowl triumph and headed for the broadcast booth. After two years, he was told by his doctors that he was healthy enough to return to the rigors of coaching in the NFL.

The Giants had just fired his replacement, Ray Handley, but there was never much serious talk of a return to the Meadowlands. Meanwhile, the Patriots' fortunes were at a low ebb. After their initial success under Raymond Berry, the team had slowly unwound and then come completely undone in Rod Rust's sole season as head coach in 1990, going 1–15 and getting outscored by 265 points. Dick MacPherson seemed to have the team heading in the right direction in his first year, but, then again, there was nowhere to go but up. It is nearly impossible to maintain the low level of play New England displayed in 1990 two years in a row. After going 5–11 in MacPherson's first season, they regressed in 1992, winning just two games while scoring just 205 points, next to last in the league. Off the field, the team had new ownership in MacPherson's second season, James B. Orthwein having bought the Patriots from Victor Kiam.

Orthwein was a hands-off owner, but he still wanted no part of 2–14 seasons, so he dismissed MacPherson and cast his eye on Parcells, who had made his professional debut with the Patriots as linebacker coach in 1980. He gave him a five-year, $6 million contract and the keys to the car. "You're the boss," he told him.

It was a good situation for Parcells in that he would have more control than he had with the Giants. On the other hand, he inherited a mess. He characterized the Patriots as having "the most down-and-out, despondent, negative atmosphere you could imagine." For many, getting used to the Parcells Way was a tough assignment.

Max Lane: Coming out of Navy, it was a seamless transition for me. A lot of guys might have had some issues with the discipline of Parcells. Stuff like, even if you're on time, you're late. I was trained to be ready for that, I was used to the structure. We had to go to class at Navy and couldn't fall asleep in them. I was used to sitting through meetings. Guys who came from other teams or college programs where their butts were kissed all the time were in for a bit of a shock and a bit of an adjustment.

Gil Santos: Here comes a guy with a couple of Super Bowl championships to take over. Bill really knows how to build a football team. He came in and immediately turned the whole program into a professionally run, my-way-or-the-highway football team. He set the tone for all of the things that have gone on since then. And, like Chuck Fairbanks, Bill was not afraid to bring in great assistant coaches, Bill Belichick among them.

Willie McGinest: I had a bunch of Dallas Cowboy representatives at my draft party. I thought they were going to move up to the fifth pick, which they were. They were going to trade Alvin Harper, and they were gonna take that Rams pick at number five and get me. I thought I was going to be a Cowboy. Bill Parcells called with that fourth pick, and I was totally surprised. At the same time, I was honored to be playing for a coach of his status.

Chris Slade: For me it was a delight. I grew up a big Lawrence Taylor fan. I knew Parcells coached him all those years with the Giants, so when I was drafted by the Patriots it was a thrill and an honor. I was just elated. To be able to play for him, to get the experiences and the life lessons learned from him; it was an honor playing for him.

The roster received a major overhaul; more than 60 percent of the personnel were turned over. In 1992, the quarterbacking had been handled by Hugh Millen, Scott Zolak, Tom Hodson, and Jeff Carlson. Of the four, only Zolak survived, and he was third string. Instead, Parcells decided that his new quarterback should serve his apprenticeship in game conditions.

Ray Perkins: The thing that impressed me the most about Drew Bledsoe in evaluating him for the draft was that him being from Washington, they had quite a few snow games, rain games, and generally just bad weather games. So, if your quarterback can't play really good in bad weather, you don't need to bring him to New England, because you're going to have some bad-weather games in Boston. That's where he impressed me the most—in the bad-weather games. He didn't let it bother him. He threw the ball just like if it was an eighty-five-degree day. He was easy to work with. He was a highly competitive guy and smart.

Max Lane: He was a pocket passer. He wasn't as mobile as some of them, and I wouldn't say Drew had the most pocket presence. I think it was more of a factor of how tough and strong he was, physically. He could get hit and it wouldn't bother him. Drew never yelled at you for getting hit. He'd yell at you because he had a guy open and he didn't get a chance to throw the pass. I'd be responsible for getting him clobbered and I'd come back and help him up. I'd be like, "Dude, I'm sorry." He'd say, "Ahh, nobody was open anyway." You'd get him hurried and rushed, he'd say, "God damn it, Max, I had a frickin' guy wide open, hold him off!" That's what he cared about.

Willie McGinest: I played against Drew in college, and in my first game against him at Washington State I sacked him a couple of times.

I'd hit him and he was still throwing the ball fifteen, twenty, thirty yards down the field. He was a big guy, like six-five or taller and over 240 pounds. He had cannon for an arm. I was so impressed with him in college that when he got drafted by New England and I ended up going there, he was one of the guys I was looking forward to playing with. I knew what type of talent he was. He was a traditional pocket passer who could put the ball anywhere on the field. He was a calm guy—real laid-back, but a natural leader.

Max Lane: Everybody always talked about how he wasn't a vocal leader, but the guy played through everything. He had that dislocated shoulder. Even though he wasn't playing his best, he still got a lot of respect for playing injured. The guy was a warrior.

Chris Slade: I don't want to use this word, but Drew was often underrated. They questioned his toughness, his work ethic. Drew wasn't a rah-rah yeller and screamer. He didn't get in your face. You see Tom Brady acting like that sometimes. Tom's an emotional guy, and that's his personality. Drew was the opposite. Drew was a lot tougher than people gave him credit for. He took a lot of hits. He took a pounding. He wanted to win as much as anyone on that team. I played with him for eight years. We came in together. He was a very good quarterback. He could throw the ball from Boston to Providence. He had a rifle of an arm. I thought he was very misunderstood. He was a lot tougher than people thought, and I tip my hat to him.

Bledsoe, the number-one overall pick in the 1993 draft out of Washington State University, was given the starting job. The results were not especially pretty. The Patriots lost their first four games before just getting past the Phoenix Cardinals. When Bledsoe strained his knee, the quarterback job fell to journeyman Scott Secules for four games, and the losing continued.

The defense was improving, though. They surrendered 171 points in the first six games and then just 72 over the next six, although all six wound up as losses and the team fell to 1–11. Bledsoe had his worst game of the season in week 12, a 17–14 loss to the Steelers in which he threw five interceptions. Then, in week 13, the defense pitched a shutout and the Patriots got their second win, a 7–2 decision over the Bengals. Bledsoe threw 22 passes without an interception. A fourth-quarter win over the Browns followed (prompting a hilariously sign-of-the-times headline in the *Boston Globe*: "It's a Streak!"), and then Bledsoe had a near-perfect day against Indianapolis in a 38–0 rout. He threw only 11 passes, but two were for touchdowns and only two were incompletions. The defense let down in week 16, but Bledsoe completed 27 passes, four for scores, and Miami was beaten 33–27 to finish the season with four straight wins.

Carryover between seasons is one of the great misconceptions in sports. A late rush does not guarantee that a successful season is just over the horizon, but, in the case of the 1994 Patriots, that's just what occurred. Parcells had his sophomore quarterback throwing more times than anyone in history. The Patriots fell one shy of 700 passing attempts, and Bledsoe threw 691 of them, which remains the NFL single-season record. He completed 400 of those throws, which, at the time, was just four shy of Warren Moon's record, set in 1991. (In the pass-happy 2000s, it has since been surpassed six times, most recently by Peyton Manning and Drew Brees in 2010, who now rank one-two all-time.) New England won its final seven games and finished with a 10–6 record. Parcells had taken them from two wins to the playoffs in just two seasons.

Although New England lost in the first round of the playoffs to a solid Browns team coached by Bill Belichick, it seemed as though the sky was the limit. Surely they would keep improving.

The ideal arrangement Parcells had with James B. Orthwein went out the window when Robert Kraft bought the team as a response to Orthwein's desire to move the Pats out of Massachusetts. Kraft soon imposed a player-personnel director on Parcells, much to his chagrin. It was the first step down the road to divorce.

Belichick and the Browns were their opening-day opponents for 1995, and there were some who were talking up Cleveland as a Super Bowl contender. They led the Patriots for most of this game until New England got the ball on their own 16 with 4:29 left and went on a 15-play touchdown drive to grab the 17–14 win. Things fell apart for both teams after that. The Browns went just 5–11 and blew out of Cleveland for Baltimore after the season. Belichick resigned and would show up in Foxborough the following season as Parcells's assistant head coach. (In their careers, Parcells and Belichick would meet as head coaches in five games, with Belichick getting the upper hand in three of them.)

New England, meanwhile, would lose its next five games and fall out of the AFC East race. Both the offense and defense took a turn for the worse. Bledsoe was still making it rain, attempting 636 passes but completing far fewer than in 1994. In his final three years under Parcells, Bledsoe threw the first-, third- and fourth-most passes in history up to that point. For a coach whose favorite slogan was "power football," it was a remarkable change of attitude. Many coaches would have tried to impose their style on a team not suited for it, but it is to Parcells's credit that he changed his tactics to fit the personnel on hand.

The Patriots rallied to a 6–8 record and were still mathematically alive for a wild-card spot when they traveled to Pittsburgh and battled the Steelers hard to a 27–27 tie before succumbing late. Another loss put the final accounting at 6–10. The good news was that rookie Curtis Martin was the real deal, gaining nearly 1,500 yards on the ground and giving New England something they hadn't had in a while: a big-game running back.

Ray Perkins: We picked Martin in the third round. I mean, he wasn't just a bargain, he was a steal! Somebody should have been put in jail for that one! And he is just as good an individual as he is a football player, too. When you've got a Curtis Martin in the game, it's a lot easier to call plays.

Max Lane: It was awesome to see him get a short pass and take off with it. He was a dynamic player. He hit the holes right. He had that natural ability to just know where to hit the hole. Once he got through, he had the moves and the speed and the strength. He was just a good all-around back.

Parcells's relationship with Kraft was getting more complicated. Behind the scenes, he had renegotiated his contract so that he was no longer obligated for the 1997 season. Unbeknownst to most, 1996 was probably going to be his last year with the team regardless of what happened on the field. A further rift developed when the owner pulled rank on Parcells over who would be taken with the team's first pick in the draft.

Troy Brown: We started the season off with Robert Kraft and Bill Parcells going back and forth on who they should have picked. Parcells was maybe looking for a defensive lineman, and they got into the whole Terry Glenn thing. It ended up working out, because Glenn was a big part of us having success during that season.

Parcells very nearly resigned over the incident, and Kraft very nearly fired him.

THE 1996 SEASON

Although the Patriots had finally snapped their long Miami losing streak a decade before and won their next three games there, they had since lost six of seven road games against the Dolphins. On opening day 1996, however, they were favored to win in Miami. The Dolphins were playing in their first game under Jimmy Johnson. In the first quarter, Bledsoe was intercepted by Louis Oliver, who appeared to be headed for a touchdown until he was stripped by running back Dave Meggett. The ball bounced right to safety Sean Hill, however, and he took it in for the score. In the third quarter, with New England trailing 17–3, the Dolphins launched a 96-yard drive that appeared to be undone when Dan Marino hit Stanley Pritchett for a 15-yard gain only to have him fumble the ball into the end zone. Receiver Scott Miller fell on the ball, and Miami went up by 17 and cruised to the 24–10 win.

In week two, the Patriots traveled to Buffalo and did a good job of keeping Jim Kelly on a short leash, picking him off three times and holding the Bills to just 231 total yards. Kelly's one touchdown pass, a 63-yarder to Quinn Early, came with 5:21 to go in the game and put the Bills up 17–10. The Pats charged right back, but Phil Hansen stuffed Meggett at the 2 to end the threat.

Starting a season 0–2 is not necessarily a death sentence in the NFL, but it's usually a prelude to irrelevance—especially since both losses were to division rivals. Fortunately for the Patriots, the Arizona Cardinals came to town for the New England home opener. The Cardinals in those years were a welcome sight on any schedule, especially as visitors, having not finished with a winning road record since 1976. (This streak stood all the way until 2009, when they went 6–2 on the road and went to the play-offs.) In the first half, New England got more first downs than Arizona ran plays (18 to 15) and cruised to an easy 31–0 victory. Week four was looking like a cakewalk too, as the second-year Jacksonville Jaguars fell behind 22–0 in the second quarter. The Jags' Mark Brunell then unloaded scoring passes of 41, 51, and 61 yards to put Jacksonville back in the game. Mike Hollis tied it at 25 with a fourth-quarter field goal.

Playing in just the fourth game of his career, rookie kicker Adam Vinatieri attempted six field goals and made five of them—both still career highs. The fifth successful kick came with 2:36 gone in overtime, evening the team's record at 2–2. (The upstart Jags under Parcells protégé Tom Coughlin would show up in New England again four months later to play the AFC Championship.) With the victory, Parcells became the 22nd coach in NFL history to reach 100 wins.

The Patriots traveled to Baltimore in week five and built a 24-point lead on the Ravens. Baltimore made it look closer than it was in the fourth quarter, with three touchdowns followed by successful conversions, making the final 46–38. Bledsoe picked apart the mistake-prone Ravens secondary for four touchdown passes. After a loss to the Redskins evened their record at 3–3, the Patriots took advantage of two Colts fumbles and beat Indianapolis 27–9. After holding off a determined Bills team 28–25, Bledsoe blew out the Dolphins with a big second half and threw for 419 yards and three touchdowns in the 42–23 win. Facing the Jets in week 10, New England staged one of the great rallies in team annals (see "The Largest Comebacks in Patriots History," on page 218), although an even better one was yet to come.

The next week, the 9–1 Broncos came to town and rolled up a 24–0 lead before New England could respond. There would be no comeback this time, as Denver finished them off, 34–8. The Patriots dispatched their next three opponents with relative ease. The Colts fell 27–13, the

Chargers 45–7, and the Jets 34–10. None of them rushed for more than 50 yards, although teams tended to throw a lot against the Patriots. (Only the Chargers faced more passing plays in 1996.) Meanwhile, the Bills were taking a powder, falling from 9–3 to 9–5 and letting New England lap them. The Pats missed a chance to clinch the division when they lost to the Cowboys, four field goals to two, with the Dallas defense grabbing three interceptions, recovering a fumble, and making a pair of key fourth-down stops to keep New England in line in the next-to-last game of the season.

The Dolphins obliged the Patriots by beating the Bills on Monday night, giving New England the AFC East title. They still had a lot on the line heading into their final game in East Rutherford, New Jersey, against the Giants—some of it relevant to the standings and some of it relevant to pride. This would be the first time Parcells would face the Giants since leaving the team. He'd been back to the Meadowlands before, but that was to play the Jets. It was not a meeting he was looking forward to; Parcells had no desire to face a franchise he still cared about. On the more practical side, the Patriots needed the win to avoid having to mess with a first-round playoff game.

There was plenty more intrigue where that came from. This was to be Giants coach Dan Reeves's last game as well. He had his gear packed and was ready to exit. The other New York coach, Rich Kotite, was also on his way out, and the Jets were not making it a secret as to who they wanted to take his place: Bill Parcells. They couldn't talk to him, though, until the Patriots were finished playing.

The 6–9 Giants were incredibly inconsistent. They had one of the weakest offenses in the league, but a solid defense, and it was that defense that put their first points on the board.

Troy Brown: We didn't look like a team that was playing for anything. In actuality we were playing for home-field advantage during the playoffs.

In the first quarter, Drew Bledsoe was pressured in his own end zone and threw the ball away. He was called for intentional grounding, and the Giants had a 2–0 lead. The Giants D frustrated Bledsoe throughout the first half as the Patriots could manage only 74 yards of offense. Cornerback Jason Sehorn also got him for a pick-six, capping a second-quarter scoring surge that saw the Giants run up 20 points. Earlier in the quarter, Charles Way had banged over from the 1 and Brad Daluiso had kicked two field goals.

Dante Scarnecchia: It was real quiet on the sideline.

Chris Slade: You know Charlie Way, my boy from Virginia—he kicked our butts in the first half. Al Groh, our defensive coordinator, came to us and said, "This guy wants it more than you. He's kicking our butts!" He wrote Way's number 30 on our board and circled it over and over, repeating, "This guy wants it." That was the turning point for us. We went in and changed our attitude.

Otis Smith: We were going into each and every game believing we could win, whether we were down by ten or two. The score didn't matter because we were prepared to battle until the end.

"I took it to our guys at halftime," said Patriots captain Bruce Armstrong after the game. "I asked them, what kind of team did they want to be? I asked them to play like something was on the line for us, which it was. I issued a challenge."

The fiery speech didn't help—at least not right away. Eleven minutes of playing time later, the Giants still had their 22-point lead. The Patriots finally got on the board when Adam Vinatieri kicked a 40-yard field goal at 4:12 of the third quarter. New England opened the fourth quarter with a drive that culminated in a 26-yard touchdown pass from Bledsoe to Terry Glenn, and the Giants, who were now being shut down by the Patriots defense, were beginning to look nervous.

What New York needed at that moment was a time-consuming drive. Instead, they went three and out and took all of a minute off the clock in so doing, and Mike Horan came out to punt the ball away, with Dave Meggett deep to receive. Meggett had spent six years with the Giants, leading the NFL in punt-return yardage in both 1989 and 1990 and running back six punts (and one kickoff) for touchdowns for them.

When Horan, a prolific and skilled punter, put one right in the center of the field, Meggett took it at the New England 40 and went right up the gut. Nobody laid a hand on him. The only Giant with even a chance to catch him was Horan, and Meggett blew right past him for the score.

Just like that, the Patriots were within six points and there was 11:09 left to play. When the Giants went three and out again and had to punt, New England got the ball at its own 25 and started driving. After Giants defensive end Chad Bratzke snuffed a reverse play in spite of a nice block by Bledsoe, the Patriots found themselves with a third-and-13 at the New York 42.

Troy Brown: I had my biggest day as a pro during that game. I came to life. I also got injured in the first half; I developed a hernia. I didn't know what it was for a long period of time. I continued to play. On that crucial third-and-thirteen situation over the middle, Drew kind of threw the ball behind me as I was sliding down. But I caught the ball on the marker for the first down to keep the drive alive. Through-out that season I had continued to grow, and I think Parcells developed more confidence in me. As the season went on, I got more and more playing time as a third-down receiver for the team.

In spite of being nearly laid out flat, Brown reached back and up and yanked the pass out of the air. It was one of his seven catches on the day, a career high to that point.

Bledsoe went for the gold on the next play and just barely overthrew Shawn Jefferson in the end zone. The Patriots were facing a fourth-and-7 at the Giants' 14 with a minute and a half to play. On the 13th play of the drive, Bledsoe took the snap and dropped back past the 20. Down at the 2, Ben Coates was tangled up with safety Tito Wooten, but he broke free and turned around and Bledsoe hit him with a perfect pass. Coates had no momentum, though, and Wooten and Conrad Hamilton stood him straight up while other defenders rushed over to keep him out of the end zone. Coates would not go down.

Chris Slade: Ben Coates basically carried the whole defense into the end zone.

Troy Brown: Dave Meggett came up and helped push for the go-ahead touchdown.

Parcells went for 2, but the pass to Keith Byars over the middle was high, meaning that a successful Giants drive would now win the game rather than tie it. There was still 1:23 on the clock, and New York had two time-outs to play with, having wasted one setting the defense prior to the 2-point conversion. Hamilton made a nice runback on the kick-off and would have had even more had he not been taken down with a textbook open-field tackle by Adam Vinatieri.

On fourth and 7 at their own 48, Dave Brown connected with Chris Calloway to give New York a first down at the New England 40 with 45 seconds left. It was only his second completion in his last 11 passes. The Patriots had most of their backs in a deep drop and lined up as though they were only going to rush the down three. Instead, they brought both outside linebackers on a blitz and Brown was wrapped up. Instead of eating the ball, however, he backhanded it to an open space in the field and was called for intentional grounding.

It was a huge break for the Patriots as the Giants moved further from the considerable range of Brad Daluiso and lost a down as well. New York was looking at a third-and-21 when Brown appeared to make their problems go away, finding Thomas Lewis open at the 32. He went up high for what seemed to be a makeable catch, only to have the ball pop off his hands and up into the air, where it was nearly intercepted before falling to the ground. Instead, after one more futile play, New England had closed out the franchise's greatest come-from-behind victory. (See "The Largest Comebacks in Patriots History," on page 218.)

"Coach Parcells was so emotional after this game that he was short of words—I have never seen Coach Parcells short of words," said corner-back Ty Law. "It obviously meant a lot to him to come back here in his first game against the Giants and to win, and especially to win like this."

Chris Slade: It was the first time I'd seen Parcells emotional. He broke down and cried.

THE TEAM

The Patriots had the best offense in the AFC in 1995 and the second best in the NFL behind Green Bay. Drew Bledsoe was at the peak of his powers, throwing 27 touchdown passes against 15 interceptions. For the third year in a row, he led the league in passing attempts, this time with 623. He completed nearly 60 percent of them (eighth in the league) for 6.6 yards per throw, which was not among the leaders but was well above league average. At 83.7, he had the eighth-best passer rating in the NFL.

Curtis Martin had a solid season, rushing for 1,152 yards (ninth overall) while scoring the second-most touchdowns in the league with 17. He caught 46 passes and got a Pro Bowl selection.

Although Parcells wanted to draft a lineman instead of Terry Glenn—who was the choice of Bobby Grier, the director of player personnel—there is no arguing with the results of his first year in the league. He caught 90 passes—including eight in the big comeback against the Giants—shattering the rookie record of 83 set by Earl Cooper of the 49ers in 1980. His stay in New England was often marked by time on the disabled list. In a bit of irony, Parcells later brought him to the Cowboys, where he would finish his career.

Second on the team in receptions was Pro Bowl tight end Ben Coates, who also scored nine touchdowns. He was helped out by midseason acquisition Keith Byars. The former Eagle and Dolphin fullback caught 27 passes in his 10 games with the Patriots. Veteran left tackle Bruce Armstrong was chosen for his third straight trip to the Pro Bowl. He would be named to a total of six Pro Bowl teams in his 14-year career, which he spent entirely with the Patriots. Dave Meggett's heroics in the comeback win against the Giants capped a season in which he, too, would be named to the Pro Bowl as a special-teams player. He had 588 punt-return yards, most in the conference.

Max Lane: On the offensive side of the ball we had Dave Wohlabaugh playing center. Bob Kratch and William Roberts and Todd Rucci handled the guard spots. Bruce Armstrong and I were the tackles. We were fortunate we didn't have too many injuries on the offensive side of the ball. We were more of a balanced team that year.

Dante Scarnecchia: We threw the ball well. Actually, I think we threw it more than we wanted to throw it, or more than Bill wanted to throw it. But, it was the formula. We didn't turn it over much.

The defense was anchored by Willie McGinest, a third-year man out of USC. He was switched from left outside linebacker to the right end in 1996 and responded with a Pro Bowl season that included scoring touchdowns on both a fumble recovery and an interception return. The young secondary, which featured future greats like Ty Law and Lawyer Milloy, got a boost when the Pats picked up Otis Smith, who had been released by the Jets.

Otis Smith: It was great for me. I went from a team that at the time wasn't very good to a team that was on the brink of breaking through. With [right cornerback] Ricky Reynolds getting hurt, they were lacking experience at the corner position. Ty Law was very young at the time, and they had Jimmy Hitchcock, who was young as well, so they brought me in for some veteran presence and a little wisdom. Not only did I come in and try and play, but I wanted to help those guys get better because they had a ton of talent there; to show them how to work in practice and motivate those guys to play better each Sunday.

Dante Scarnecchia: On defense we played the way Bill and Al wanted us to play. We had good techniques. We were opportunistic. We were good at creating turnovers. All those things paid huge dividends for us.

Max Lane: Lawyer was a rookie, but he was an impact player. Tedy Bruschi was an impact role player. Todd Collins got off the truck farm and came back that year. We had a good linebacking corps: Ted Johnson, Tedy Bruschi, Chris Slade and Dwayne Sabb. Up front we had Mike Jones, Mark Wheeler, and—God bless his soul—Pio Sagapolutele. Willie McGinest was playing good. Ferric Collons fit in there, too. We had a lot of good players and we had a lot of depth.

Dante Scarnecchia: Willie McGinest is a special guy; a great leader and a good football player. A tough guy. He's got an infectious personality and we he speaks a lot of people listen. Ted Johnson was a tough-minded guy. A big hitter. A guy you can count on in the middle to keep things plugged up. We had a lot of good players that carried us into the next era.

The Pats were very good against the run (only 3.5 yards per attempt, fifth in the league) and slightly worse than league average against the pass. While their overall statistics don't look that impressive, the D unit really put it together down the stretch. After their worst loss of the season in Denver, the Patriots ball stoppers allowed just 11 points a game over the last five games—and this dominance continued into the playoffs.

THE STEELERS

The Central Division champion Pittsburgh Steelers were the best defensive team in the conference. Led by linebackers Chad Brown and Levon Kirkland and cornerback Rod Woodson, Pittsburgh had proven it could handle any defensive eventuality. Against the run, the Steelers allowed the third-fewest rushing yards in the league in 1996 and the second-fewest yards per carry. No team rushed for more than 130 yards on them in a single game. Against the pass, only the Super Bowl champion Packers allowed fewer net yards per throw. They were known for their zone blitzing, a tactic that allowed them to lead the league in sacks per pass attempt.

Pittsburgh was coached by Bill Cowher, who was in his fifth season with the team and his fifth trip to the playoffs. (Only Paul Brown and Chuck Knox before him had ever pulled off that feat.) In their first-round playoff game, the Steelers outdid themselves on both sides of the ball, tying their season high in points scored, 42, while bettering their season-best defensive performance in holding the Indianapolis Colts to just 146 total yards. They had actually let a 13–0 second-quarter lead slip away, but roared back for the 42–14 win as Jerome Bettis bulled in for two touchdown plunges and multi-threat Kordell Stewart, still in "Slash" mode, scored two of his own.

Bettis rushed for 1,431 yards on 4.5 yards per carry, the second-best average of his career. The good news for the Patriots was that "The

Bus" had injured his groin against the Colts—some of whom suspected the injury was the result of a touchdown celebration.

The Pittsburgh quarterback was Mike Tomczak, who, at the age of 34, had just had the best season of his career, setting personal bests in just about every counting stat category. The downside was that one of those categories was interceptions, of which he'd thrown 17 to just 15 touchdown passes. Very adept at the play-action pass, his favorite targets were Andre Hastings, who led the team with 72 receptions, and Charles Johnson, who had 60 and was good for 16.8 yards per reception.

THE GAME

For only the second time in their history, the Patriots would be hosting a playoff game. It had been nearly 20 years since the first one, the 31–14 loss to the Houston Oilers in Chuck Fairbanks's bizarre finale at the end of the 1978 season. The Patriots were keenly aware that their fans had never seen them win a playoff game at home.

Max Lane: We had that bye week, so we had some time to let it sink in. But we were young and hungry, so we were like, let's just win. Sometimes when you get caught up in the historical perspective of things, you lose focus on the task. Parcells did a good job keeping us focused so that we knew what was going on, but we didn't think about it too much.

Willie McGinest: We were hearing it from everybody that we didn't have a chance. I think that's what gave us the motivation. Parcells was saying all week that nobody was giving us a chance. He made us feel like the underdog, which we were. I think guys got tired of hearing him, but that was part of his mental game—to tell us that this team was too tough for us. He'd say that they had too many weapons, that they were too this and too that. The type of guys we had, we were really resilient. Guys didn't want to hear that. We felt we had a point to prove. On paper, they probably *did* have a better team, but as far as heart and determination went, we knew we were going to win that game.

A lot of the pregame talk was dedicated to how Cowher would use his two quarterbacks. The Kordell Stewart gambit, in which he would sometimes line up as a wideout and sometimes over center, was an exciting wrinkle in the NFL of the mid-nineties. Fifteen years later (and thanks to some of Bill Parcells's later work), the wildcat is a feature of many offenses, but back then it seemed revolutionary—regardless of how much it owed to the early days of football, when skill players might do just about anything on a given play.

Otis Smith: We felt we could stop Jerome and the running game. If not stop them, at least slow him down and not let him into the secondary. If we could corral him and not let him loose, we stood a chance there. And keeping Kordell Stewart in the pocket and not letting him scramble and use his legs, as well as his arm, to create time to find receivers down the field. It put a lot of pressure on us not only to stop the Bus from running but to stop Kordell Stewart and keep him in the pocket.

Willie McGinest: To have any success on defense, you have to stop the run. If you can't stop the run, it opens up the whole playbook for an offense. We wanted to turn this into a one-dimensional game for them, so we had to take away the Bus. We were accustomed to playing against big backs, but we actually preferred that to playing against the little, fast backs. We had Marion Grier on our team. In our practices, he played the role of the Bus and he gave us a good look. Our number-one mission was to stop Bettis and then take away Kordell and a couple of other weapons. You can't stop everybody, but we wanted to stop two or three of their most viable weapons to give ourselves the best chance to win.

When analysts weren't talking about Stewart, they were focusing on "Blitzburgh" and whether or not the Patriots could handle the pressuring schemes of the Steeler defense. All of that Steelers talk was not sitting well with the Patriots. Talking about his teammate Bruce Armstrong, Bledsoe offered this insight to the Associated Press: "He wasn't too happy with the fact that everybody was giving Pittsburgh the ballgame, yet we were the ones with 11 wins and the bye and the home game. There were a couple of guys on our line that played with a chip on their shoulder."

Max Lane: Pittsburgh was the defending AFC champions. They had beaten us in '95 at their place. I think they felt they had our number. Pittsburgh looked at New England like, "What are they doing here? They haven't earned anything yet." They had that attitude, but we knew the kind of team we had.

Game day found Foxborough experiencing unseasonably warm conditions. With the temperature at 46 degrees and the humidity at 95 percent, a fog had descended on the land. Visibility for those in the upper reaches of Foxboro Stadium was dim.

Chris Slade: It was actually kind of neat to play in a situation and environment like that. It was unlike anything I'd ever been involved in. It is what it is: playoff football in New England, and anything can happen.

Gil Santos: I had to try to broadcast that game through the fog. There were portions of the field that I couldn't see because the fog was so dense. On punts and kickoffs, I had to wait for the ball to come out of the higher fog and try to gauge where it was going to be by watching where the return men were going. Once it was kicked, it got lost in the fog and I'd pick it up again just before it came down to the player to return it, or hit the ground and go into the end zone for a touchback or whatever the case was. It was a very difficult game to broadcast.

"It just made it extra interesting to me to go out there and see all that fog," said Curtis Martin after the game. "I wondered whether they'll be able to see me when I'm running."

Chris Slade: Lucky for me, on defense all I had to do was look for the guy with the black hat and the football in his hands. For the offense, catching the football was tough in that fog.

Down on the field, the Steelers were soon put into a fog of their own. Starting from their own 23, Pittsburgh was penalized for an illegal shift and started in a 5-yard hole. In spite of that, they gave the ball to Bettis for two slams right into the center of the line, which netted 4 yards. Tomczak dropped back into the shotgun on third and 11, but his pass to Jahine Arnold was incomplete.

After an 8-yard punt return by Meggett, Bledsoe stepped up to the line at his own 45 to start the Patriots' first possession of the day. It would turn out to be of very short duration.

Max Lane: On the first play from scrimmage, we ran a play action; I think we called it Ride 136. We faked an off-tackle to Curtis, giving us a chance to fire off the ball, then go for a big-play strike to Terry Glenn down the sideline.

Glenn got two steps on Rod Woodson, and Bledsoe hit him.

Troy Brown: Young Terry Glenn against an aging Rod Woodson. He'd had his knee reconstructed the year before. It did look like Terry Glenn left him in the dust—left him standing still there.

Max Lane: We couldn't see where Terry was because of the fog. It was weird. I don't know how Drew saw him; maybe he had a better vantage point. It set the tone for the game.

Woodson recovered enough to save the touchdown, but it was a 53-yard gain down to the 2-yard line. On the next play, Curtis Martin went off right guard and in for the score. Three minutes into the game, the Patriots were up 7–0.

A near disaster for the Steelers on the ensuing kickoff turned in their favor when Arnold lost the ball at the 2, but his teammate Ernie Mills scooped it up and brought it out to the 19. Stewart's first appearance came on third and 1 of the series that followed, and it did not go well. McGinest and Todd Collins hauled him down for a loss as he tried to go around right end, and Pittsburgh had to punt it away once more.

Meggett returned this one 14 yards to the New England 41, where

Bledsoe went right at Woodson again, hitting Glenn for 12 yards. Martin caught a short pass and made a nice run, getting the Patriots 13 yards closer on the two plays. Bledsoe dropped back and waited for the screen to develop before dumping the ball off to Byars. He rumbled 34 yards for the touchdown. The Patriots had held the ball all of three minutes and had a 14–0 lead.

How well were things going for New England? They had already declined three penalties because they'd gained more yardage on the plays they ran than the penalties would have provided.

After both teams had fruitless possessions to close out the first quarter, the Steelers got some movement going with a first down on their next series, but stalled at their own 37. Josh Miller dropped back to punt, but the snap went to up back Fred McAfee instead, and he took off around right end for 10 yards. When Bettis cut loose for 11 yards across midfield to the New England 42 on the next play, it appeared as though the Steelers were finally getting on track. Instead, Chris Slade—who'd had seven sacks during the regular season—dropped Tomczak on each of the next two plays, assisted by Chad Eaton on the first one and Mike Jones on the second. Pittsburgh was hurled back 15 yards on the plays.

Chris Slade: This was the same year I went through a platooning thing with Parcells. He had decided midway through the season he was only going to put me in on passing downs. His reasons for doing that was typical Parcells playing mind games, telling me he needed me rested for the stretch run. He had to motivate me. I had something to prove to him and I wanted to help the team win. It worked. Good job, Parcells!

Miller lined up to punt again, this time following through with an actual kick. With the ball at the Patriots' 22, Martin lined up in a very deep set behind Bledsoe, who took the snap and handed him the ball.

Max Lane: We were so jacked for that Pittsburgh game, because we knew we had the best offensive game plans. Pittsburgh plays a 3-4. We put in a little bit of a blocking scheme, where you blocked the guard. [Right guard] Todd Rucci would block out the guy covering me. I would fold around underneath him. It's called a tug. It was a tackle under guard. Guard would block out, I'd pull around up end for the linebacker in the hole. We ran that play for Curtis, and he went forever.

Martin went right up the middle. Seconds later, he was standing in the Pittsburgh end zone, the author of the second-longest touchdown run from scrimmage in a playoff game.

The Steelers would get the ball back four more times in the quarter. On one of the series, they used Stewart exclusively, but he was sacked and threw two incompletions. The Steeler defense had better luck against Bledsoe on the subsequent New England possessions, sacking him and forcing an intentional grounding to kill one drive and intercepting him to end another. The half ended with New England up 21–0.

The teams exchanged possessions to open the second half. On the second New England series of the third quarter, they had moved from their own 15 out to the 40, where, on first and 10, Bledsoe tried to dunk a pass to Martin but was intercepted by linebacker Chad Brown. Before the defense could get used to being back on the field, Tomczak hit Hastings for 23 yards down to the New England 14, where he was wrapped up by Lawyer Milloy and Ty Law. If the Steelers were going to claw their way back into the game, this was their chance.

Instead, they played small ball. A short pass to Bettis garnered 2 yards before Law dumped him. On second and 8, Tomczak tossed one out to Bettis behind the line of scrimmage, where he was met by McGinest and brought down for a 3-yard loss. On third and 11, Stewart tried to go around right end but was stopped after 4 yards by Slade and Michael McGruder. Norm Johnson came on for the 29-yard field goal. The Patriots had lost their shutout, but the defense had kept it a three-score game.

New England went three and out on their next possession, but got the ball right back. In contrast to their conservative approach in the red zone on their previous possession, the Steelers went long on first down from their 36, which resulted in a Milloy interception at the New England 39.

The Patriots embarked on a six-play, 61-yard drive that, save for a

9-yard pass to Shawn Jefferson, was all Curtis Martin. He capped it with his third touchdown of the foggy afternoon, a 23-yard jaunt off right guard that gave New England a forbidding 25-point lead.

The Steelers tried some razzle-dazzle on the kickoff, with return man Mills faking a reverse to Stewart, only to keep it himself for a 36-yard gain. Showing once again that he was willing and able to do more than run off the field after kicking off, Adam Vinatieri was in on the stop. Lining up exclusively out of the shotgun, Tomczak drove the Steelers from their own 40 to the New England 15. On the 12th play of the drive, he tried to hit Corey Holliday at the 1-yard line but was picked off by free safety Willie Clay, who brought it out to the 15. It was the last Pittsburgh threat of the afternoon, although they would get the ball back two more times.

The Patriots had dinged the Pittsburgh defense for the most rushing yards they had surrendered all season by far: 194. Of those, 166 belonged to Curtis Martin. "We'd heard a lot about their defense and, quite frankly, our players were a little tired of hearing that," said Parcells after the game.

The New England defense had limited Bettis to 42 yards on 13 carries and held the Steelers to just 213 total yards. Tomczak was 16-for-29 with two interceptions, while Stewart was 0-for-1. The Patriots very nearly shut him down completely. His one tangible contribution was a 10-yard run. Gerald Eskenazi of the *New York Times* very presciently wrote before the game, "If Stewart has to play more, his effectiveness is in question. Right now, defenses become unsettled because of the dramatic shift in rhythm he brings—his ability to run the option, or simply run. The longer he stays in the game, the more accustomed to him opponents can become."

In dominating fashion, the Patriots had given their fans something they had never had before: a playoff win in their own backyard.

THE AFTERMATH

With their first home playoff victory on the books, New England would embark on an 11-game home winning streak in the playoffs, the second-longest of all time. (See "All-Time Home Playoff Records," on page 216.)

The following week, the Patriots doubled their number of home playoff wins when the defense turned in another solid performance and suppressed the upstart Jacksonville Jaguars, 20–6. The second-year Jags, who played New England much tougher than the Steelers had, were driving for the tying touchdown with under four minutes to go in the game when Willie Clay intercepted Mark Brunell in the end zone. On Jacksonville's next possession, the Patriots defense came up big once again.

Chris Slade: James Stewart was running and I knocked it out of his hands and Otis picked it up.

Otis Smith: I picked it up and scored off of it.

Smith's 47-yard trip to the end zone gave the Patriots some breathing room with a 14-point lead. Brunell threw one more interception just past the two-minute warning to ice it.

What little good was left in the Parcells-Kraft relationship disintegrated completely during the playoffs. By now, there was no chance Parcells was returning, but another aspect of their renegotiated deal had come to light. There was a clause that prohibited Parcells from coaching elsewhere in 1997. When he asked the owner to let him leave free and clear, Kraft refused. Eventually, the league brokered a deal between the Jets and Patriots in which New England was compensated with draft picks.

Chris Slade: We as players tuned it out, because there was nothing we could do about it. It was a situation where you had a head coach and owner with different agendas and they never could get along. It was unfortunate, but it happens all the time in sports.

Troy Brown: Personally I didn't mind Parcells's yelling and screaming. I didn't have a problem with Parcells. He was a different guy off the football field. I didn't always agree with him, but I respected him. He was a caring guy. I hated to see him leave, because we were on to something good. It was a difficult time for the players, because rumors were circulating the whole season that he was going to leave the team. We never got an official announcement, but we knew he was leaving.

Max Lane: We handled some questions during the week of the Super Bowl. We'd say, "We don't really know what's going on. We're just here to play a game. We don't care." After you lose a game, all the excuses come out. I remember hearing guys say it was a distraction. That's a bunch of hogwash. As we said before the game, we really didn't know a whole lot of what was going on. There are always personalities that don't get along. That's true everywhere. Parcells's quote that week—"The Packers are here to make history; we're here to win a game"—became our motto. He did a good job keeping us focused. The contract dispute wasn't a factor.

Once again, the Patriots met a team of destiny in the Super Bowl (See "The Biggest Mismatches in Super Bowl History," on page xxx), and once again things ended badly for them.

APPENDICES

The Most Years Without a Home Playoff Victory

Playoff wins are great, but they're even nicer when executed in front of the home folks. For 36 years, the Patriots deprived their followers of such joy. That is nearly a record for a team in one geographic area (considering that the record holder split its time in three cities). The following franchises have gone the longest periods without winning a playoff game at home.

61 years: Chicago/St. Louis/Phoenix/Arizona Cardinals
From 1947, a 28–21 victory over Philadelphia in the NFL Championship, to 2008, when they beat Atlanta 30–24. (Home playoff losses in that period: 0.)

39 years: Pittsburgh Pirates/Steelers
From the beginning of the franchise, in 1933, to 1972, when they beat Oakland 13–7 in the Immaculate Reception Game. (Home playoff losses in that period: 1.)

36 years: Boston/New England Patriots
From the beginning of the franchise, in 1960, to 1996, a 28–3 victory over Pittsburgh. (Home playoff losses in that period: 1.)

34 years: Detroit Lions
From 1957, a 59–14 victory over Cleveland in the NFL Championship, to 1991, when they beat Dallas 38–6. (Home playoff losses in that period: 0.)

33 years: Baltimore/Indianapolis Colts
From 1970 (victories over Cincinnati, 17–0, and Oakland, 27–17) to 2003, a 41–10 defeat of Denver. (Home playoff losses in that period: 3.)

33 years: New Orleans Saints
From the beginning of the franchise, in 1967, to 2000 and a 31–28 victory over the Rams. (Home playoff losses in that period: 3.)

31 years: Dallas Texans/Kansas City Chiefs

From the inception of the franchise, in 1960, to a 10–6 victory over the Los Angeles Raiders in 1991. (Home playoff losses in that period: 1.)

30 years: Washington Redskins

From 1942, when they won the NFL Championship 14–6 against Chicago, to 1972, when they beat Green Bay 16–3. (Home playoff losses in that period: 0.)

27 years: New York Giants

From 1958, when they beat Cleveland in a tiebreaker, 10–0, to 1985 and a 17–3 victory over San Francisco. (Home playoff losses in that period: 1.)

23 years: Los Angeles Rams

From 1951, a 24–17 defeat of Cleveland for the NFL Championship, to 1974 and a 19–10 win over Washington. (Home playoff losses in that period: 1.)

22 years: Chicago Bears

From 1963, a 14–10 victory over the Giants in the NFL Championship, to 1985 and a 21–0 victory over the Giants again. (Home playoff losses in that period: 0.)

22 years: Green Bay Packers

From 1939, a 27–0 win over the Giants for the NFL Championship, to 1961, a 37–0 rout of New York. (Home playoff losses in that period: 0.)

22 years: San Francisco 49ers

From 1949, a 17–7 triumph over the New York Yankees in the final year of the AAFC, to 1971, a 24–20 win against Washington. (Home playoff losses in that period: 0.)

All-Time Home Playoff Records

The 11-game home playoff winning streak the Patriots started with their 28–3 win over Pittsburgh is second only to the Green Bay Packers,

Football programs had a long tradition of caricaturing the mascots of the participants, and this Phil Bissell classic for the AFL inaugural was in line with that approach. As assistant coach Joe Collier points out, "It was fifty cents and half of it was devoted to write-ups on the Patriots owners." Indeed, each of the ten got his own page.

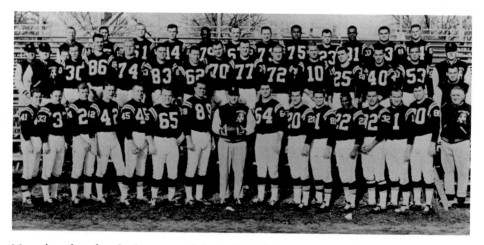

More than three hundred men passed through the first Patriots training camp, and this was the result. Head coach Lou Saban holds the ball for his charges, who include, to his left, Gino Cappelletti (20), Ron Burton (22), and thirty-six-year-old rookie quarterback Butch Songin (11).

A three-time AFL All-Pro, defensive end Larry Eisenhauer assessed himself like this: "I was kind of a free spirit. If you told me to go left, I'd go right. If we had to go to bed at curfew at ten o'clock, I'd go to bed at five in the morning. In those days, things weren't as structured as they are today. Emotionally, I loved the game. I loved the excitement. I loved the rush of the game."

A devastating runner at his peak, Jim Nance battled weight issues throughout his life. Defensive tackle Houston Antwine once said to him, "Hey Nance, you better lose that weight or you'll find yourself on this line next to me."

Gino Cappelletti attributes his place on the very first Patriots roster to his versatility. In 1960, he kicked and played defensive back, while also dabbling in offense—a job that would become full-time in 1961. (Courtesy of the Sports Museum, Boston, MA)

It can't, as they say, get any better than this—and it rarely ever did in the Jim Plunkett era. He and the Patriots finished off the powerful Oakland Raiders 20–6 on September 19, 1971, christening their new stadium and their new name in Plunkett's very first professional game. Ron Sellers reaches for the handshake.

Patriots legend Mosi Tatupu. At his peak, he averaged 5.5 yards per carry and was a hellion on special teams.

New England made some very savvy draft choices between 1973 and 1976, and linebacker Steve Nelson was one of them. The highest pick ever out of North Dakota State, he gave the Patriots fourteen solid seasons.

The Patriots went 32–32 under Bill Parcells (seen here with Pro Bowler Bruce Armstrong) and went to the playoffs in 1996 with Parcells having already agreed to a job with the New York Jets. It was the second time in team history that the Patriots were in the postseason with a lame duck coach.

When Robert Kraft bought the Patriots, it didn't take long for him to run afoul of the delicate sensibilities of Bill Parcells. His relationship with longtime Parcells colleague Bill Belichick was much more cordial, not to mention productive. (Courtesy of the Sports Museum, Boston, MA)

Adam Vinatieri had so many clutch kicks for the Patriots, it's nearly impossible to pick a standout. This one won the tuck rule game in overtime and got him carried off the field by his teammates, although his earlier 45-yard field goal to tie it was twice as long and even more dramatic, in that if he missed, New England's season would have been over.

In the first half of Super Bowl XXXVI, Antwan Harris forced a fumble and Terrell Buckley was there to grab the room-service hop. Fellow defensive backs Lawyer Milloy and Tebucky Jones look on.

Of the small percentage of players who've played in back-to-back Super Bowls, an even smaller percentage have strung together two performances like those of Deion Branch, seen here hoisting the MVP trophy after the Patriots took down the Eagles 24–21 in Super Bowl XXXIX.

Rodney Harrison made two key interceptions in Super Bowl XXXIX. The first snuffed a drive in the red zone in the first quarter, and the second sealed the Eagles' fate with nine seconds to go in the game.

Tom Brady has two of the top five single-season passer ratings in history (second in 2007 and fifth in 2010). No other quarterback appears in the top ten more than once.

This was a common sight in 2007: Randy Moss getting separation on coverage. In this case, it's against safety James Butler of the New York Giants. Moss is about to score the touchdown that would set a number of records and give the Patriots a 29–28 victory in the final game of their perfect regular season.

who went undefeated in the first 13 postseason games they hosted. Since the NFL began scheduling playoffs in 1933, host teams have enjoyed a daunting advantage. Through 2011, they've won 296 games, against 138 losses, for a .682 winning percentage. As you can see from the chart below, only two teams have losing records. The Patriots *did* have the second-best record until their one-and-done performances in 2009 and 2010 pushed them further down a very competitive list.

Franchise	W	L	Pct.
Chicago/St. Louis/Phoenix/Arizona Cardinals	4	0	1.000
Houston	1	0	1.000
Boston/Washington Redskins	13	2	.867
Detroit Lions	5	1	.833
Green Bay Packers	14	3	.824
Denver Broncos	13	3	.813
PATRIOTS	**13**	**3**	**.813**
Oakland/Los Angeles Raiders	19	5	.792
Seattle Seahawks	7	2	.778
Buffalo Bills	10	3	.769
Dallas Cowboys	19	7	.731
Miami Dolphins	15	6	.714
Pittsburgh Steelers	20	9	.690
Cleveland Browns	13	6	.684
Philadelphia Eagles	13	6	.684
San Francisco 49ers	19	9	.679
Carolina Panthers	2	1	.667
Jacksonville Jaguars	2	1	.667
Minnesota Vikings	13	7	.650
Cleveland/Los Angeles/St. Louis Rams	11	6	.647
Cincinnati Bengals	5	3	.625
New Orleans Saints	5	3	.625
Atlanta Falcons	3	2	.600
Chicago Bears	12	8	.600
New York Jets	4	3	.571
New York Giants	12	9	.571
Tampa Bay Buccaneers	4	3	.571
Baltimore/Indianapolis Colts	9	7	.563

Franchise	W	L	Pct.
Houston Oilers/Tennessee Titans	6	5	.545
Baltimore Ravens	2	2	.500
Los Angeles/San Diego Chargers	6	8	.429
Dallas Texans/Kansas City Chiefs	2	5	.286

The Largest Comebacks in Patriots History

The 22-point deficit overcome by the '96 Patriots on the last day of the regular season was very nearly the largest they ever bridged. What follows are the biggest point obstacles the team has ever overcome to salvage a win or tie (through the 2010 season).

23 points: Patriots 38, Seattle Seahawks 23 (September 16, 1984)

When Kenny Easley picked off a Steve Grogan pass in the second quarter and returned it for a touchdown just after his teammate Paul Johns had returned a punt for a TD, it seemed like all Seattle had to do for the rest of the game was punch the clock and sit on their 23–0 lead. Instead, coach Ron Meyer replaced Grogan with Tony Eason with nine minutes to go in the first half and things slowly began to turn around for the Patriots. Just past the two-minute warning, Eason scored on a 25-yard run to make it 23–7 at the break. The second half was all New England as Derrick Ramsey and Mosi Tatupu both scored to bring the Pats within 2 before Tony Franklin put them ahead to stay with a 32-yard field goal with 6:31 to go. The extra gravy was added when Tatupu and Irving Fryar scored touchdowns in the waning moments.

22: Patriots 23, New York Giants 22 (December 21, 1996)

This and the team's biggest all-time comeback belong in a separate category of revival. In most of their other big comebacks, the Pats had scored at least 3 points before beginning their surge, but these were both "standing-start comebacks"—they were being shut out at the moment of their largest deficit. What makes this game a "greater" comeback than the game listed above is that it didn't get started until the third quarter was nearly over.

21: Patriots 31, New York Jets 27 (November 10, 1996)

The 1–8 Jets (they would go on to finish 1–15) surprised their home fans by busting out to a 21–0 lead on the 6–3 Patriots. New York scored on its first three possessions, while the Patriots didn't get on the scoreboard until there were two minutes left in the half. Bledsoe had a rough first quarter, throwing two picks and fumbling the ball away on a sack. He recovered and, at one point, had 11 consecutive completions. The Patriots set up one score on an end-around to Terry Glenn and another when Glenn caught a 28-yard pass on a flea-flicker. They also benefited from a terrible spotting error by line judge Charles Stewart, who handed them a first down when they were still trailing 27–24. They had come all the way back to tie it at 24, but lost the lead on a Nick Lowery field goal. The go-ahead touchdown was scored on a Bledsoe–to–Keith Byars pass late in the fourth quarter. Even with that, the Jets would not go quietly. Their starting quarterback that day was Frank Reich, a man who knew from comebacks, having engineered the greatest example in league history when he led the Bills from 32 points down to beat the Oilers in the 1992 playoffs. This time, he drove New York from their own 24 to the New England 11 with just under a minute to play. Reich's next four passes were incompletions, however, with Otis Smith and Lawyer Milloy tipping away one each to preserve the comeback victory.

21: Patriots 31, Indianapolis Colts 28 (September 19, 1999)

Since Peyton Manning joined the Colts in 1998, this has been a rivalry that has seen a number of thrillers. This, the first truly classic Colts-Pats encounter of the Manning era, is one of the standouts of the series. Indianapolis had gone just 3–13 in Manning's rookie season, but was clearly a team on the rise in 1999. This became all the more apparent when Manning hit Marvin Harrison for three touchdown passes in the first half for a commanding 28–7 lead. Rookie Edgerrin James also scored a touchdown, but his fumble with 2:32 left in the game proved costly. By then, Drew Bledsoe had heaved his fourth touchdown pass of the day to tie the score at 28 and the Patriots defense had stiffened, surrendering just 79 yards in the second half, an improvement over the 265 they'd given up in the first. The James fumble gave New England the ball at the Indy 37. With 26 seconds left, Adam Vinatieri completed the comeback with a 26-yard, tiebreaking field goal.

21: Patriots 33, Chicago Bears 30 (November 10, 2002)

When the 2–6 Bears got a 27–6 lead on the defending world champion (albeit 4–4) Patriots in the third quarter, an upset appeared to be in the offing. Instead, Tom Brady and the Patriots came roaring back. Brady would finish the game with 36 completions on 55 attempts. Adam Vinatieri had started his day with a team record 57-yard field goal. His fourth kick put the Pats within 8 at the top of the fourth quarter. The Bears added an insurance field goal, which they were glad to have when Brady hit Kevin Faulk for 36 yards to make the score 30–25. With less than a minute left, instant replay became a factor not once but twice. Bryan Robinson appeared to have intercepted a Brady pass before fumbling it to teammate Rosevelt Colvin. The call on the field was reversed, however, and the ruling was changed to an incompletion. On fourth and 1, Brady ran a sneak for the first down and avoided a sack on the next play, underhanding the ball to Kevin Faulk for a 7-yard gain to the 20. He then fired a pass into the back of the end zone, where David Patten laid himself out and hung on to the ball for the score. But did he manage to scrape his second foot in the end zone on the way down? Tense moments passed as the play was reviewed, but the news was good for New England, and the comeback was complete.

20: Patriots 43, Oakland Raiders 43 (October 16, 1964)

What is definitely one of the wildest games ever played ended not with a Patriots victory but with the highest-scoring tie in pro football history. Unlike all the other games on this list in which the Pats got way behind early, they were right in this thing well into the second quarter. Furthermore, they had to mount a second comeback late in the game when the Raiders regained the lead. With Boston trailing 17–14, the 0–5 Raiders began to pull away. Cotton Davidson had one of the best games of his career, bombing the Patriots for four touchdowns. By the time Mike Mercer kicked his second field goal in the middle of the third period, the Raiders had a 34–14 lead and seemed to have things well in hand. Boston then poured in 21 unanswered points, though, as

Larry Garron scored twice and Art Graham once. Babe Parilli would finish his day with four TD passes as well, while putting in the first 400-yard passing performance in team history, although he was also intercepted four times.

The Pats saw their short-lived lead die when Powell hauled in his second touchdown catch of the day. Raiders coach Al Davis then made a decision that is easy to second-guess in hindsight. Instead of going for the kick, he chose the 2-point conversion, which failed, leaving the score at 40–35. With time running out, Parilli drove the Pats down the field and hit Garron from 11 yards out with 48 seconds showing. Unlike Davis's choice, Mike Holovak's decision to go for 2 was more obvious. Parilli found Jim Colclough for the deuce and the Pats had a 43–40 advantage with almost no time remaining. This lead would have an even shorter shelf life than the previous one. Oakland drove to the Boston 31, where Mercer launched his third field goal of the day, knotting the game with five seconds to go.

20: Patriots 26, Minnesota Vikings 20 (November 13, 1994)

It seemed only natural that the 7–2 Vikings would be up 20–0 on the 3–6 Patriots, a team that had lost four in a row. Drew Bledsoe had thrown seven interceptions in his two previous games without even a single touchdown strike for balance, so it made sense that the team was getting blanked. What happened next, though, remains in the record books. The Patriots went to the air and stayed there: Bledsoe threw 70 passes and completed 45 of them—both numbers are still counted as the most ever. What is more, he wasn't sacked or intercepted. As the clock wound down, he drove the Patriots to Matt Bahr's game-tying field goal with just 23 seconds left in regulation. New England received the opening kickoff of overtime and never relinquished possession. Bledsoe was a perfect 6-for-6 in OT, the last one a 14-yard touchdown strike to Kevin Turner for the win.

17: Patriots 28, New York Titans 24 (September 17, 1960)

You might as well make your first win a memorable one, and the Patriots did just that. Gordon White Jr. of the *New York Times* put it this way: "If the American Football League lasts a hundred years the Titans,

New York's entry in the circuit, may never again be the victims of as rude a jolt as they received last night." In an ending somewhat similar to what fans of a different New York team would endure 18 years later, the winning touchdown was scored by Chuck Shonta as the final gun sounded. He came into possession of the ball when Titans punter Rick Sapienza fumbled the snap on what was supposed to be the last play of the game. In the era before taking a knee was allowed, teams with leads were often forced into situations like this. Most of the time, it didn't matter, but on this occasion, Shonta outhustled Sapienza for the loose ball, picking it up at the Titans 25 and sprinting into the end zone. (Sapienza was cut immediately and never played in the AFL again.)

Boston had fallen behind 24–7 before rallying in the third quarter when Tom Greene hit Oscar Lofton to make it 24–14. Butch Songin connected with Jim Colclough to cut the lead to 24–21, but by then there were less than two minutes left in the game. When the Patriots attempt at an onside kick failed, it seemed academic that the Titans would hold their lead by running out the clock, which they very nearly did. Nearly.

17: Patriots 24, San Diego Chargers 20 (October 19, 1962)

Among their big comeback games, this one is unique in that the Patriots got on the scoreboard first. After their opening drive stalled at the six-yard line, they settled for a Gino Cappelletti field goal and the 3–0 start. The Chargers made that go away fast and led 20–3 at the half. The Patriots were terrorizing San Diego's pair of first-year quarterbacks, though, picking off Dick Wood three times and John Hadl once. Boston was still being stymied until about halfway through the third quarter, when they exploded for three touchdowns in an eight-minute burst. Babe Parilli–to–Jim Colclough accounted for the first two, while Jim Crawford went off tackle from the 1 for the go-ahead score. The defense kept things in check for the final 13:45, securing the win.

17: Patriots 30, New York Jets 20 (October 28, 1984)

In spite of a 5–3 record, Ron Meyer had worn out his welcome with the Patriots after he fired defensive coordinator Rod Rust, a move that did not sit well with general manager Patrick Sullivan. Calling it the "straw that broke the camel's back," Sullivan replaced Meyer with Raymond Berry just hours after the Rust firing. Berry was not on the coaching staff, but lived a stone's throw from the stadium. No longer a spectator, as he often was at Patriots games, he now found himself on the sidelines, coaching against the Jets. (Ironically, Berry worked as a motivational speaker, and had been scheduled by the Jets to talk to the team that very week. Obviously, his speech had to be canceled.) Berry's New England debut was not going well as his new team had fallen behind by as much as 20–3 in the second quarter. Jets coach Joe Walton then made the curious decision to elect to kick off to start the second half, even though they had the right to receive.

"We had a good lead," Walton told the *New York Times*. "The team was playing as well as I've seen it play, and I thought it would be a good idea to have the wind with us in the fourth quarter."

The worm really began to turn when Luke Prestridge lifted a 40-yard punt that took a Patriots bounce and just kept going . . . and going. It was finally downed at the Jets' 1-yard line, 82 yards from the line of scrimmage. Meanwhile, Jets punter Chuck Ramsey put the Patriots in excellent field position two different times with bad kicks. Berry made no fiery speeches at halftime, but what he did do was send Craig James into the game. Primarily a backup under Meyer, James cut loose for 79 yards on just 10 carries, including a 25-yard touchdown run—he would gain 1,227 yards the next year and be selected for the Pro Bowl—and the Pats outscored the Jets 24–0 in the second half.

Oakland Raiders at New England Patriots

DIVISIONAL PLAYOFFS
January 19, 2002

	1	2	3	4	OT	F
Oakland Raiders	0	7	6	0	0	**13**
New England Patriots	0	0	3	10	3	**16**

St. Louis Rams vs. New England Patriots

SUPER BOWL XXXVI
February 3, 2002

	1	2	3	4	F
St. Louis Rams	3	0	0	14	**17**
New England Patriots	0	14	3	3	**20**

They weren't even supposed to be there, the team with the castoff head coach and the sixth-round draft pick at quarterback. The Patriots' amazing 2001 season starred two men who would go on to become not only icons in New England but indelible forces in the game of football as a whole in the early part of the 21st century: Bill Belichick and Tom Brady. But what that team accomplished in that season transcended

those two men as individuals; it was a true team effort, one that reso-
nated all the more because it came at a time when, to paraphrase team
owner Bob Kraft, we were all Patriots.

THE PATRIOTS

As the year 2001 progressed, it seemed like a transitional time for the
franchise, not necessarily the start of a dynasty. In March of that year, the
face of the franchise was Drew Bledsoe, who had just signed a record-
breaking mega-deal with the Pats: 10 years for $103 million. Following
Bill Parcells's departure, Pete Carroll was brought in as head coach in
1997. New England made the playoffs his first two years, but he was let go
after a late slide in 1999 caused the team to miss out on the playoffs.

Troy Brown: My career kind of took a break during the Pete Carroll
era. I never could win him over and convince him I was a starting
receiver. But I played my role pretty well. I liked Pete Carroll. I thought
he was coaching the wrong team at the wrong time. Say what you
want to say about him, but he never had a losing season as the Patriots coach.

Nick Cafardo: First of all, I hated to see Pete Carroll go. I thought he
was one of the greatest people I met in sports. I think he was a terrific coach. He wasn't able to fit his team with the right personnel to
suit his coaching style. He was trying to coach with Parcells's players.

The next chapter in Patriots coaching history was another journey
into the bizarre. Bill Belichick had been named as Bill Parcells's successor to coach the New York Jets (where Parcells had landed after his
Patriots stint, taking many of his coaches, including Belichick, with
him). But minutes before the very press conference arranged to officially herald Belichick's hire, he quit. Shortly thereafter Belichick became the Patriots' head coach. Parcells and the Jets were understandably
confused and upset, since Belichick was still under contract to New
York, and they asked for and received compensation for the Belichick
signing: a first-round pick in the 2000 draft.

Nick Cafardo: Belichick was the right choice, given all the people that were out there. He's always going to be a PR disaster. He was the defensive guru, a genius. He was definitely the guy to go get. They made a great hire. They knew they'd struggle a year or two and then take off.

Willie McGinest: When I met Belichick, I was impressed. I heard a lot of things about how he doesn't relate to the players well, how he didn't communicate, was a little standoffish and all that. Of course, it's true he's not the most outgoing guy you'll meet. But I was impressed with his knowledge of defenses, and how he got us prepared, on the field and mentally, and also with his teaching ability. How through his preparation he could put the right people on the field at the right time.

Troy Brown: I was excited about the discipline of Belichick coming into the organization. We knew we were going to work hard every day.

Willie McGinest: We were excited. We knew our defense was going to rise to another level. We knew what he brought to the table. Guys automatically knew we were headed for something special. He was going to make sure we had the right players there. He was going to keep the foundation of players that he knew what they could do. Everybody else was going to have to prove themselves. If you couldn't do what he wanted you to do how he wanted you to do it, he was going to find somebody who could. With his demeanor and the way he approached everything, we knew we were in for something special. We just didn't know exactly what.

The earliest phase of the Belichick era didn't deliver on its promise.

Troy Brown: We got off to an 0–4 start with Belichick and we couldn't get it going.

The Patriots finished Belichick's first year, 2000, in last place at 5–11.

Willie McGinest: After we had that bad season, Belichick gave us a tough, tough camp. Guys were a little beat up and a little sluggish coming out of camp. It's not an excuse. It made us better physically and stronger mentally. He'd say "You get through this camp, and you go hard. There's nothing you're going to see or go against that's going to be tougher than this." And he was pretty much right.

Troy Brown: People were saying he wasn't the right guy for the job. They couldn't believe the Patriots gave up a first-round pick for this guy. That wore on us.

Willie McGinest: We knew we were a better team than what we showed. We had a bunch of guys who said, "We need to rededicate ourselves. We need to work harder. What we're doing is not getting it done." From taking care of your body, hydrating, weight room, conditioning, to practice and film—whatever it took, guys made an overall commitment on this team. That's what we were going to do—to get better and try and turn this thing around.

Troy Brown: We worked hard and we thought we'd have a better start the next season. Wouldn't you know it, we start out 0–2 in 2001?

The early 2001 season is remembered not for anything that happened on the field but for events that happened off of it. One Patriots player was even more affected by the September 11 attacks than his teammates.

Joe Andruzzi: Everybody remembers that day. I was at the dentist's office. I have three brothers who are New York City firemen. At first, the report was that a small plane hit the tower. Then, by the time I was leaving, it was a 747. Then another plane hit. By the time I got home and put the TV on, the two towers were burning. I was calling from the time I was in my car for the next six hours total, trying to call New York, trying to get hold of my parents, trying to get hold of my brothers. I had a gut feeling one of them was there. And I was right: One of my older brothers was one of the first responders. He was in tower one.

He was running out of tower one when tower two fell behind him. I'm thankful to have him back in my life. There are a lot of other people who weren't as fortunate as my family was.

The aftermath was just as hard. It was a struggle. For a lot of people I'm sure it's still a struggle. My brother made it through, and he realized there was a reason why he made it. He's still a firefighter to this day. He loves his job. My other brothers were called in. My other older brother was called in. My little brother just broke the academy the Friday before. September eleventh was his first day on the job. He was supposed to start on Thursday the thirteenth, and he was called in on the eleventh.

After they canceled the game that week, I drove down to New York and spent the weekend. I left my wife and kids here. I didn't want my kids to be a part of it. My brother held his fingers closely together. No words were said. He walked into the house and held his two fingers together. That's how close he was. I gave him a big hug.

The games scheduled for the weekend after the attacks were canceled. The Andruzzi brothers all went up to Foxborough for the next game, on September 23rd against the New York Jets. They stood on the field as honorary captains for the coin toss, at the request of Bob Kraft.

Joe Andruzzi: It wasn't an easy decision for them to come up there. They knew what they represented. They didn't represent me, they didn't represent themselves—they represented all who perished that day. Patriots fans and Jets fans were holding hands. When they called my name, I came running out with two flags that were hanging in the locker room. I wanted to rev the crowd up, because everybody needed it that day. I truly believe that sports were a way for people to get their mind off things for a little bit—three or four hours. I wanted to be out there and help people get through the day. My dad was there, too. He's a retired detective for the New York City Police Department. All four of them are city workers. I look up to them. They're running into burning buildings when everyone else is running out. To have them at that game after what happened is something I cherish.

The game against the Jets featured an unexpected turning point for the Pats, one that at the time had the potential to doom the season. Jets linebacker Mo Lewis pancaked Bledsoe on a hit near the sideline, knocking him out on his feet. It was a hit Bledsoe's backup called the hardest he'd seen in his entire life. The backup was an obscure sixth-round pick in the 2000 draft out of the University of Michigan. Skinny, awkward and slow in his rookie year, he'd gained 30 pounds of lean muscle and spent a lot of time practicing under the tutelage of Bledsoe. Now it was his job to fill his mentor's shoes. His name was Tom Brady.

Otis Smith: After Drew got hurt, everyone was nervous: Where do we go now?

Adam Vinatieri: I'll admit, when he first came in I didn't know what to expect. When Bledsoe went down in that Jets game I said, "Oh shoot, is this the beginning of the end?"

Kevin Faulk: Injuries are part of the game. It's a blow to your team. But when it's the quarterback, it's a really big blow. You don't understand what's going to happen. You're wondering what the mind-set of the backup is. You prepare for a game every week like the starter does. But you don't play every week. My concern was, Is this kid ready to play?

Joe Andruzzi: Here comes this scrawny guy who was a fourth-string quarterback in 2000. Belichick saw something in him. Through the off-season he was in the weight room every day, and the film room. He was there trying to make himself better. He was pushing himself to make himself the backup quarterback that year.

Nick Cafardo: Brady wasn't very polished. People who say they knew he was going to be great from the beginning—I don't buy it. I don't think anyone thought that. Brady was platooning with Drew Henson at Michigan. There was no reason to think he could be a great quarterback.

Troy Brown: When I saw the guy, I didn't think much about him at all. He was nothing special. He was a frail kid, not highly touted. Then his leadership skills started to emerge and he told us what he expected of us. And he was a good guy and we respected him. We had to make him comfortable, because he has the most important position on the field. He was ready for the opportunity when it presented itself.

Nick Cafardo: One day as a rookie, Brady had a pizza in his hand and walked by Bob Kraft and said, "I'm gonna win a championship for you one day." He was the third-string quarterback. He was behind Michael Bishop in those days. Kraft just looked at him and said, "Really?"

Getting the right players for the right roles became a hallmark of Belichick and his player-personnel guru, Scott Pioli, who had worked with Belichick dating back to his days as the head coach in Cleveland. Pioli started off as assistant director of player personnel for the Patriots in 2000 and had the "assistant" dropped from his title before the 2001 season. He and Belichick essentially shared the GM role for the Pats.

Nick Cafardo: The one thing we didn't know about Belichick was how would he be with personnel, drafting players. He was kind of a mixed bag in that department in Cleveland. As it turned out, he made some very good moves and identified players outside the box. Adam Vinatieri was undrafted, kicking in the World League. Stephen Neal was a wrestler in college, also undrafted. Belichick always seemed to find the right older veteran to fit into a certain role. He did this brilliantly, more brilliantly than I've seen anyone do it. Another thing he was able to do was introduce young kids to veteran players and have them learn from the veterans. They fit right in. That was the beauty of Belichick. It turned out that personnel was his strong suit, and that's why that team became what they became.

Scott Pioli shares the credit for that as well. And there's no better example of Pioli and Belichick's personnel work than their decision to draft Tom Brady. Just because Brady was drafted so late didn't mean he wasn't qualified.

Willie McGinest: There's a bunch of guys like that. Terrell Davis of the Broncos was another sixth-round pick. He was a Super Bowl MVP and NFL MVP. You can't really rate a guy by his draft status. It's determined by what he does on the field. You probably have more high-round picks that go out and don't produce than you have low-round picks that have opportunity to go out and play and really show off.

Dante Scarnecchia: After [quarterbacks coach] Dick Rehbein went out to Michigan to work out Tom, he came back and talked about him in glowing terms. He thought he had the arm strength and the ability to play in this league or he never would have recommended him so strongly. Dick really sold Tom to Coach Belichick and the rest of us. Was he ready for primetime when we got him? No. For instance, in his rookie year, we had him out there for a preseason game. The Giants nearly killed him. He didn't see the pressures very well.

Gil Santos: In 2000 he was a rookie and played during the exhibition season. Both Gino Cappelletti and I were saying, "This Brady kid might be pretty good down the road. He's got something." When he took over in 2001 after the Bledsoe injury, it was like, "Holy smoke, what do we have here?" [In week four] the Colts thought they we're going to blast the Patriots off the field. It was the other way around. It set the tone for the rest of the season.

Ty Law: When he got in the game and he took control he knew it. We had a team dinner and Tom said, "Ty, I'm not ever sitting back down." We found that this boy could play. Tom took it and ran. Look at him now!

The team started to improve, blowing out the favored Colts the next week and going on a 5–2 run over the next seven games to pull above .500.

Otis Smith: Brady had a great mentor in Drew. Drew helped him develop and helped him stay focused. That shows you what kind of a guy Drew Bledsoe is: a good guy and a good player. Unfortunately for him, he got hurt. Tom took the reins and did a hell of a job. I was glad to have him.

Willie McGinest: Belichick always gave us hope, he always said, "Look around the league: Nobody's jumping out that far ahead. If you guys really want it you can get it. You've just got to play one week at a time." Guys believed in that and had a lot of pride, and we challenged each other and turned it around.

In week ten, the 5–4 Patriots took on the preseason Super Bowl favorites, the St. Louis Rams. The Rams won 24–17. Belichick made a mental note about how well the Rams picked up the Patriots' blitzes in the game.

Willie McGinest: We played against the Rams and took a tough loss there. It left a sour, sour taste in our mouths. Those guys were so cocky, and they talked so much. I remember saying, "Don't worry, we'll see you guys again down the road."

Gil Santos: Antowain Smith was going to the end zone to tie the game just before the half, but he fumbled on the 1-yard line. The Rams came down and kicked a field goal and the Patriots ended up losing the game by just a touchdown. In that game, the Patriots proved they could play with the Rams or anybody.

Kevin Faulk: Playing the Rams helped us a lot. We were measuring up against a team that was the best in the NFL at the time. We went toe to toe with them. Even though we lost, that gave us confidence as a team.

Nick Cafardo: The Patriots had been on a nice run, but it looked like they met their match with that Rams team. The great Mike Martz had the New England defense on their heels all day. You could tell who the better team was. After watching that, you thought, Okay, the Rams are going to win it all.

There was a great debate the following week. The team had been winning with Brady. But Drew Bledsoe was medically cleared to play, and Bill Belichick had a decision to make.

Kevin Faulk: From a players' standpoint, we had confidence in both of them. We knew that was a decision the coaches had to make. Drew played well for a long time in the NFL. You leave it up to the coaches to make that decision and you hope for the best for both guys.

Otis Smith: Brady came in and sparked a whole lot of interest, and we were on a roll with him, so the coaches saw no reason to change.

Nick Cafardo: I remember going on TV and arguing that they should give the job back to Bledsoe after what he'd done for this franchise. I'm glad no one listened to me.

Gil Santos: At the time, I thought it was a mistake. Bledsoe was the starter, and he had them in the Super Bowl in '96. I wasn't so sure it was a good idea to keep this kid going when you have a proven guy coming back from injury. Once again, it proved why I'm a broadcaster and Belichick's the head coach.

As Bill Belichick said on Fox, "Brady's had most of the snaps, he's got the timing with the offensive line and the receivers. I thought that gave us the best chance. We've got two good quarterbacks—three good ones with [Damon] Huard. You can't have too much depth at that position."

It was clearly the right decision. After that, the Patriots won their last six regular-season games, and Brady made the Pro Bowl, maturing in front of his teammates' eyes.

Willie McGinest: Physically, he wasn't one of most dominating guys. One thing he had was a big heart. He had a great work ethic. He had a good attitude. He never bitched about being a backup or complained. He did what he had to do, learned the game, and when he got his opportunity he surprised everybody. He took advantage of it, because he played like no one else.

Joe Andruzzi: He controlled the huddle. He's a very calm, cool, collected type of quarterback. Always a big smile on his face. He gets a little feistier now, I see. He was still feisty back then.

Willie McGinest: His skill set was never in question. It was just a thing where nobody expected him to play as well as he played. To be as mature and confident and do the things that he did.

Adam Vinatieri: He made a believer out of me. The thing that he has above anyone else, there's this coolness about him. People mention Joe Montana as one of the greatest ever. Brady has that Montana coolness. He enjoys playing the game. He has fun at it. When he's in the huddle calling plays, he's not stressed out about it. Not everybody can say that.

Foxboro Stadium had initially been slated for demolition on December 23, 2001, the day after the Patriots' final home game. In fact, after dispatching the Dolphins that Saturday afternoon, the team and coaches celebrated with fans around the stadium, victory-lap style. But Foxboro got a stay of execution. After the season's final week, in which the Pats romped in Carolina and the Jets beat the Raiders in Oakland, the team whose season looked over in week two had secured a bye and a home game in the divisional round of the playoffs. Their opponent ended up being their old rivals, the Oakland Raiders.

THE RAIDERS

Coached by Jon Gruden, Oakland won the AFC West with a record of 10–6. Their offense was built around Rich Gannon, who had thrown for 3,000 yards three years in a row and threw the fewest interceptions in the NFL in 2001. Gannon was joined on the team by fellow All-Pros wide receiver Tim Brown, right tackle Lincoln Kennedy, cornerback Charles Woodson, and punter Shane Lechler. The previous year the Raiders had made it all the way to the AFC Championship Game. For the 2001 season, they had added seventeen-year pro and future first-ballot Hall of Famer Jerry Rice to their already potent offense, which also featured a big year from running back Charlie Garner. In the wild-card round of the playoffs, the Raiders avenged a defeat from the previous week by beating the New York Jets 38–24 and punching their tickets for New England. Little did they know what awaited them weatherwise. It would come to be known as the Snow Bowl.

Gil Santos: It was a recipe for disaster: a night game in New England in January. The snow was supposed to start by four o'clock. I parked and got out of my car at four o'clock, and sure enough the snow had started. By game time it was a winter wonderland.

Belichick arranged for the tarp to be removed from the field a little early, thinking the snow would favor his team over the California invaders.

Willie McGinest: Nobody wants to play in those conditions. But, if we have to, we want it to be to our advantage. Oakland was not a cold-weather team. And that was to our advantage: to have them out on our field, worrying about the conditions instead of the game. Mentally, guys are thinking about everything else, so they're spending less time focusing on the game. That turned out to be big for us.

Kevin Faulk: We knew the weather was supposed to be bad. Coach told us to go out before the game, find spots that were slippery and we'd need to avoid. Go over it in our heads so when the game started we'd know where not to go.

Otis Smith: We figured if we could get up and bump those guys at the line of scrimmage, it would be difficult for them to get down the field. They had two great receivers in Jerry Rice and Tim Brown. We felt like the conditions played into our hands. We had played on icy fields before. We knew how to play in those types of conditions and how to keep our feet under us. That's one thing Bill Belichick always taught us.

Willie McGinest: We knew it was going to be a short-pass game, quick routes, maybe screens, flare routes, angle routes, slants. A lot of those deep threats and different things were out of the picture.

Adam Vinatieri: I thought, This is going to suck. It snowed buckets the entire game. It doesn't get worse than that as far as field conditions. The ball was wet. There wasn't any traction. We were sliding all over the place.

THE GAME

With the snow still heavy at game time, the Raiders got the ball first. During that first drive, in an amazing example of the bad old days of instant replay, the action halted for nearly 10 minutes as the officiating crew attempted to ascertain whether a Tim Brown catch had been good enough for a first down. It wasn't, and in a moment of foreshadowing, Gruden was unhappy with the officials. Gruden elected to punt on fourth and 1 from the New England 48. Lechler kicked the ball into the end zone.

Brady showed no signs of nervousness on the first possession, and the team began to drive down the field, at one point completing three straight screen passes, smart play-calling indicative of the way Charlie Weis and the Patriots offense had gotten Brady going throughout his strong season.

Kevin Faulk: Our offense was more about not letting Brady lose. We wanted to try to control as much as we could on offense, because he was a young guy. We didn't want to throw everything at him, so we did a lot of stuff—a lot of screen passes, a lot of draws—to try and keep him confident and to keep the offense confident.

The Pats got the ball down to the Oakland 30, but the Raiders defense stuffed Faulk on a third-and-short. Too far away for a field goal and too close for a punt, Belichick went for it on fourth down. Receiver David Patten was initially left uncovered, but Charles Woodson, Brady's old teammate from Michigan, noticed this before the snap and ran over to him. Brady missed his much-diminished target, and it was Raiders' ball.

The rest of the first quarter was marked by punt after punt as both teams could not get anything going offensively.

Troy Brown: We were really struggling. We expected to come out and play better at home against a team from California.

Willie McGinest: The vision was terrible and the footing was horrendous. That slowed the game way down. It was back to basics for us.

The snow was unrelenting. CBS, broadcasting the game, cut to Armen Keteyian down on the field. He looked like Frankie Carbone in the meat truck at the end of *Goodfellas.*

Joe Andruzzi: I remember cut-blocking a guy and getting snow down my neck and into my shoulder pads. It was tough to stay warm on the sidelines.

Near the end of the quarter, Charles Woodson was back to receive a punt and called a fair catch. Je'Rod Cherry bumped him a second early and was called for it. The Raiders got the ball at the 50-yard line and they finally got things going from there. On a key third down, Jerry Rice made a nice grab on a slant, getting the first down and putting him over 2,000 yards receiving in his playoff career. The drive culminated in a 13-yard pass from Gannon to James Jett, who had come in when starter Jerry Porter hurt his shoulder earlier in the half.

Adam Vinatieri: I thought the conditions would be a big advantage for us. It would be difficult for me, but it would work to our advantage as a team. How drastically was I wrong? The funny thing was, Oakland did very well. I thought, Are you kidding me? How are they moving the ball and we're not?

Brady appeared to be pressing on the next sequence. He tried a tricky pass in the general area of Troy Brown that was picked off by Johnnie Harris.

Nick Cafardo: Brady made some throws in the first half of that game where I know he had no grip on the ball. He probably had no idea where it was going.

It was Oakland's ball in Patriots territory, and given the conditions, the game was very much on the line. The Patriots' defense managed to hold, with Gannon missing Tim Brown on a huge third-and-5, thanks to an amazing bat-down by Otis Smith.

Otis Smith: Just standing in front of Tim Brown is scary. I figured if I could get my hands on him and to corral him, so to speak, and not allow him to get downfield, it would screw up their timing, and that's what I did.

On the ensuing punt, the Raiders' Derrick Gibson had the opportunity to down the ball at the 1, but he was confused by the snowy field, lost track of where he was, and allowed the ball to bounce into the end zone for a touchback. This was a huge play, as Brady, looking a little shaky for one of the few times all year, was spared having to operate from under the shadow of his own goalposts. From there, the puntfest continued, and the teams went into the half with the score 7–0 Raiders. So far, Shane Lechler had a 6–5 lead over Ken Walter in the punting battle.

Kevin Faulk: The game was not out of reach. We knew all we had to do was play good football for 30 minutes and we'd win.

Charlie Weis faced a challenge. Brady had already thrown one pick and nearly threw another in the second quarter. He ended the first half 6 for 13 for 74 yards, half of those coming in the last two minutes with the Raiders in somewhat of a prevent. The Patriots offense looked stagnant, and the crowd was getting restless. Weis needed to come up with some plays to get Brady back into the game.

Kevin Faulk: We were very confident in Charlie. He was a guy who came up with a lot of stuff for his offensive guys. He was going to make sure you were in a position to make plays.

Nick Cafardo: Charlie Weis got Brady on the right track. I give him so much credit for what happened that year, and I'm not sure he gets enough of it. At first, he didn't want to overwhelm Brady, but once he realized that Brady *couldn't* be overwhelmed, he threw the kitchen sink at him. Brady responded well.

The Patriots got the ball to start the third and they came out throwing, attempting to build off the success Brady had on the Pats' last drive before the half. Two huge completions to David Patten got the ball all the way down to the Raiders' 9-yard line, but Brady missed on two passes into the end zone from the 5 and Adam Vinatieri was called on to kick a 23-yard field goal, making it 7–3.

The Raiders answered the Patriots with a nine-play drive down to the New England 20. It resulted in an impressive 38-yard Sebastian Janikowski field goal, which made the margin 7 points once again.

The Pats attempt to answer was in serious trouble before it even started: Regan Upshaw stripped Brady on first down. The Patriots were able to keep their hopes alive by recovering the ball at their own 15. The Pats had a great screen set up on second and 17, but tight end Jermaine Wiggins dropped the ball, yelling at himself so demonstratively afterwards that he could be heard on the broadcast.

The Pats went three and out, and the Raiders got excellent field position, starting at their own 49. Gannon made a 22-yard third-down completion to Rice, and Janikowski came on to make it a two-score game, this time with a 45-yard field goal. It was now Raiders 13, Patriots 3. The cold-weather team was not capitalizing on the conditions.

The Pats managed a couple of first downs on the ensuing drive, but shortly after the fourth quarter began, they were in a familiar position: Ken Walter came on to punt the ball back to the Raiders for the seventh time that evening. But the Patriots' defense came up with a big stop, not allowing the Raiders a single yard, and getting the ball back at their own 33. With 12:29 left, the running game went out the window. Brady found his rhythm and took over.

Kevin Faulk: Before the regular season was over, you could see him sort of take charge as the quarterback, becoming the leader in the huddle. That's how he was, and that's how he is now.

The game data tells the story best.

- First down: Brady 14-yard completion to David Patten.
- First down: (shotgun) Brady 7-yard completion into Oakland territory to Kevin Faulk.
- Second down: (shotgun) Brady 3-yard completion to Jermaine Wiggins for a first down.
- First down: (shotgun) Brady 8-yard completion to Troy Brown.

- Second down: (shotgun) Brady 4-yard completion to Jermaine Wiggins for a first down.
- First down: (shotgun) Brady 11-yard completion to David Patten.
- First down: (shotgun) Brady 4-yard completion to Jermaine Wiggins, deflected off David Patten.
- Second down: (shotgun) Brady 6-yard completion to David Patten for a first down.
- First down: (shotgun) Brady up the middle for 6 yards (Touchdown).

Nick Cafardo: At that point, his throws were tight and accurate. That blew me away. As great as he had been all year, this seemed to be too much for him to handle—only it wasn't. In the second half, the weather didn't faze him in the least.

For the drive, Brady went 9 for 9 for 60 yards, with 6 yards rushing and a touchdown pass. First-year starters aren't supposed to produce career-defining drives in their playoff debuts, let alone when their playoff debuts coincide with blizzards, but that's what Tom Brady did. However, his celebration wasn't exactly worthy of the moment. His plan was to emulate Tom Rathman and spike the ball as hard as he could into the ground.

Gil Santos: After Brady's touchdown, he tried to spike the ball, and he fell down. The guys razzed him about: He ought to come up with a better celebratory act then falling on his face in front of seventy thousand people.

Kevin Faulk: He was so excited he couldn't keep his balance.

Nursing their 3-point lead, the Raiders went back to work, securing two first downs and grinding the ball into New England territory. But the Pats managed to stop Garner for a 1-yard loss on first down, and passes to Jon Ritchie on second down and Jerry Rice on third fell helplessly to the snow.

Lechler needed all of his All-Pro skills to avoid having his punt blocked by Je'Rod Cherry, and the Pats got the ball back at their own

20. Brady picked up where he'd left off, completing a 12-yard pass to Wiggins, who made a great extended two-hand grab. Then they stalled, thanks in large part to a great defensive play on second down by Tory James, and Walter punted the ball back to the Raiders at their 35. There was 2:41 left. A Raiders first down at that point would have been the game, and after Garner rushed for a total nine yards on the first two carries, they were one yard shy of getting it.

As Gruden wrote in his book *Do You Love Football?*:

We had a third-and-one from our own forty-four. We were a yard away from winning the game. We went to our signature short yardage play, 14 Blast. It's supposed to work like this: Rich Gannon hands the ball as deep as he can to Zack Crockett, our short-yardage specialist. Zack runs right behind the lead fullback, Jon Ritchie, around the horn to block the backside linebacker. It's a great play. At least we thought it was. Much to our surprise, Bryan Cox came up to stuff it. No gain. We were still playing.

Gruden figured that with Lechler's skills, the Raiders would be able to pin the Pats inside their 20, if not their 10, and thought Brady had pulled enough rabbits out of enough hats for one evening. Surprisingly, the Patriots didn't go after the punt, but Lechler's kick was nothing like what Gruden had in mind. It was a low-liner in the middle of the field, easily returnable. Troy Brown took it at the 19 and brought it back 27 yards, but then nearly undid it all by losing the ball. Larry Izzo made the fumble recovery for the Pats, his second of the game.

On first down, Brady found Faulk for 7 yards to take the Pats into Oakland territory on the final play before the two-minute warning.

Kevin Faulk: As the night went on, I wasn't cold. The game itself warmed me up. The game was so intense that you didn't think about the temperature.

The second-and-3 play saw Brady make an awkward scramble through the snow that resulted in a first down. Then came the play that defined the game and gave it a place in NFL history.

Joe Andruzzi: It was a dual protection that we called. I was right guard. I had both of those guys. It's a dual read; if both of them come, it would have to be a hot read. When I set out, I saw the edge guy coming. The blocker who usually gets to him first is the guy up the middle, but the middle linebacker was coming, too, so I kind of stutter-stepped and reached for one. The other one hit Brady.

Belichick later told NFL Films, "Woodson wasn't blocked, and really Tom should have read that, but he was looking on the other side of the field and Woodson stripped him."

Kevin Faulk: First and foremost, we should have had Tom protected. Secondly, they had a good call defensively and Charles Woodson got free. He sacked the quarterback. In my eyes, we fumbled the ball. I thought, Uh-oh, the game is over.

Willie McGinest: I grabbed my helmet and I was headed to the field.

"We saw Tom Brady fumble," Gruden would later write. "We saw Greg Biekert recover it at our forty-eight. Our players are celebrating. We're going back to the AFC Championship Game! But what we saw wasn't what the replay official upstairs saw. He challenged the fumble that the officials on the field had ruled. All of a sudden the game wasn't over."

Troy Brown: We were walking off the field and I was thinking, "Man, is this the last time we get this good of an opportunity to make it to the Super Bowl? We had a prime opportunity and we blew it." Next thing I knew, the play is stopped and we're on the sideline and they are going to review the play. I was thinking there was no way they're going to overturn this play.

Joe Andruzzi: I was sitting there in the snow. Looking up, trying to figure out what was going to happen as we waited for the refs to go for the review. I prayed that it would go our way. All we wanted was that ball back in our hands.

"Once I saw the play replayed, I saw the play in much more detail," Bill Belichick would tell NFL Films. "And I thought that Tom was tucking the ball and I thought this was going to be an incomplete pass. Interestingly, it was a very similar play to what had happened earlier in the season when we played the Jets and Anthony Pleasant hit Vinny Testaverde and it was the same thing: We hit him, the ball came out, we recovered, and we felt like it was our ball. But Vinny was bringing the ball back to his body. It was a very similar play to the Oakland play. So when I saw the replay I knew what the ruling should have been, because we had dealt with that play earlier in the year on the other side of it.

Sure enough, the call was reversed. Many watching thought it was karmic payback for the Ray Hamilton roughing-the-passer call from 25 years prior.

Nick Cafardo: I talked to Ray that week. I think everybody talked to Ray that week. Things do balance out, even if it takes a while. As bad as that moment was for Ray Hamilton and the Patriots back in 1977, this one was the sweetest thing that ever happened to them.

Was it the right call? Mike Pereira, the former director of officiating for the NFL, later told NFL Films: "What the rule says is if the forward motion of the arm continues, even in the process of attempting to tuck the ball back into your body, it's incomplete. If the ball is knocked out of his hands, if he loses it on his own, as long as the ball is not tucked completely into the side of his body, that's an incomplete pass. It was a very good call. Under the rule the way it's written, overturning the fumble was the right call."

There's a bit of video floating around the Internet where Gruden, talking informally at the Greatest Bar in Boston and very obviously half-kidding, looks at the camera and says, "When you watch TV and you see Mike Pereira in the Fox command center, tell him to kiss my ass: It was a fumble."

In his book, he takes a more philosophical view, writing, "Sure, if you coach, play or root for the Raiders, you can be all teary about the 'tuck rule,' but I wasn't going to put that one on the officials. In my opinion, the outcome of the 'Snow Bowl' will always come down to 14 Blast. You make that first down, the game's over. We got stuffed."

Even Brady himself wasn't fully convinced about what had happened, saying in a postgame interview on CBS, "I'm just glad they called it the way they did."

There was still football left to be played, and as easy as it is to say with hindsight that the game was over after the tuck-rule call, that simply isn't true. The Pats still had a mountain to climb.

Kevin Faulk: Now we had to get ourselves back up as players. We were brought to the lowest of the low, but now it was our turn again.

The Pats didn't waste their turn. As Jon Gruden's head nearly exploded on the sideline, Brady made another completion to David Patten to bring the Pats down to the Raiders' 29, seemingly on the cusp of Adam Vinatieri's range at best, given the conditions. Brady threw two incompletions, then, with no one open on third down, he scrambled for a short gain up the middle, setting up a Vinatieri attempt at a tying field goal.

Adam Vinatieri: It was definitely a mental roller-coaster ride. It went from, "Dang it, we lost" to "Hey, we got a chance here," but there were still no guarantees. Forty-five yards in those conditions is a really low-percentage kick—I don't care who you are.

The stats didn't look good, even with the wind behind him. (While many recent accounts suggest the kick was into the wind, a review of the game footage confirms that it was not.) Vinatieri had missed four of his last five attempts at this range, but his teammates had faith.

Joe Andruzzi: Adam had played in those conditions before. He played in South Dakota. He knew how not to let it get to his head.

Adam Vinatieri: Where I went to school in South Dakota, it was cold, and it was windy every day. You had to have the mental fortitude to be able to deal with those conditions.

Gruden did not resort to the NFL's cliché freeze-the-kicker gambit, and for a very good reason. He wrote, "We had one time-out left, but I wasn't going to use it. As a result, the Patriots had to send out their kicker, Adam Vinatieri, to try a forty-three-yard field goal with a moving clock. I didn't want to try and 'ice' the kicker because I didn't want to give the Patriots' ground crew time for the same thing that happened in that same stadium in 1982.

Otis Smith: We had a lot of confidence in Adam. He actually taught me how to kick a ball. The kid has ice in his veins. He was always calm. It didn't bother him. When I met him his rookie year, I'd mess with him. He'd set up the ball to kick and I'd knock it down. He'd never say anything, he'd just put it back up. He always put his foot on the ball at the right place at the right time.

Vinatieri lined up and let it loose. Even knowing the outcome years later, when watching it on video, one still expects the kick to fall short. It didn't get nearly as high as the Janikowski kicks from earlier, and it never approached the center of the uprights. But, somehow, the kick snuck over the crossbar as Vinatieri did his best Carlton Fisk. Then Gary Glitter's stadium anthem filled the stands and the Patriots' season continued. Jon Gruden and the Raiders looked like they wanted to go home.

Adam Vinatieri: At the time, I said in an interview that I'd make that kick sixty-five percent of the time. I look back at that and laugh, knowing what I know now. If I had a hundred shots at it, I might make it ten times.

Dante Scarnecchia: That kick to tie the game was unbelievable. When I saw the ball, I was thinking this is the Snowplow Game all over again. When the ball left his foot, I said, "It's too low. It won't go that far." The ball kept going and it powered through. How do you do that? Really? I'd never seen a ball kicked that way. Adam made huge kicks for us. Name them—there is a whole bunch of them, but I've never seen a kick like that before. For him to get that ball through in those conditions with that length—it was the greatest thing I've ever seen.

"[That call] was like a vacuum [that] just sucked the life out of all of us," Lincoln Kennedy later told NFL Films. "From that point on, we just weren't the same team. We no longer had that swagger. We no longer felt that we were the better team. I knew after that ruling we were not going to win this game."

Adam Vinatieri: Once we tied it, I felt we were going to win this game. Nothing was guaranteed, but somehow in my mind I knew we were going to win. The momentum swung, and we had the energy at that point.

But regardless of what the players were feeling, the game still wasn't over. Gannon knelt to end regulation and it was time for sudden death. The Patriots won the toss, the Raiders took the wind, and Brady was back at it, completing seven passes in a row to begin overtime, highlighted by a 20-yard gain to J.R. Redmond, most of it after he broke a tackle. Three of the catches were by Jermaine Wiggins, making his earlier drop a distant memory.

With 10 minutes left in overtime, the Patriots were looking at a fourth and 4 at the Oakland 28. The wind was against them, making a 45-yard field goal attempt a scoring dead end. So, with the game on the line, Brady came through yet again, hitting Patten for 6 yards and the first down, making him 8 for 8 in the overtime period. It was unclear if he was throwing to Patten or Wiggins initially, but Patten made a great grab while already on the ground.

Four runs from Antowain Smith (including a huge conversion on third and 5) brought the ball down to the Oakland 9-yard line. Brady barreled ahead for 2, and it was time for Vinatieri once again. This time, Gruden did call a time-out. With Mark Henderson nowhere in sight, the Patriots as a team cleared a spot for Vinatieri that would make a John Deere 314 blush. "Spirit in the Sky" by Norman Greenbaum blared throughout the stadium until the referee blew his whistle. This time the kick was textbook: high and right down the middle.

Gil Santos: The Raiders had played the first game ever played in Foxborough at then–Schaefer Stadium, and the Patriots beat them pretty good. Then they played the last game ever played at Foxboro Stadium, and the Patriots won again.

"It was the greatest hour in New England football history," Gruden wrote. "I was the first victim of Tom Brady."

The next week, the Patriots were underdogs on the road against the Pittsburgh Steelers in the AFC Championship Game. Before the game, Bill Belichick busted out an oldie but goodie from the Bill Parcells motivational playbook.

Kevin Faulk: He told us that they had their bags packed for the Super Bowl, and he told us the name of the hotel where the Steelers were going to be staying. It was just enough to get the hair on the back of your neck up.

Joe Andruzzi: They had their bags packed. They thought they were automatically Super Bowl bound.

Troy Brown: Yeah, Bill Cowher was on TV saying he gave his guys the day off so they could get their families ready for New Orleans. Everybody picked Pittsburgh to win; we weren't supposed to have a chance.

Willie McGinest: Pittsburgh were a really good team, but we didn't like each other too much.

And those feelings didn't improve at all when the Steelers knocked Brady out in the second quarter. Fortunately for the Patriots, they had a very overqualified "backup" quarterback who was dying for the opportunity to show what he could do.

Troy Brown: Bledsoe came in off the sideline with a big smile on his face. On one of his first plays, he rolled out to the right, same sideline, and got blasted. But this time he got blasted by a smaller guy by the name of Chad Scott. But you just couldn't help but worry if he was going to get up or not. But he jumped up and he was full of energy, high-fiving guys and patting guys on the head. That's when we knew he came to play. He finished that drive off with a touchdown pass to Patten in the corner of the end zone.

The Patriots won the game 24–17 and were headed to New Orleans.

Otis Smith: Drew was a highly competitive player. When he got his opportunity again, he made the best of it. He showed us and the rest of the world just how good of a quarterback he was.

Nick Cafardo: I think anyone who was a Drew Bledsoe fan cherished that.

Joe Andruzzi: Bledsoe was able to put it together and triumph for us. He did a great job and helped us get to the Super Bowl.

THE RAMS

The 1999 Rams were known as the Greatest Show on Turf. They won the Super Bowl behind an amazing offensive attack led by first-year starter and league MVP Kurt Warner, running back Marshall Faulk, and wide receivers Isaac Bruce and Torry Holt. The offense was special again in 2000, scoring 540 points, but the defense was porous and the team was bounced in the wild-card round of the playoffs by the New Orleans Saints. For the 2001 season, Lovie Smith was brought in from the Tampa Bay Buccaneers to be defensive coordinator. He was an excellent complement to offense-minded head coach Mike Martz, and the team improved greatly defensively. They scored 500-plus points for the third year in a row while slashing almost 200 points allowed, going from a league-worst 471 to a seventh-best 273 in 2001. Their 14–2 record was the best in a very competitive NFC. Warner once again captured the MVP award (Marshall Faulk had won the year before), meaning a Rams offensive player was named league MVP three years running. If the team had an Achilles heel, it was turnovers: Warner threw for 22 interceptions, and the team ranked 26th overall with a minus-10 turnover differential, a very high number for a good team.

In the playoffs, Warner dominated in his showdown against Bret Favre and the Packers in the divisional round, winning 45–17. In the NFC title game, the Rams overcame a halftime deficit and held off the Philadelphia Eagles 29–24, thus setting up a Super Bowl showdown against the Pats.

Otis Smith: These guys had weapons across the board. They seemed to have weapons coming out of the stands—they were that good. We posted some pretty good defenses against offenses like that. It was an atmosphere that they were used to: indoors on turf. Those guys did a tremendous job preparing themselves, and we knew we had an uphill battle. We needed to step up our game tremendously.

The Patriots had won an amazing eight games in a row heading into the Super Bowl, and yet the Rams were perceived as such a juggernaut that the Pats were still massive underdogs, plus 14.

Troy Brown: They played in a dome environment. They had all the swagger, talent, big names. You name it, they had it. We weren't even supposed to be there.

Willie McGinest: All the so-called experts said we'd be losing by thirty at halftime.

Nick Cafardo: A lot of people picked the Rams, even in Boston.

But others had faith in their team.

Gil Santos: I gave the Patriots a very good chance. From the middle of the season to the end of the regular season right through the play-offs, no team had scored more than seventeen points on the Patriots. The last team to score more than seventeen against the Patriots was the Rams. I was confident that the Patriots could stay with them, and if things worked out right, could beat them.

And most important, the Patriots had faith in themselves.

Adam Vinatieri: Yeah, they beat us during the year, but we knew we could play with them. It was kind of like fighting Muhammad Ali. The fear factor, his aura, and his reputation would be so scary to start with. That's how it was with those guys. It was like, "Oh my God, how are we going to do this?" As the game went along, we figured if we played them again and did a few little things differently, we'd have a chance. That's the great thing about Coach Belichick: It's hard to beat him once, but it's really, really hard to beat him twice. He had this amazing knack of being able to throw together a game plan that the other team would not expect. That's what he did. We played a different way than they expected us to. It wreaked a lot of havoc on them.

Belichick was famous for having designed the Giants' defensive game plans that led the team to Super Bowl glory in Super Bowl XXV against the Bills and their amazing K-Gun offense. He and defensive coordinator Romeo Crennel faced no less a challenge coming up with a way to stop the Rams. As he told Fox, "We knew we had to cover more than rush. We rushed them with everything but the kitchen sink in the first game, and they did a great job and Warner got rid of it quickly, so we needed to do a little more covering."

Willie McGinest: His defenses were always catered to whichever team we were playing against. We had a base defense, but we just didn't have one defense. We could give so many looks and do so many different things. That would allow him to plug different players in to do different jobs to make it look like there was something else going on. We'd give the illusion that there was something else going on—but there really wasn't.

Otis Smith: He wasn't only a motivator on the field. He challenged you *all* the time, on the field *and* in the classroom. It was an ongoing thing. He was trying to get better, trying to diagnose what other teams were doing to us. He was helping me and other players understand situational football. I think he did a great job. It still helps me at this point in my career now.

Belichick once again used the Patriots' underdog status as an advantage.

Troy Brown: We had to get a different hotel. We were offended by that. The other hotel was ready for the Pittsburgh Steelers. We were told it was decorated in Pittsburgh Steelers colors and they couldn't get it down in time. We had to get these rooms at the Fairmont, which was sort of off the beaten path. We were offended by that, too, and Bill played it up. We had a chip on our shoulder all week.

Willie McGinest: They thought the Rams were too explosive for us, that they had too many weapons. We took that in all week long and used that as motivation.

The Patriots made a statement before the game even started, eschewing the usual individual player introductions and electing to come out as a team, as they had done all season since a logistical foul-up in week one in Cincinnati.

Joe Andruzzi: That's how we'd done it all year. But for the Super Bowl, they wanted us to come out individually. Our captains were adamant about not doing it. "We're not individuals. We are a team and we're going out as a team." They gave in, and that's what we did.

Ty Law: Coach Belichick came to us and said, "Look guys, the network paid a lot of money and it's about timing and we have to go out as individuals." And we said, "Oh, no we ain't. They can call us out individually, but we won't go."

Troy Brown: That was the biggest play in the game. We sent a message to them. We are coming out united. Our mission was to go out there and play the game together, like we had all year. They got the message loud and clear. It sent a tone and a theme for the rest of that decade that this is a team sport, that one person is not going to win the game for you.

Adam Vinatieri: Belichick would tell us, "Just do your job and I'll get us in position to succeed." You had to rely on your teammates and do your thing. They really taught me what it meant to be a member of a team. He instilled the concept of *team* in me. We were such great friends. We really did it together. We loved each other so much that we didn't want to let each other down. We held ourselves and each other accountable. It's hard to beat a group of men who are that committed to one goal.

The Patriots held on the first series, after a 38-yard kickoff return by Yo Murphy and an 18-yard completion to Torry Holt got the ball into New England territory. The Patriots' pass coverage looked strong right from the start.

Willie McGinest: One of the things Belichick did in practice was to put all the receivers two yards in front of the line of scrimmage so they would have a head start. Their receivers were so fast, they would get into their routes very quickly and Kurt would get the ball out of his hands really fast. We wanted to simulate that.

A good punt by John Baker pinned the Patriots down at their own 3-yard line. No sooner had John Madden stated on the Super Bowl telecast that the Patriots would have to run the ball out from there than they came out with an empty backfield. Brady dropped back and hit Troy Brown for a 21-yard gain. It wouldn't be the only time Madden underestimated Brady that night. The Patriots drove the ball to the St. Louis 48, far enough, at least, to reverse field position.

After Walter's punt went into the end zone, the Rams started at their own 20 and successfully drove downfield. One of the key plays was a 14-yard completion to Marshall Faulk, who was run out of bounds by nose tackle Richard Seymour.

Otis Smith: Marshall Faulk is in the Hall of Fame. He presents problems as a receiver when he's lined up against guys who aren't as fast as him. It was a dangerous situation. I thought our guys did a tremendous job trying to keep him in the box.

The drive stalled at the Pats' 32, and Jeff Wilkins hit a 50-yard field goal, giving the Rams a 3–0 lead. In a way, it was a moral victory for the Pats. The drive was marked by more tough hitting from New England, especially from the secondary. They also bloodied Warner's lip.

Nick Cafardo: You could tell the difference between that game and their previous meeting with the Rams. They knew they had to beat them up a little bit, literally smash-mouth. They did that right from the get-go.

Troy Brown: The only way we had a chance to beat the Rams was to be physical. On defense, we had a bend-but-don't-break mentality.

Willie McGinest: We knew we were a more physical team than they were. If we were going to have a chance at winning this game, we were going to have to slow them down by beating them up. Belichick said, "I want everybody hitting. I don't want anybody crossing the line of scrimmage without getting hit. Before you rush, jam. Jam Faulk, jam the tight end, jam the receivers—jam everybody. I want to beat them up. I want to wear them down physically." That's how we approached the game.

The Pats went three and out on the ensuing drive, and when the Rams got the ball back, Marshall Faulk rushed three times for a first down. The first quarter ended with a Bobby Hamilton sack of Warner, but he came back with a long completion to Az-Zahir Hakim to start the second quarter and the Rams were on the edge of field goal range once again. Defending at their own 34, the Patriots held on third and 5, and Wilkins came on again. This time, he missed a 52-yarder, wide left.

Once again, the defense featured extra defensive backs playing tight, physical coverage, and no blitzing.

Troy Brown: Our guys were just lighting them up. Their receivers would be fixing up for a ball and they'd pull their hands back and look at the defender before they got hit. We wanted to send the message that "if you guys are going to beat us, you're going to pay the price for doing it."

The Patriots managed a first down on the next possession, crossing into Rams territory, but the drive went in reverse after an offensive-holding penalty, and Walter had to punt it away. The Rams took over at their own 19. On second and 5, Faulk scampered for 15 yards and a first down at the Rams' 39, which led to one of the game's key plays.

Ty Law: For our game plan, we were going to do the same thing we did the first time we played them. They were so fast, we just backed off of them in that game and played more rushing zones. I said, "We can't keep sitting off on these boys and let them run. Let's blitz their asses and get in their faces." I said, "I got Isaac Bruce. If he goes to the bathroom, I'm going with him." Otis Smith said, "I got Torry Holt." Everybody claimed somebody and the coaches scrapped the old game plan right there. We put in the game plan to get in their faces like we did in Indianapolis. If they're going to beat us they will beat us like this. The coaches listened to us.

Troy Brown: Early on, we had them on the ropes and they couldn't get into a rhythm. Ty Law came up with a big interception off of pressure from Mike Vrabel off of the edge, forcing them to throw the football without seeing where Ty was. It was a great read by Ty.

Ty Law: Isaac Bruce was in motion so I couldn't get my hands on him, but Vrabel had a clear shot to Warner and altered his throw. I jumped in front of it. At the time we were so intense that everything was going in slow motion. That's when you know the game is going good, when the play slows down. It was like the ball took forever to get there. It was amazing.

Vrabel's hit on Warner's helmet would have been a penalty by 2010 standards, but it wasn't called in those somewhat more permissive days. The hit was just enough to alter the throw. Law grabbed it out of the air at the St. Louis 47 and brought it in for 6 points, then reinvigorated himself at the oxygen tank on the sidelines. Vinatieri's extra point made it 7–3.

The teams traded unsuccessful possessions, and it was the Rams' ball on their own 25 with 1:52 left. This was plenty of time for Warner to run the no-huddle and try to retake the lead. Except that's not what happened. The Patriots secondary struck again.

Otis Smith: We would study an individual guy and understand what that guy brought to the table. It helped us out, because Ty Law and I could play both left or right corner. We had a great secondary with Terrell Buckley, Tebucky Jones, and Lawyer Milloy: guys that didn't take losing for an answer.

Ricky Proehl caught a pass for a 15-yard gain, but the ball was knocked loose by Antwan Harris. Terrell Buckley picked it up and returned it to the St. Louis 40. To this point, Brady hadn't looked great, but now he got to operate out of his favorite formation, the shotgun. He hit Troy Brown for 16 on first down after a couple of nifty run-after-catch moves.

On second and 2 from the 16, Brady tried an out for David Patten against Dexter McCleon. It was very similar to a play the Eagles had run successfully against the Rams the week before in the NFC Championship Game. McCleon stayed with the play, and it fell incomplete. After Kevin Faulk picked up the first down, the original plan was to go back to the out for Patten against McCleon from under center. But on a last-second overrule of Charlie Weis by Bill Belichick, the play was changed to an out-go instead of just an out. Sure enough, McCleon was once again in perfect position to defend the out, but Patten spun around him and was open to make a corkscrew leaping grab right at the pylon. Brady had struck again.

The score was Patriots 14, Rams 3, as Bono made his way through the crowd to the stage singing "It's a Beautiful Day" and U2 performed a memorable halftime show, which included a tribute to the victims of 9/11.

The Patriots got the ball to start the third, looking for the knockout blow. They got the ball into Rams territory, but Brady overthrew

Patten on a play that might have been a touchdown. Grant Wistrom blew up a J.R. Redmond rush attempt for a four-yard loss, and a screen for Troy Brown on third down wasn't enough, so Walter punted it back away.

The Rams started at their own 16, and Warner started to flash the skills that made him great, hooking up with Hakim for a 20-yard gain and then Bruce for 22. A pass interference penalty on Otis Smith gave the Rams three first downs on three plays.

Otis Smith: Kurt Warner's a great quarterback. He had a hair-trigger release. It was quick and pinpoint all the time.

Usually, a team with a defense like the Patriots', up 11 in the second half, would look a pretty certain winner—no team had ever come back from such a deficit in a Super Bowl before—but with the way the Rams offense was quickening, the lead was anything but secure. But another huge play from the Pats' D righted the ship. Warner didn't have time to get the ball to an open Torry Holt downfield because Seymour and Vrabel descended on him for the sack. On the next play, Warner tried Holt again, but the pressure and coverage were just enough that Holt was out of bounds when he made the catch.

On third down, Roman Phifer came off a delay and clobbered Warner just as he threw, forcing an incompletion, and the Rams had to punt.

Willie McGinest: One of the things we discovered was that nobody really jammed these guys. Because of the talent and the speed, teams played off them coming off the line. We knew if we played that finesse game, giving them a head start, we couldn't beat them.

The Patriots' ground game asserted itself on the next series: Antowain Smith ran off the right end for 17, and David Patten ran a reverse for 22 yards, advancing the ball to the Rams' 42. Smith got five more up the middle on first down, and once again the Pats looked to be on the verge of getting a lead that even the Rams' vaunted offense wouldn't be able to eliminate. But the Rams' defense stepped up its game and stopped Smith on second down, and Dré Bly had blanket coverage on a slant to Patten on third, forcing another Walter punt. This time, he slightly overkicked his teammates, who were looking to down the ball inside the 5, and the Rams got the ball at the 20.

Marshall Faulk carried the ball on the next four plays, bringing the ball out to the 50. Warner had been dealing with an injured thumb all season, and he appeared to aggravate it at some point, perhaps on the Phifer hit on the previous sequence, or maybe on one of the handoffs to Faulk. But banged-up thumb or no, the Rams were once again on the make.

It was then that their Achilles heel came into play once again. On second down, Otis Smith made a great open-field tackle on Torry Holt to stop a big play, and then, on third and 5, he made a big play of his own.

Otis Smith: We were playing in cover-two-type coverage. I got up and played man-to-man. I hit Torry Holt in the chest, and when I did that Warner threw the ball, and when I looked it was in my arms. I couldn't help but catch it.

Smith ran the ball back to the St. Louis 33. Five plays later, Vinatieri booted it through the uprights and the two-touchdown underdogs had a two-touchdown lead, 17–3.

Adam Vinatieri: When we played in the Super Bowl five years earlier, I never had an opportunity to kick a field goal. This time I wanted to have a souvenir. I said to my equipment guy, "Johnny, if I kick a field goal, can you get the ball for me?" But he forgot to get the ball.

The fourth quarter started with the Rams driving again, this time all the way down to inside the Patriots' 10-yard line after a vintage Warner-to-Faulk connection for 22 yards. St. Louis couldn't get the ball to the end zone on the next three plays (the Pats almost got picks on second *and* third down), setting up a must-make fourth-down situation and the strangest sequence of the game.

Warner scrambled toward the goal line and got hit by Roman Phifer, and the ball came loose. Tebucky Jones picked it up and ran 97 yards for an insurmountable 21-point lead and a certain Super Bowl victory. Patriots fans everywhere were going wild. But the cameras picked up a flag on the play: holding on the defense. The result was nullified and the tension returned to the stadium.

Willie McGinest: Tedy Bruschi and I had a play called Banjo. I had Faulk outside. Bruschi had him inside. So I jammed him. Warner started to scramble the opposite way. Faulk was on the opposite side of where all that took place. Bruschi started running with Warner and everybody else the other way. Marshall ran an angle route inside. So I had to do something, because he would have been wide open in the end zone. I wasn't going to let him run in there free.

Still, McGinest and the Patriots didn't like the call.

Willie McGinest: It really should have been a no call. He wasn't even in the play. The play was dead on our side. He wasn't even on the side of the ball. I was surprised. I know I held him a little more than I had prior. To me, why would you make a call like that? It had no effect on the play.

The result was first and goal from the Patriots' 1, and, on second down, Warner took it in himself for the touchdown. 17–10. The Rams not only had a new lease on life, but with their offense, a 14-point swing, and 9:20 left, the seconds-ago-over game was once again a contest. And after the Pats went three and out, taking only about 1:30 off the clock, the Rams appeared to have every chance.

A holding penalty on the punt pinned the Rams back on their own 7-yard line. Warner moved them forward, passing for a first down before connecting with Ricky Proehl for 30 yards, which took them to near midfield. On the next play, Warner checked down to Jeff Robinson for 12 yards and another first down. It seemed only a matter of time before the Rams tied the game.

For most of the game, Warner had been effective in avoiding sacks, even when the Patriots pass coverage was excellent. But on second and 9, his luck in that department ran out. Warner started the play by deftly eluding Richard Seymour's initial sack attempt, but Willie McGinest redeemed himself for the hold by planting Warner back at the Rams' 45, a 16-yard loss.

Willie McGinest: I felt like I had to do something. I felt like I let my team down. I told myself I had to do something to get that play back and help us out.

On fourth down, Baker's kick floated into the Patriots' end zone, and the Pats took over at their own 20. The Pats' play calling turned super-conservative, and the Rams' revitalized defense looked strong as New England went three and out again. Worse yet, a bad punt by Walter set the Rams up at their own 45, with 2:12 left, plenty of time for the Greatest Show on Turf to do its thing and set up the possibility of the first overtime game in Super Bowl history.

Sure enough, for the first time that evening, the Rams' offense looked like the juggernaut that had been terrorizing opponents for the past three seasons: three plays, three completions, 55 yards, one Warner–to–Proehl touchdown catch, 7 points. The whole thing took 21 seconds, and the game was tied with 1:51 left.

Adam Vinatieri: After the Rams tied the game, I said to Johnny, "They screwed up. They left us too much time."

After Troy Brown danced the kickoff return back to only the Pats 17, John Madden speculated on the broadcast that the Pats should just kneel down and take their chances in overtime.

Joe Andruzzi: I'm glad we didn't listen to him.

Madden certainly wasn't the only one who thought that was the best course of action. In an interview in *America's Game*, Tom Brady recalled being of that mind as well. "It's 17–17. My first thing is I go up to Charlie and say, 'What are we doing?' And he says, 'We're going.' I said, 'All right, what's the first play?' And I'm sure Bill said in his ear, 'He better take care of that ball.' So Charlie yells at me, 'Hey! Take care of that ball.' And Drew was standing next to me and he said, 'F——that. Go out there and sling it.'"

Otis Smith: Defensively, we were starting to wear down a little bit. I was breathing hard. I know I didn't want to go back out there and face their offense. We had a minute-plus left on the clock. There was enough time to drive the ball down and try to score.

Willie McGinest: We knew what Brady and our offense could do. Not only that, we knew what Adam could do. Our attitude was, "We're not going to give them nothing. If they are going to get the ball, they're going to have to take it from us. We're going to try and score a field goal."

Joe Andruzzi: Tom comes in the huddle with a big smile on his face. The other ten guys all sense his ease. If you had a guy who went in there and was all nervous, biting his fingernails, that's not going to go over well with everybody else. He comes in with his big smile and says, "Let's go do this damn thing; let's get it done."

On first down, Madden nearly looked like a prophet: Brady was almost strip-sacked, which could have handed the Rams the win in the worst case for New England. But he eluded the grasp of defensive end Leonard Little and found Redmond for 5 yards. On the Super Bowl telecast, Madden reiterated that the Pats should be looking to overtime. On second down, Brady went to Redmond again, this time for 8 yards and a first down to the 30. The Pats hustled to the line and Brady clocked the ball with :41 left. Meanwhile, Vinatieri was on the sideline, practicing with his net.

Willie McGinest: We knew Adam's range. We just had to get within Adam's range.

Adam Vinatieri: As a kicker, you have to feel like every game is coming down to your foot. That was the way the game was playing out.

A screen pass to Redmond produced another first down, and, more important, he just barely managed to get out of bounds to stop the clock. Thirty-three seconds remained. Madden recanted on the spot: "Now I kinda like what the Patriots are doing." Pat Summerall, doing his final broadcast as a team with Madden, likened the game to one he'd played in with the Giants, the famous 1958 Championship Game against the Colts.

Kevin Faulk: We practiced that situation so many times. When it came up at the end of the game, we said to ourselves, "We've been through this with our defense in practice and we're ready for it, so here we go!"

Brady threw the ball away on first down, just getting outside the tackles, preventing a grounding call and preserving time on the clock. On second down, Brady completed a pass to Troy Brown for 23 yards and a first down at the Rams' 36.

Troy Brown: As players, you get a vibe and get into a rhythm with the quarterback. Whatever mood or zone he was in, sometimes you fall into that, too. He was upbeat about it, and we were ready to make some plays for him.

Otis Smith: Brady hit Troy Brown on a route out of bounds, and here comes Mr. Ice-in-His-Veins.

Adam Vinatieri: At that point I was over at the net thinking, "It's time to win this thing." I was just trying to clear my mind, which was hard to do in the Super Bowl. I tried to tell myself that it would be the same kick as it was on the practice field. I didn't think about the ramifications of a make or a miss.

But it wasn't Vinatieri's turn just yet. They were close enough for him to at least try, but not enough to feel very confident. And, with 21 seconds on the clock, there was still enough time for one more play. Brady managed to hook up with one of his fellow Snow Bowl heroes.

Troy Brown: That last play by Jermaine Wiggins was huge for insurance; he got us six yards closer.

Brady clocked the ball again with seven seconds left on the clock.

Adam Vinatieri: A 48-yarder wasn't a chip shot. Inside, in a dome, there wasn't going to be any wind or conditions. I knew I had the distance. I had to make good contact.

Kevin Faulk: As a football player, you always talk about kickers and punters, how they don't actually play, they just kick; but at that point in time, you're on his side. Whatever he's been doing while we've been practicing has got to work right now. With the kicker we had, whatever the situation, I would have bet the house on him!

Troy Brown: We were feeling much more confident than the kick in the snow, but I still couldn't look at it.

Dante Scarnecchia: Until the ball goes between the posts, coaches are the worst as far as having confidence. We've been on the sidelines a long time and we've seen the good and bad. Once the ball goes through, then you can express your feelings.

Adam Vinatieri: It was like a golf swing. It seemed like everything slowed down for me. Once I got out there, when I kicked the ball, it felt so good leaving my foot. I had to look up and make sure it was going where I wanted it to go. At that point I think I already had my hand in the air looking at my sideline before the ball was three quarters of the way through. I was celebrating before it hit the net. It was the greatest moment of my professional career.

Troy Brown: I remember sitting on the bench with Ty Law, holding hands, with our heads down, waiting for the crowd to make some noise one way or another to let us know if it went in or not. Sure enough, the crowd was going crazy and a couple of guys were screaming around us. I looked up and saw the ball going into the net. At that point, I was like, "We're the world champions!"

Willie McGinest: I just thought about what it was like to get back there and to win. The most gratifying thing for us was that nobody gave us a chance.

Troy Brown: That's what you start every season for. It brought tears to my eyes. You think of all the pain you went through and the hard training you went through and the summers spent getting ready for that moment, and you feel for guys who don't make it, the disappointment of not fulfilling the dream. It's like climbing to the top of Mount Everest.

Adam Vinatieri: Before I kicked it, Johnny said to me, "Adam, you hit it and I'll get it." When it went into the net, he ran down there and had to fight off a few people. I think he got a shiner and a kick in the groin. I got the ball, and that might be one of my greatest possessions. What a great friend, to take a beating to get the ball for me.

Dante Scarnecchia: I had been through two losses in Super Bowls that were both in the same venue. It hadn't been a very good place for us. I looked up and saw that they had all the Super Bowl scores on these banners. I thought to myself: "Oh my god, please don't make it a third." It worked out for us.

Queen blared, David Patten made a faux snow angel in the end zone, and red-white-and-blue confetti rained down on the field. In his postgame speech, Bob Kraft delivered his famous line, "We are all patriots, and tonight, the Patriots are world champions."

Joe Andruzzi: It's kind of weird when you look at it like that. How our colors are red, white, and blue. The symbol for the Super Bowl was the flag that year. Everything kind of fell into place. We were happy to hold up the trophy for us and everybody else.

APPENDICES

The Stumblers: Champions Who Got Out of the Gate Poorly

Teams that lose on opening day of the NFL season, be forewarned: Fewer than one in five titleholders have started their seasons at 0–1. Only four of those teams moved to 0–2, only two of those were 1–3, and only one of them was still under .500 seven games into the season. The team that managed to do all four of those things and still bring home the biggest trophy is the 2001 New England Patriots. What follows is a list of eventual champions that were under .500 past the first three games of the season.

1938 New York Giants

After opening the season with a 27–14 road win in Pittsburgh, the Giants ran into a rough patch. In their second game, they beat the Eagles everywhere but the scoreboard. New York outrushed and outpassed Philadelphia, but two key mistakes cost them the 14–10 contest. Bob Pylman and Joe Carter both scooped up Giants fumbles and ran 90 yards for touchdowns. In an early version of *Monday Night Football*, a week later, the Pittsburgh Pirates visited the Polo Grounds under the lights, playing with the white ball the NFL used to trot out for night games. Frank Filchock, first coach of the Denver Broncos, picked apart the Giants defense with deft passing and also had an interception while on defense. Future Supreme Court justice Byron "Whizzer" White cut loose for 191 yards out of the Pirates' backfield. The Giants became so frustrated at one point that a fistfight ensued and Pittsburgh's Armand Niccolai was knocked cold by Chief Johnson, who was thrown out of the game. New York lost 13–10, but from that point forward, the defense went into high gear, allowing just 38 points as they went 7–0–1. The Giants then beat the Green Bay Packers 23–17 in the title game.

1952 Detroit Lions

Thanks to the 49ers, the Lions got off to a 1–2 start. With Frankie Albert running their vexing T formation at foggy Kezar Stadium, San Francisco took game one, 17–3. Two weeks later, a Detroit record crowd of 56,822 showed up for the Lions' home opener, only to see them humbled 28–0 by the 49ers. Y.A. Tittle came off the bench for San Francisco and engineered two touchdown drives, while the Lions didn't get a first down until late in the third quarter. This game set the record for the worst shutout defeat of a team that would eventually become champion (see "Shutout Losses by Championship Teams," on page 298); a mark that would stand for over 50 years. The Lions got rolling the next week with a second victory against the Rams—the team they would later beat in the tiebreaker. They would go on to score more than 40 points on five occasions and finish at 9–3. After dispatching the Rams, they did what they often did in the fifties: beat the Cleveland Browns for the NFL title.

1954 Cleveland Browns

In the Browns' opener, the Eagles' defense held Otto Graham to 130 yards passing as he was just 9 for 23, while Adrian Burk and Bobby Thomason had two touchdown passes each for Philadelphia, who won 28–10 going away. Cleveland bounced back against a wretched Cardinals team in week two, only to run into disaster in week three at Pittsburgh. The 55–27 Steelers victory represents the most points ever surrendered by an NFL team destined to win the championship. (See "The Worst Defeats Inflicted on Championship Teams," on page 132.) Over the next eight games, the Browns rebounded, outscoring their opponents 248–58 and running their record to 9–2. They didn't lose again until the last week of the season, when they were downed 14–10 by their nemesis, the Detroit Lions, whom they then crushed in the NFL Championship, 56–10.

1961 Houston Oilers

The defending AFL champions got off to a great start with a 55–0 drubbing of the Oakland Raiders. Then the roof caved in: San Diego and Dallas got out to big leads on the Oilers in weeks two and three and never looked back. In week four, the Bills scored 15 unanswered points in the fourth quarter, beating Houston 22–12. On October 13, the 1–3 Oilers were visiting the 2–3 Boston Patriots (who had just fired Lou Saban and replaced him with Mike Holovak). It is no wonder that nobody had a clue that the AFL Eastern title was on the line. With :05 on the clock in the fourth quarter and the Oilers trailing by 3, George Blanda kicked a 25-yard field goal to tie the game at 31. Had the Pats been able to hang on to their lead, they would have finished 10–4–0 and the Oilers—who immediately replaced coach Lou Rymkus with Wally Lemm and tore off nine straight wins—would have also finished 10–4–0, forcing a tiebreaker game. Instead, Houston nipped Boston by a game, beat the Chargers in the title game, and completely overcame their disastrous start.

1980 Oakland Raiders

The Raiders were 2–1 when they were stymied by the Bills in week four, 24–7. In week five, their quarterback, Dan Pastorini, was knocked out for the season when he broke his leg against the Chiefs in the first quarter. In came Jim Plunkett, a quarterback familiar to New England fans. By 1980, he had fallen on hard times, having been released by the 49ers in 1977 and throwing just 15 total passes in 1978 and 1979. In relief of Pastorini, he unloaded 52 passes, completing only 20 and getting picked off five times. The Raiders were 2–3, but the news was mostly good from that point on. Oakland went 9–2 the rest of the way and then won four postseason games, capped by a 27–10 runaway victory over the Eagles in Super Bowl XV, for which Plunkett was named the MVP.

1981 San Francisco 49ers

The Niners began their season 1–2, losing to Lions and Falcons teams that were much better than their eventual respective 8–8 and 7–9 records would indicate. The Detroit game was lost with 18 seconds to go when Billy Sims scored from the 1-yard line. After the Falcons took them out 34–17 in week three, San Francisco nearly ran the table, losing only a close one to Cleveland in week 11. They seemed even more like a team of destiny when Dwight Clark and Joe Montana hooked up for The Catch to win the NFC Championship Game. They then got an early lead on the Bengals in Super Bowl XVI and held on for the 26–21 victory.

1993 Dallas Cowboys

Fresh off one of the most convincing Super Bowl wins ever—a 52–17 smackdown of the Bills—Dallas looked like a good bet to get off to a hot start in that their first two opponents were the Redskins and the Bills again. Instead, they were without the services of Emmitt Smith and were forced to use the long-forgotten Derrick Lassic at running back instead. Washington, which would finish at 4–12, humbled the Cowboys 35–16, and Buffalo got some mini-vengeance when Steve Christie kicked the go-ahead field goal with a little over two minutes remaining. Troy Aikman threw an interception to end the contest, and rumors began flying that coach Jimmy Johnson was headed for Miami. Johnson did bolt for the Dolphins, but not before the Cowboys finished out the season at 12–4 and ran the table in the playoffs, beating the Bills again in the Super Bowl.

2001 New England Patriots

The '01 Pats hit all the low spots that title winners almost never do. Lost first game? Check. Lost second? Check. Then they rebounded in game three only to get bounced 30-10 by the Dolphins in week four. Just when they'd battled back to even their record, they traveled to Denver in week seven and turned the ball over to the Broncos five times, blowing a 20–10 lead in the process. A 3–4 record was undiscovered territory for championship teams. No other club has ever stood on the bad side of .500 that far into a campaign and recovered to win a league title or Super Bowl.

2007 New York Giants and 1934 New York Giants

Though they operated seven decades apart, these two installments of the Giants had quite a bit in common. Both had less-than-inspiring regular seasons, and both took down undefeated superpower teams in the championship game after having lost to them in the regular season. The '34 Giants were blanked 9–0 in their opener and then managed only six points the following week. They went 7–3 the rest of the way, winning the title in an Eastern Division in which no other team was over .500. They met the 13–0 Bears for the title and prevailed 30–13 in the famous Sneaker Game. The 2007 Giants surrendered 80 points in their first two games, losses to Dallas and Green Bay. They went 10–4 the rest of the way, but registered a point differential of just plus 22, the second worst ever for a Super Bowl champion.

Starting at 0–1

The only other future championship team that still had a losing record beyond the first game was the 1932 Chicago Bears, who lost their fourth game after tying the first three. The champions who started 0–1, but were never again under .500 were as follows: the 1925 Chicago Cardinals, 1948 Philadelphia Eagles, 1955 Cleveland Browns, 1957 Detroit Lions, 1960 Philadelphia Eagles, 1961 Green Bay Packers, 1986 New York Giants, the 2002 Tampa Bay Buccaneers, and the 2011 New York Giants.

The Patriots in the Snow

According to the *Boston Globe,* the Patriots have never lost a game in the snow since moving to Foxborough in 1971. In addition to the other snow games discussed elsewhere in this book, we can't forget this sampling of wintry contests.

Patriots 36, Chicago Bears 7 (December 12, 2010)

The final score might not look that impressive, but it's mitigated by the fact that it was 33–0 at the half and that New England really took its foot off the gas after the break. Not only that, but this was a *road* game, played against a 9–3, playoff-bound Bears team that had won its previous five games. Tom Brady registered a passer rating of 113.4 as he and the whole team played as though there were no adverse conditions whatsoever, while the Bears struggled with the elements and the Patriots both. New England's only concession to the blizzard was a missed extra point after Deion Branch's 59-yard touchdown reception.

Patriots 59, Tennessee Titans 0 (October 18, 2009)

Talk about a game out of time. First of all, there was the snow coming down in vast quantities just a couple of weeks after the Red Sox finished playing. Then there were the throwback uniforms: the Pat the Patriot helmets and bright red jerseys for New England and the Houston Oilers derrick helmets and blue socks for the Titans. The referees were wearing the red-striped shirts of early AFL times, too. Randy Moss got into the spirit of it after one of his three touchdowns by casually tossing the ball to a ref like you see them do in the highlight reel from the 1963 AFL Championship Game. Brady had a near-perfect 152.8 passer rating and, had Bill Belichick been so inclined to let him, could have tied the NFL record of seven touchdown passes in a single game. Instead, Brady sat down in the third quarter, giving way to Brian Hoyer, who scored the final Patriots touchdown on a quarterback sneak. In addition to the three scores to Moss, Brady hit Wes Welker twice and Kevin Faulk once. Laurence Maroney's 45-yard sprint started the scoring for New England in the first quarter. It was the single largest Patriots win ever, and it is not hard to imagine that they could have set the league record for single-game points as well had they not taken it easy after their last score. As it was, they set the record for the biggest half-time lead in history, 45–0.

Patriots 47, Arizona Cardinals 7 (December 21, 2008)
Had the Cardinals managed to hang on to their late lead in Super Bowl XLIII, this game would have gone down in history as easily the worst regular-season defeat ever by a Super Bowl champion. (The Cardinals would have also tied the record for most points surrendered by a champion, in their 56–35 loss to the Jets.) Having already clinched the title in the noncompetitive NFC West, Arizona came to snowy Foxborough and played like they wished they were back in the desert. Kurt Warner had one of the very worst games of his career, throwing for just 30 yards before being mercifully pulled in favor of Matt Leinart, who, at least, helped Arizona avoid a shutout with a 78-yard TD pass to Larry Fitzgerald. That the Pats didn't make the playoffs and the Cardinals did was one of the ironies of this game, one of the three in 2008 in which their backup quarterback, Matt Cassel, threw for 300 yards.

Patriots 20, Indianapolis Colts 3 (January 16, 2005; divisional playoff)
While the snow never accumulated to any great extent in this game, it did come down steadily throughout the contest, mixing with sleet at times. Tedy Bruschi recovered two fumbles and the Colts gained just 46 yards on the ground while New England frustrated MVP Peyton Manning's attempt to get his team into the game.

Buffalo Bills 30, Patriots 28 (October 21, 1974)

It wasn't a snow game in the true sense of the phrase, in that there were only flurries on this gray afternoon in Orchard Park, New York, but it sure served notice that a long, cold winter was arriving for the Patriots. For the first five games of the season, things had just kept getting better and better. New England went 5–0 as their opponents' scores kept dropping; from 24 to 20 to 14 to 3 to 0, it was the best start to a Patriots season to date. But O.J. Simpson scored twice and the Bills built a 27–14 lead and won going away, tying the Pats at the top of the AFC Eastern Division standings. Both teams would be eclipsed by the Miami Dolphins, though, as the Pats would go 2–6 the rest of the way while Buffalo was going 4–4.

Buffalo Bills 24, Patriots 14 (December 20, 1964)

What a difference a year makes. Unlike the previous December, when the Pats ran circles around the Bills in the snow, it was Boston's turn to struggle on the white stuff—this time at home. With the Eastern Division title in the balance (Boston was 10–2–1, while Buffalo was 11–2–0), the teams waited through a 30-minute delay of the opening kickoff while four inches of snow was scraped off the turf. Jack Kemp hit El Dubenion on a 57-yard TD pass to get the scoring stared early. The Pats answered, but, when Gino Cappelletti slipped on the 2-point conversion, they missed a chance to go up 8–7. The Bills scored 17 unanswered points, the last set up when Charley Warner intercepted a Babe Parilli pass and returned it to the Boston 17. In a set more reminiscent of the modern game than that of the early AFL, Parilli was using two wide receivers and two tight ends on many plays with just Larry Garron in the backfield, while the Bills responded by rushing just three men and dropping the rest back on coverage. The biggest crowd to see the Patriots to that point (over 38,000) braved the elements.

Patriots 26, Oakland Raiders 16 (October 21, 1962)

Wouldn't the NFL be more fun if there were no kicking specialists? What if there was a rule that said that all kickers had to play at least 50 percent of the snaps on either offense or defense as well? We'd go back to having games like this one, where Gino Cappelletti broke the team record for field goals with four and also scored a touchdown and kicked 2 extra points for a total of 20 points scored on the night. Only 12,514 hardy fans braved wet snow and rain to watch this battle in the mud.

New England Patriots vs. Carolina Panthers

SUPER BOWL XXXVIII
February 1, 2004

	1	2	3	4	F
New England Patriots	0	14	0	18	**32**
Carolina Panthers	0	10	0	19	**29**

Super Bowl XXXVIII was a game full of surprises, not the least of which was the NFC representative or the wardrobe malfunction that took place at halftime. What was a mismatch—on paper at least—turned into a dogfight; and what started out as a defensive battle wound up as one of the Super Bowl's higher-scoring entries, concluding with the most points ever scored in a Super Bowl quarter.

THE 2003 PATRIOTS

The purpose of the exercise is not to dominate, of course, but to win. And while the 2003 Patriots didn't do much of the former, they certainly did plenty of the latter. After falling to 9–7 in 2002 and missing the playoffs on tiebreaking procedures, New England rode their defense to a big improvement in 2003, surrendering 100 fewer points than they had the year before.

The Patriots led the league in interceptions with 29, a feat made more impressive by the fact that they allowed only 11 aerial touchdowns. Left corner Ty Law had six picks, as did Tyrone Poole. Nine different Patriots had at least one, and they returned five of them for touchdowns, including two by Tedy Bruschi. In all, the Patriots' defense put

42 points on the board and the special teams added 7. Combined, they accounted for 20 percent of the team's scoring.

On the ground, they allowed just 3.6 yards per carry, much better than the league average of 4.2. They surrendered only 4.9 yards per pass, the best in the league. All this success against the opposition's passing game came in a season that saw them release veteran strong safety Lawyer Milloy when they could not renegotiate his contract to make it fit the salary cap. It seemed like a blow at the time, both on the field and off, in that Milloy was a fan favorite and, so people thought, one of Bill Belichick's favorites as well.

Nick Cafardo: It was a move I widely criticized. I was a big Lawyer Milloy fan. I thought he was the heart and soul of that defense. Another statement made by the coach: He wanted to get younger and faster. He made a tough choice there. I thought it would backfire, but in the long term, it turned out to be another outstanding move.

Willie McGinest: Lawyer was one of the guys I took under my wing when he first got there. He was a helluva player and teammate. It was tough for us to see him go. It was surprising, especially the timing. No one thought he was going to go right then—and to the team we opened against, no less.

Joe Andruzzi: We had dealt with the same thing the year before with Terry Glenn. When Lawyer's issue came up, it was Lawyer's issue. None of us knew the ins and outs of what was going on unless you were with Lawyer, right next to him. Basically there was no reason for us to focus in on that as a team. The season has to go on—that's what it came down to. We let management handle it without us having to worry about anything.

Kevin Faulk: I think that was the moment that I realized that football and the NFL was more of a business. That's what it is and that's what we do.

New England replaced him and moved on. It was the Belichick era in microcosm, one in which the individual parts are subservient to the greater good, no matter how seemingly painful it might be to replace them. Since the win in Super Bowl XXXVI, the defensive backfield had been made over nearly completely as part of the continuing quest to keep from getting too old and to stay within the confines of the salary cap. The defense thrived, though. Safety Rodney Harrison (a free agent pickup from San Diego), tackle Richard Seymour, and Law were named All-Pro, Willie McGinest went to the Pro Bowl, and Tedy Bruschi should have.

Joe Andruzzi: When he was on the other team, you hated to play against Rodney Harrison. It was great to have him on our side. Rodney was a great team leader. Real football minded; he loved the game. He really glued the defense together. Getting him was one of the things that helped move us forward that season.

Dan Koppen: There's not enough I could say about Rodney. The way he practiced and the way he played his game—he was a great guy to have. [It was great] to be able to come into that locker room as a rookie and be on that team with guys like Rodney and twenty other people I could mention who carried themselves the way NFL football players should.

The offense struggled with its ground game, posting one of the lowest yards-per-carry numbers in the league. Only five teams threw fewer interceptions, though, as Tom Brady turned in another solid performance. Kevin Faulk caught 48 passes out of the backfield and led the team in all-purpose yards. Deion Branch had the most catches, with 57. It was a quiet year for the offense as they scored fewer than 300 points. Tellingly, nobody from the New England O unit was named to the Pro Bowl.

Not apparent from the team's record, it was also a year with many key injuries: Rosevelt Colvin was brought in from Chicago to bring speed to the left-side linebacker position, only to be lost after two games. Another Bears free agent, nose tackle Ted Washington, was lost to a broken leg after the second week. Guard Mike Compton went down for the count, too. Ted Johnson broke his foot, and his fellow linebacker

Mike Vrabel would miss seven games and the first round of the play-offs. Wide receiver David Patten would be felled for good with a knee injury that limited him to five games and nine catches, down from 61 the year before. Injuries befall every team, but this was an inordinate amount. It was a testament to the roster-building technique of the Bill Belichick/Scott Pioli braintrust that gave them the unique depth to thrive in this adverse situation.

Dan Koppen: You get opportunities and you have to make the most of them. To make it in this league you have to have a little bit of luck, but you have to do something with that luck to show the team and the coaches that you can handle that spot. Woody hurt his sternum in the first game. That allowed me to step in and start the second game. Then Mike Compton realized he had a broken foot that he had been playing on. He was done for the season after that. My luck was that Compton got hurt. I played well enough obviously, where they were comfortable enough to move Woody to guard and me into center. It was one of those things that happened so fast. As a rookie, you don't know anything and are not expected to know anything. You just put your head down and go. It was a heck of an experience. Fortunately, Tom Brady is definitely a lineman's quarterback. We felt comfortable with each other. On the field, our trust developed pretty quickly.

The Patriots started the season with one of the worst losses ever by a title-winning ball club (see "Shutout Losses by Championship Teams," on page 298), traveling to Buffalo, where they ran into their previous quarterback and the recently departed Lawyer Milloy.

Christian Fauria: We got our butts kicked by Buffalo in the opener. We were embarrassed, really. London Fletcher knocked out Damien Woody, and Drew Bledsoe was hanging out like it was a graduation party.

Troy Brown: That happens to a guy when a division rival picks him up: The guys on his new team are going to be fired up to get him a win. He's giving them information about players and things we do, that type of stuff. Damien Woody was bleeding out of his ears because they cranked him so hard on that Sam Adams interception for a touchdown. I had never seen a guy bleed out of his ears before that. He was out for a couple of weeks. It was an ugly game for us.

Dan Koppen: That was my first game as a pro. Everybody was making it into a big deal, [trying to paint it like] the locker room was rebelling and that the coach lost his team. It wasn't that; the fact of the matter was we just played like crap. We got blown out and we deserved to get blown out because we didn't play very well. It was one of those things where you get your butts kicked and you have to learn from it and play again the next week.

Now that the Pats were lying prone, there were some who wanted to kick them. Most famously, ESPN analyst Tom Jackson stated with great conviction that the Patriots hated their coach. It was pure invention in that he hadn't actually spoken with any players. The comment came just prior to New England's late-afternoon game in Philadelphia. For another franchise, Jackson's words might have been divisive, but the Patriots' defense roared back from the Buffalo debacle with a devastating performance. They made life miserable for Donovan McNabb, sacking him seven times, forcing him to fumble three times, intercepting him twice, and tipping 14 of his 46 passes. The 31–10 victory over the Eagles rendered Jackson's ill-considered but emphatic statement moot. In the end, it was he who came off worse, not Belichick.

There followed a tense battle with the Jets that finally opened up when Asante Samuel ran back an interception for a touchdown. In week four, the 2–1 Patriots traveled to Washington and let the Redskins get out in front 20–3 before hustling back to make a game of it. Brady was intercepted three times, but engineered a comeback that had them within a 55-yard field goal attempt of tying the game. Instead, Bill Belichick chose to go for the first down on fourth and 3 with 43 seconds left to play. The rally ended when Brady's pass to Daniel Graham was knocked away.

Christian Fauria: I played for Washington after I left the Patriots, and we talked about that game. That Redskins team sucked. They couldn't believe they won. They were just throwing stuff out there. Tom got a concussion, but he kept playing. No one knew he had it. I remember at the end of the game, walking off the field with Tom going, "What the hell?" The whole team just buckled down after that.

Dan Koppen: Coming out of that game there was a disappointment about it. We felt we were the better team and should have won it. But sometimes you can learn a lot more from losing than winning. I think we grew up a lot after that game.

The 3–1 Tennessee Titans came to town and an epic seesaw battle ensued. There were no fewer than seven lead changes, but the Patriots came up with the most important of them: the last one.

Christian Fauria: I'll say it until I'm blue in the face about that Tennessee game: It made everyone accountable. I remember watching something on the History Channel, about a battle where not everyone had a gun and those guys that didn't would follow behind the ones that did, and if someone got shot, they'd pick up the gun and start fighting. You have to be that guy; you need to take another person's role and excel at it. That's where backups have so much value. Look at the injury list from that game; look at the guys that didn't play. After the game I said to Tom, "That's the way we're going to play the rest of the season. This is who we are." People use the "the lights went on" expression. It was more than that. Collectively we knew that this was what it was going to be. What we lacked in physical skill we made up with toughness and a smart coach who put us in the best position to win. Same with the coordinators. It's like they were saying, "Here are some ingredients: Make something out of it." And something good always came up.

Two weeks later, the Patriots found themselves deep into overtime on the road against the Dolphins. Although New England had long since broken their Miami losing streak, they had still *never* beaten the Dolphins in Miami in either September or October. The presiding theory was that the northerners just couldn't handle the south Florida heat at that time of year. This one went on so long, though, that both teams were dragging.

Troy Brown: It was incredibly hot, and we were miserable. We got a blocked Olindo Mare field goal from Richard Seymour; that was huge for us. From our own eighteen, we ran a play that we had practiced all week long. It was designed to work like this: When Tom would roll out to his left, the corners and the safeties would come toward him, and I would come up and take the middle of the field. On this play, I got behind those guys and Tom laid it out for me. I caught the ball and took off downfield. As I went past our sidelines, I could see Steve Burton jumping up and down and Belichick throwing his headphones in the air. It was a reason to celebrate down there: Our wins in Miami were far and between.

Heading into week nine, the winning streak stood at four. It was in their next game that Belichick had one of his most inspired moments. The Patriots were in Denver for a Monday night game and found themselves trailing 24–23 with 2:49 to go, having fallen behind after giving up their first touchdown punt return in a decade. Worse, they were looking at fourth down from their own 1-yard line. Rather than risk a blocked punt and possible touchdown or giving the Broncos excellent field position, Belichick called for snapper Lonie Paxton to shoot the ball over punter Ken Walter's head and out of the end zone. It was a simple case of trading two points for better field position, and it worked to perfection.

Now trailing by 3, Walter boomed a free kick that left the Broncos at their own 15. New England's defense forced them into a three and out, and the Patriots got the ball back at their own 42. From there, Brady drove them to the game-winning touchdown, hitting Kevin Faulk for 18 yards from the Denver 36 and then Givens for the final 18 to make it 30–26.

The winning continued after the bye week. There were shutouts of the Dolphins and Cowboys and a late rally in Houston that forced an overtime in which Adam Vinatieri kicked the game winner. There was a Patriots-Colts classic in Indianapolis in which New England zoomed to a 31–10 lead only to watch Peyton Manning throw three touchdown passes to tie it before the Patriots got back out in front.

Kevin Faulk: I call the games against the Colts our soap opera games. They're like professional basketball games where both teams were pressing and no one could stop anyone. Whoever gets the ball at the end of the game is going to win the game. They're fun when you're on the field, but it's not so much fun when you're on the sideline.

Dan Koppen: Anytime we go into their stadium or they come to us, the game is picked up a level. You can sense it with the fans. You can sense it on the field. Every time we play them it's a playoff atmosphere and it seems every game comes down to the last possession.

With New England leading 38–34, the Colts drove down to the doorstep of victory with just over a minute to play. On first down, Willie McGinest went down and the referees called time-out. Even though the Patriots had none left to spare, they were not penalized. The Colts were convinced it was a conspiracy.

"I would never fake an injury," McGinest said at the time. "I would never fake it and get off the field and miss plays in a game like that."

The Pats held on, bringing up fourth and goal from the 1-yard line with just 11 seconds to go. The epic battle all came down to this.

Willie McGinest: I had twisted my knee and had to sit out two plays. On fourth down, they had split receivers out. I walked out like I was in coverage. I kept my eyes on Peyton. I saw him audible the run to our side. He does that a lot. I was rushing the whole time. Our theosophy with him was to move around. When the ball was snapped, I came off the edge and killed the play.

McGinest nailed Edgerrin James for a 1-yard loss, icing the win.

The regular-season finale saw the Patriots hosting the rematch with the Bills and having their way with them. If you ever thought that teams at the professional level don't think about milestones, symbolic final scores, and revenge, think again.

Troy Brown: This was one of those games we wanted to send a message back to the Bills. They had beaten the crap out of us to start the season, and we had a chance to shut them out. We were up by thirty-one, and our defense was down on our goal line. Larry Izzo was playing linebacker for us along with a couple of our other backups. Bill ended up sending some starters back into the game to keep them from scoring. I was like, "What are we doing? It's the last game of the season!" But it worked for us again. I thought it was the perfect way to end our season. We started out by losing thirty-one to nothing to Buffalo and finished it off by beating them thirty-one to nothing. That's how we turned our season from beginning to end.

Izzo's interception in the end zone with 13 seconds remaining preserved the shutout and with it the season's delicious symmetry. The Pats were on a roll. They had set a team record for fewest points allowed per game and were heading into the playoffs with a 12-game winning streak.

For New England's divisional-round game, the Tennessee Titans came back to Gillette Stadium for a second visit, only this time the thermometer was barely above zero and the windchill made it feel much colder than that.

Kevin Faulk: I don't think anyone played in that type of temperature before, but what we're supposed to do is block everything out and play a good, sound football game.

Christian Fauria: I'll take a cold night over a rainy, snowy night anytime. I played in Colorado, but I'd never been that cold before. I remember thinking that as long as my hands stayed warm I knew I was going to be okay. I melted a pair of cleats because I kept them too close to the burner they have on the sidelines. Even though the ball was heavy and hard, it was easy to catch. I didn't mind it. I was not one of those guys who wouldn't put sleeves on—I put sleeves on. I stayed warm.

Joe Andruzzi: The heated seats we had felt like they weren't even on. It was absolutely the coldest game I've ever played in. Going out for warm-ups and taking a deep breath feeling your esophagus and your lungs just freezing . . . knowing that it's going to be a long one . . . trying to stay warm as best you can . . . not feeling your toes, fingers, or your hands by the end of the game.

Troy Brown: I don't know how I caught the ball, because my fingers wouldn't bend. I put my hands up and the ball stuck to them.

The teams combined for half as many points as they had in their first encounter, but still managed to deliver the drama. Adam Vinatieri broke a 14–14 tie with 4:06 to play, only to have the Titans respond by moving right down the field behind the running and passing of Steve McNair. Tedy Bruschi then pressured McNair into an intentional grounding and the Titans were called for holding. On fourth and long, McNair hit Drew Bennett in the hands, but he could not hang on and the 3-point lead survived.

Troy Brown: Tennessee played us tough. They were a well-coached team, and we were able to hold them off.

The AFC Championship Game would be a rematch with the Indianapolis Colts, a team that was flying high after not having to punt a single time in their two playoff wins. As it happened, the Patriots didn't wait around for the Colts to punt them the ball. Instead, they recovered a fumble and stole four Peyton Manning passes—three of which were by Ty Law—and generally manhandled the Colts receivers all day. The result was a 35.5 passer rating for Manning, which was a few incompletions away from being the worst of his career. The Patriots gave a lot of credit to their third-string quarterback, Damon Huard, a man who threw one pass all year and didn't even appear in the game. It was his job to mimic Manning in practice.

Willie McGinest: We got a lot of help from Damon. He did a great job; his disguises and everything. We credit a lot of our wins to our practices and our preparation. If Damon came to practice and put on a number eighteen jersey, you'd have thought he was Manning.

He studied him. He had him down pat—how he taps the center, everything he did. It gave us a tremendous look.

Dan Koppen: He got the way Peyton runs that offense: the hurry-up, calling plays out on the field, his hand signals, and the way he's always talking and changing things.

Christian Fauria: Backup quarterbacks don't usually dive into the role like that—they just sort of dip their toes in the water. Damon did, though. He had him down cold. He even got the game ball. That was a big reason why we were able to confuse Manning and why he threw some picks.

Troy Brown: Because of that game, they changed the rules about the contact thing. I don't think we did anything illegal, but we planned to be physical. On one particular play, Ty Law had Marvin Harrison in his team's Gatorade over there. I think they found it unfair that we could jam the receiver as well as we were. So they changed the rules on that, which is why you see the seven-on-seven style of play today, where guys can't really touch the receiver. I think it dilutes the game a lot.

In addition to Manning's struggles, the Colts punting unit, perhaps rusty from disuse, yielded a safety on a poor snap. The Pats' only touchdown drive was kept alive by a gutsy fourth-and-1 quarterback keeper in their own territory. All their other drives stalled in the red zone, but Vinatieri tied his career-best mark of five field goals and New England won comfortably, 24–14.

The Patriots had subdued the two highest-rated passers in the NFL to get to the Super Bowl.

Nick Cafardo: They beat two great players: McNair and Manning. They always got up for those guys. McNair posed so many problems with his legs. They had to take him out of the game or they would lose the game. In Belichick's wisdom, they cut off his options; they had a spy on him. They did everything they had to do. That was part of the genius [of the plan]. The fact that they had players that could execute the plays as well as they did, to me, that was amazing. You could have all the best players in the world, but if one guy makes a mistake, it's over. They didn't make mistakes. It was amazing to watch that be in sync as often as it was. These guys had so few breakdowns it was incredible.

Christian Fauria: There were co-MVPs that year: McNair and Manning. We played them in succession, and both defensive plans were good. These were areas where Bill and Romeo Crennel really shined. I was happy that they were MVPs, because it made us play better.

THE PANTHERS

After four trips to title games against teams of extreme quality, the Patriots finally seemed to have caught a break for Super Bowl XXXVIII.

The Carolina Panthers had had as mediocre a regular season as any team that ever managed to make it to the Super Bowl to that point. (See "The Biggest Mismatches in Super Bowl History," on page 323.) Their 11–5 record hid the fact that just about everybody played them close; Carolina won only two games by more than 10 points. They ended up in overtime four times during the regular season and once more in the playoffs. To their credit, they came away 4–1 in those games. You could say they were good in the clutch, but then again, they were getting tested a lot, and not always by elite teams. They were a middle-of-the-pack offensive team and slightly above average in defense, with their pass defense being the team's strongest suit. To their credit, in the playoffs they upset superior Rams and Eagles teams on the road to the Super Bowl.

One of the biggest changes for the '03 Panthers was the addition of Stephen Davis, a free agent signed after some very good years with the Redskins. He averaged 103 yards a game in his 14 starts and scored eight touchdowns. Steve Smith led the team in receptions with 88, which put him just inside the NFL's top 10. He was also ninth in the league in all-purpose yards. Muhsin Muhammad was the number-two receiver, and Ricky Proehl, late of the Rams and Super Bowl XXVI, was on hand as well.

Quarterback Jake Delhomme had come from near obscurity to lead the Panthers to the big game, becoming only the second undrafted quarterback to start a Super Bowl—Kurt Warner, whom he backed up while playing for the Amsterdam Admirals in NFL Europe, being the first. Delhomme was 28 and had started only two NFL games prior to 2003. He made the most of his big chance, posting a yards-per-pass figure of 6.46, good for eighth best in the league. Furthermore, he led seven fourth-quarter comebacks in the 2003 season and added another in the playoffs.

The big stud on defense and probably the most talented player on the team was Kris Jenkins, the only Panther to be named All-Pro. He anchored a talented front four that included Mike Rucker, who had 12 sacks and a Pro Bowl invite, Julius Peppers, who added seven sacks, and nine-year veteran Brentson Buckner.

Nineteen members of the Panthers roster had been on the 2011 team that won its first game and proceeded to lose their remaining 15. The turnaround was engineered by first-time head coach John Fox, who had most recently been the defensive coordinator for the Giants. Under his direction, the Panthers cut their point differential by 113 and improved to a 7–9 record in 2002. By getting his team to the Super Bowl in such a short time after their one-win season, he was treading ground that only Vince Lombardi—who took over the 1–10–1 Packers in 1959 and brought them to the NFL championship in two years—had walked before him.

THE GAME

Christian Fauria: Our preparation was kind of light. We never practiced in pads. Practices were short and light. It was business as usual. I had a messed-up calf and I couldn't walk. I ended up making it into the game.

During pregame warm-ups on the floor of Houston's Reliant Stadium, things got a little heated.

Willie McGinest: Carolina had a bunch of guys that did a lot of talking. They were known for that. We were going to let them know we're not backing down to nothing. It's all-out war. We weren't one of those teams that got caught up in that.

Troy Brown: Carolina gave us some ammunition. They did quite a bit of talking, though, over the course of the week.

Christian Fauria: The whole week Carolina fans were doing a lot of talking. We weren't saying anything. We were being held down. It was almost like if you hold a ball underwater, the harder it is to hold it down. The farther it goes up, the bigger splash it makes. Our emotions were getting to us because we couldn't say anything. I think Bill gave one of his best pep talks I'd ever heard. This is personal now. We were like a bunch of crazy dogs. When they let us out there, both teams were really antagonistic. We were ready to rip their heads off.

Joe Andruzzi: Belichick did his pregame speech in different ways through the years. One year, he broke out the trophy. We wanted to be able to hold up another one of those. The one after this he asked if anyone wanted to go to the Philadelphia Eagles' victory parade. He gave us the route. In 2001, he had asked if anyone wanted to order the Rams Super Bowl hat and shirt. He said, "They're online; go ahead and order them." Stuff like that.

Willie McGinest: Bill Belichick—the [so-called] guy that never speaks, the guy with no personality—delivered one of the most intense inspiration speeches he ever gave us. Everybody said it. That game started in the room right then and there. We had never seen that. He does so many things and then he always has a twist. That was one of his twists, and that got us going.

Adam Vinatieri: The roles were reversed from two years before. This time, we were expected to win. We weren't shocking anybody at this point.

Joe Andruzzi: We were the team to beat. They didn't look at us like that in '01. We had definitely raised the bar. It was good to be an underdog, but it was also good to be the team to beat.

Christian Fauria: Even though we had won all these games, we still had a chip on our shoulders. That's really the Patriot way: playing with a chip on your shoulder even though people are giving you nothing but respect.

Kevin Faulk: Bill said to us, "No one expected these guys to be here. Once the ball is kicked off, just play the game and don't worry about that."

THE FIRST QUARTER

Adam Vinatieri's opening kickoff was taken at the 18 by Rod Smart, who had earned fame with the ill-fated XFL, where he adopted the nickname He Hate Me and had it stitched on his Las Vegas Outlaws jersey. Now wearing his given name on his Carolina jersey, Smart got five yards on the return. The first Panthers possession was a three-and-out, and Todd Sauerbrun punted the ball away to Troy Brown, who caught it at the Patriots' 25, cut to the left across the 30, paused, and looked upfield. Seeing a seam, he burst straight through the charging Panthers and crossed the 50 before being slammed down by special-teams captain Karl Hankton at the Carolina 47. New England was well positioned for its first possession.

Dan Koppen: It was a huge point of emphasis to be sure we protected Tom. Carolina had a formidable defensive line.

Brady threw on first down and found Deion Branch for 16 yards. After Kevin Faulk picked up five, Brady threw to Brown, who had gotten wide open at the 21. After the catch, he eluded the grasp of Greg Favors and picked up seven more yards. The drive stalled there, though, as Brady threw one away under an intense rush, got called for illegal movement, and then missed over the middle in the end zone.

Then, to everyone's surprise, Vinatieri misdirected his 31-yard attempt. For a kicker who had made five such seeming chip shots two weeks earlier in the AFC Championship to miss a shorty like this was fairly surprising.

Adam Vinatieri: It was a frustrating situation. I believe you learn from experiences in life. That first one, I just missed it. They painted the field, and I'm not making excuses, I slipped and I just missed it.

It was to be the closest either team got to scoring for the rest of the quarter. The Panthers never got any farther than their own 23, and the Patriots managed to get back across midfield one more time before stalling. The best scoring opportunity belonged to Panthers safety Deon Grant, who had a Brady pass in his arms with clear sailing ahead but couldn't hang on to it.

Although nothing happened on the scoreboard, one player in particular had a memorable first quarter. Troy Brown experienced good, bad, and ugly in the space of the first 15 minutes:

- An excellent punt return to start New England's first possession.
- Good yards after catch to sustain the first drive.
- Getting fallen upon by six-five, 275-pound Mike Rucker. While flat on his back, Rucker's knee went right into Brown's nose, rendering him bloody. They packed his nostrils to staunch the flow, and back out he came.
- A fumble on a fair catch, which he recovered himself.
- A failed end-around that took the Patriots out of field goal range on third and 3 at the Carolina 31.

Delhomme was just 1 for 7, and his one completion was for 1 yard. The Panthers managed one first down—and that came on a penalty. It seemed at this point that Carolina's offense was completely overmatched and it wasn't going to take many points to beat them.

SECOND QUARTER
While the Patriots' number-one-rated defensive unit was stifling the Panthers, the Carolina defense was holding its own as well. The quarter

opened with them forcing the Patriots into a three and out. After a poor 22-yard punt by Ken Walter gave the Panthers their best field position of the day, the New England defense hurled them back. On third down, Willie McGinest dumped Delhomme for an 11-yard sack, and the Panthers were done in three once more.

New England then started the first sustained drive of the day. Brown caught three passes, while Antowain Smith and Kevin Faulk did the groundwork. Then David Givens dropped a first-down pass at the 9 on third and 8 and Vinatieri came on to try the 36-yard field goal. This time, the kick had a low trajectory and lineman Shane Burton reached up and tipped it. The ball rolled uselessly into the end zone.

Twenty-four minutes of football had now passed without any points. None of the previous 37 Super Bowls had ever gone this long without either team getting on the scoreboard. Then, just as it was beginning to look like a Super Bowl would make it to halftime at 0–0 for the first time ever, the Pats forced a turnover deep in Carolina territory, unleashing a scoring frenzy by both teams that would change the nature of the game.

On second and 12 from his own 25, Delhomme dropped back to pass, only to have his pocket collapse around him. Mike Vrabel got around Todd Steussie and hit Delhomme from the blind side, causing a fumble. Richard Seymour covered it for New England at the 20.

After two runs by Antowain Smith, Brady went into a deep drop on third and 7. He immediately saw the entire center of the field come wide open and took off. He took it down to the 5, his longest run of the season. On the next play, Brady suckered the Carolina linebackers on a play-action and found Deion Branch all alone in the back of the end zone. With just over three minutes to go in the half, the scoreless tie was finally broken.

Receiving the kickoff, the Panthers were called for both holding and unnecessary roughness. The Pats accepted the latter, burying Carolina at its own 5. Given the complete nonperformance of the Panther offense to that point and the fact that they had already lost a time-out to a failed challenge, the chances of them scoring before time expired were remote. When Delhomme's first-down bomb to Steve Smith was expertly defended by original Panther Tyrone Poole, those odds got even longer.

On third and 5, though, Delhomme finally completed another pass, a juggling near miss by Ricky Proehl good for 13 yards and their first earned first down of the game. After the two-minute warning, Delhomme hit another one, this time to Muhsin Muhammad for 23 out to the Carolina 46. On the next play, the Panthers got another first down when Proehl caught one over the middle in New England territory. On third and 10 from the 39, an entire half of Carolina frustrations were wiped away when Steve Smith beat Poole down the right sideline and Delhomme dropped a perfect pass over his shoulder to tie the game.

The Patriots started from their own 22 with less than a minute to play. After Givens got a first down at the 34 on a sideline route, Brady dropped back on second down and was afforded lots of time by his line. Down at the 25, Branch had been allowed to get free in the middle of the field and Brady hit him on the run. Ricky Manning chased him down at the 14 to save the touchdown. New England quickly called its second timeout with 37 seconds left. David Givens got wide open in the right corner of the end zone on first down, but Brady overthrew him. He got Givens the next time, though, nailing him at the 6. After taking its last time-out, New England faked a handoff to Faulk and caught nearly every Panther crowded near the line of scrimmage. Only Manning was deep, and he was nowhere near Givens when he hauled in the touchdown pass over the middle.

There were just 18 seconds left on the clock when Vinatieri punched a short kick to the Carolina 35, where it was scooped up by Kris Mangum, who went outside and covered 12 yards before going out of bounds. On the CBS broadcast, Phil Simms reminded viewers how many times in the past he had railed against the squib kick, a very relevant complaint given that its use had just handed the Panthers excellent field position.

Adam Vinatieri: I personally hate squib kicks. I hate everything about them. In my opinion, they are used more often than they should be. For me, we're breaking our sword and giving up the fight by doing that. We're automatically conceding field position, and that drives me crazy.

With just 12 seconds on the clock, the standard routine at this point would be a sideline pass. You've seen it done dozens of times. Instead, with the Patriots spread all over the field in anticipation of a pass, Fox called for a handoff. Stephen Davis sprinted right up the middle, untouched until he was brought down at the New England 32 by Vrabel and Rodney Harrison. With five seconds left on the clock, John Kasay buried it in the first row of the end-zone seats from 50 yards out, making it 14–10 at halftime.

THE SECOND HALF

Dan Koppen: Before games I always got the nerves. After the first snap, though, they usually went away. Not in the Super Bowl. My arm was still shaking in the third quarter. It's a different game; a *completely* different game. It's an amazing feeling.

One of the best hits of the day was made at halftime. While the teams were lining up for the opening kickoff, Patriots reserve linebacker Matt Chatham leveled an onfield intruder who had been dancing at the 30-yard line in just a G-string before running from security. The inebriated man had snuck onto the field dressed in a referee's uniform held together with Velcro for easy disrobing. After getting laid out, he was hog-tied by the police and carried from the field. Unfortunately, it was not a career-ending hit for the man, who was fined just $1,000 and has continued his pursuit of sad infamy at other major sporting events throughout the world.

For the first 12 minutes of the second half, the teams returned to the scoreless state that had characterized most of the first half. Both teams got the ball twice, and all four possessions ended in punts. The difference between the first and third quarters was that Delhomme was playing with much more authority than he had in the early stages of the game.

With 3:57 to go in the third quarter, the Patriots got their third possession of the half, starting at their own 29. Brady got things started with a 16-yard gainer to Branch. Antowain Smith got them their next first down with two good runs before Brady hit Branch yet again for 8. After Joe Andruzzi was called for holding, Brady ran a play-action on second and 12 and the linebackers bit on it, allowing Daniel Graham to slip into the open at the 25. He tacked on another 16 yards after the catch, giving the Pats a first and goal on the 9. As the quarter ended, Smith plowed his way to the 4.

The fourth quarter started with Brady lofting a pass to Christian Fauria in the left corner, but the tight end couldn't stay in bounds. The Panthers were flagged on the play, however, because Favors had grabbed Brown coming across the middle. With a first and goal from the one, defensive tackle Richard Seymour lined up in the backfield with Antowain Smith. Were the Patriots going to let him score a touchdown, the way the Bears had with William Perry in Super Bowl XX? No, this was no novelty act. Seymour ran interference on the give to Smith, pushing aside safety Mike Minter and clearing a path for the touchdown and the 21–10 lead.

On the next series, Delhomme continued to improve, hitting on passes of 13 to Muhammad and 18 and 22 to Steve Smith. On second and 10 from the New England 33, DeShaun Foster took a delayed handoff, cut to the left, got sprung by a pulling block from guard Kevin Donnalley, and went unscathed down the sideline for 6. Fox then went against standard doctrine and called for a 2-point play. With over 12 minutes to play, it seemed early for such a move, and it looked even more suspect when Delhomme's pass to Muhammad fell incomplete.

Their lead cut to 21–16, the Patriots started from their 26 after Bethel Johnson's 14-yard kickoff return. Brady got first downs on passes to Branch and Brown, moving the ball across midfield. After another first down, the give went to Faulk, who glided through a gaping hole provided by Andruzzi and Tom Ashworth, taking the ball from the 33 down to the 10. On third and goal, Brady tried to connect with Fauria in the end zone, but was picked by cornerback Reggie Howard. He was brought down by center Dan Koppen at the 10.

On third and 10, Delhomme ran a play-fake to Foster and moved to his left as his line gave him plenty of time. When he looked downfield, he found Muhammad getting past Eugene Wilson across midfield. The pass hit him in stride at the 35. Wilson caught Muhammad at the 15, but a well-placed stiff-arm sent him sprawling, and the 85-yard touchdown play was on the books as the largest gain from scrimmage in Super Bowl history. The Patriots of 2003 were an unlikely team to achieve this dubious distinction, as throughout the regular season and the playoffs they had not allowed an offensive touchdown of more than 30 yards. In this game, though, they had just been dunned for their third. Up by only one, Fox's decision to go for 2 this time was a no-brainer, but the attempt failed when Delhomme's pass sailed over Kevin Dyson's head.

After Johnson's 29-yard return to the New England 32, Brady led the Patriots on a short-gain march just past midfield. On first and 10 from the Carolina 47, Givens lined up opposite Manning wide right and tossed him to the side to get open. He was knocked out of bounds at the 25 for a gain of 22. Three plays later, the two hooked up again, this time for 18 yards down to the 3. For second down, linebacker Mike Vrabel lined up on the left end and cut across the middle just inside the end zone. The cross caused two Panther defenders to collide, leaving Vrabel free to take Brady's pass for the go-ahead score.

For the 2-point conversion, offensive coordinator Charlie Weis called for some nifty misdirection as a quick snap went directly to Faulk while Brady pantomimed the ball going over his head. Faulk went right up the gut for the deuce, giving New England a 29–22 lead with just 2:55 left on the clock.

Kevin Faulk: It was something we practiced all the time, never knowing when it could come up.

Troy Brown: That's Tom's favorite play: a direct snap to Kevin Faulk.

The Patriots' drive had taken 11 plays and consumed 4:05 off the clock. In spite of having over 1,300 multipurpose yards during the season and playoffs, the conversion marked the first points Faulk had scored all year.

The injury bug that had plagued the Patriots throughout the season was now in evidence again. Eugene Wilson was out, and by the two-minute warning, Rodney Harrison would be, too. Steve Smith's excellent kickoff return was halved when Lester Towns was called for holding. It was Carolina's 12th penalty of the day, but it didn't matter. Jake Delhomme executed a drive that exorcised all the demons that had plagued him in the first quarter.

On first down, Foster caught a 9-yard reception, then ran for 7 yards to the 36. Harrison made the tackle and immediately realized he had broken his arm. The Panthers were in hurry-up mode, though, so he didn't have time to get off the field. When Delhomme hit Muhsin Muhammad and he crossed midfield, it was Harrison who pushed him out of bounds at the New England 45, exacerbating his injury. The two-minute warning finally got him off the field for some proper medical attention.

Back from the break, Delhomme nailed Proehl at the Patriots' 25 and he took it down to the 15. Fox called time-out and, in hindsight, it might have served the Panthers' needs better if they had let the clock run. On third and 8, the Patriots blitzed and found themselves reliving a nightmarish moment from their recent past. Delhomme threw a timing pass and, for the second time in three years, Ricky Proehl had tied a Super Bowl against them with under two minutes to play.

New England then caught a huge break when Kasay pushed the kickoff out of bounds. It was a case of the game-tying drive being *too* efficient, and that, combined with the poor kickoff, left the Patriots 68 seconds and three time-outs to get the ball close enough for Vinatieri to ice another one.

Adam Vinatieri: At that point I had three years of watching Tom Brady do his thing. He had done it in the past, so I knew we had a good chance.

Joe Andruzzi: It was déjà vu from Super Bowl XXXVI. We had more time on the clock than in New Orleans. Our offense knew what needed to be done.

Willie McGinest: When we got the ball in our hands we didn't worry about anything.

Nick Cafardo: No matter what, if there was more than a minute left, you thought Brady could do it. I've never seen a quarterback who makes better use of the clock than he does. The level of his awareness—knowing exactly what he has to do to get it done—is incredible. How often does a quarterback get that done? Brady does it all the time. It's routine. He doesn't have to think about it. He had 1:08 left and the ball at the 40: *come on!*

Brady hit Brown for 13 yards on second down and called his team's first time-out. On the next play, Brady went right back to Brown and hit him. He had pushed off, however, and the penalty not only negated his 20-yard catch but pushed the Patriots back nearly to their starting point. Looking at a first and 20 from their own 43, Brady went to Brown again, this time for 13.

Dan Koppen: I looked up and saw him go up there with one arm and make that catch and it was like, "Oh my goodness!" In that situation, it drives everybody forward. If you look up the definition of New England Patriot, Troy Brown's picture will be there.

A short pass to Graham brought the ball to the 40 with 15 seconds to go and the Patriots expended their second time-out. Now New England was running out of downs, seconds, and time-outs.

As he had nine times previously that evening, Brady found Deion Branch in space and nailed him. Branch had gotten between coverage on the right side. As he tried to get out of bounds, Branch was knocked to the ground by Minter, forcing the Patriots to take their last time-out.

Out came Vinatieri. "If you got to have one kicker with everything on the line, he's the guy I want kicking it," said Belichick after the game.

Willie McGinest: The big story of that game was that they had a prolific pass rush—a number of guys that could get to the quarterback. Our offense took so much heat leading up to the game. They'd get asked, "How are you guys going to stop their D line from penetrating?"

Joe Andruzzi: We knew they were a tough team, though. We knew we were a good offensive line and we had to go out there and do our best.

Willie McGinest: Well, they didn't give up any sacks, and the offense were able to move the ball a lot. Tommy is Tommy; he's going to create that magic and do his thing. We had all the confidence in the world. Once we got the ball to where we needed to be for Adam to go out there—nothing is for certain, but I liked our chances.

Adam Vinatieri: When you're in a Super Bowl, you don't want to have negative thoughts, but since my second kick had been blocked, I was going into this one at zero for two.

Christian Fauria: The last thing I was thinking about was Adam. I wanted to make sure I got my block. I was concerned with blocking the edge. Once I knew I was secure, *then* I turned and watched.

Kevin Faulk: With Vinatieri kicking, bet the house on it.

At that point the Panthers, following the script that has become standard in the NFL, called a time-out just as he was lining up to kick. Although there is no evidence that this gambit does anything more than force broadcasters to freestyle while everyone stands around waiting for the restart whistle to blow, teams continue to do it. To build some drama, Greg Gumbel pointed out that the only place Vinatieri had ever missed an indoor kick was in this very building.

Finally, the unnecessary delay came to an end. The Patriots' regular long-snapper, Lonie Paxton, has spent more than a decade with the Patriots and missed only six games due to injury. Unfortunately, those included the postseason of 2003.

Adam Vinatieri: [After Paxton got hurt] Brian Kinchen had to come in on short notice to be our snapper. It was a difficult situation to say the least, but everyone did a nice job. The snap and hold was perfect on that last one. It was a tough situation for a guy like Brian

Kinchen to come in a couple weeks before the playoffs and have to pick up the slack. It was tough on him, but everything worked out well.

Kinchen, who had accidently cut a finger on his snapping hand earlier on Super Sunday, whipped the ball back to Walter, who set the ball down. Vinatieri planted and swung through it with his powerful right leg and banged it home from 41 yards out. The tie was broken!

Troy Brown: Mr. Clutch again. Made himself a lot of money playing football.

With :04 on the clock, the kickoff was going to be the last play. When the Panthers dropped back both Smith and Smart, one would be forgiven for assuming they were either setting up for some razzle-dazzle or, at the very least, a desperation rugby-style lateral-fest. Instead, Smart took the kick at the 2 and headed directly up the right side into traffic, where he was swarmed under at the 22.

Willie McGinest: That was definitely one of the most physical games of my career.

Joe Andruzzi: Out of all three Super Bowls, that was the hardest one. It was also the most physical game I ever played. We left it all out there. I was sore for a week or two after the game; I was feeling every play.

Nick Cafardo: It was one of most exciting games you'll ever see. It built up to a crescendo. It was fun to watch the quarterbacks go back and forth exchanging touchdowns and all the great catches. Everybody brought their "A" game in the second half. The way it was going, you had no idea how it was going to end up.

Adam Vinatieri: I had never been body-slammed by anyone, but Tedy Bruschi picked me up and crushed me on the ground. I guess he laid me down pretty soft, but he ragdolled me pretty bad. When I think of that game, I think of big Tedy giving me a big hug and slamming me.

Kevin Faulk: The feeling is different each time. You didn't get there the same way; you did it with different people and situations.

Christian Fauria: No matter what, you're always going to have "Super Bowl Champ" in front of your name.

APPENDICES

Shutout Losses by Championship Teams

No eventual champion ever started a season with a louder thud than did the 2003 Patriots. They traveled to Buffalo to face a Bills team featuring recently released safety Lawyer Milloy and their former quarterback Drew Bledsoe, whom they had beaten twice the year before, in his first season away from the team. On the first play from scrimmage, defensive tackle Sam Adams dumped Tom Brady for a 9-yard loss. From that point on, he and the Bills defense harassed and hurried Brady into throwing four interceptions. One of them was returned by Adams for a touchdown, making the score 21–0 in the second quarter. Brady was eventually benched in favor of Rohan Davey in what would be his only appearance of the season.

It was not only the worst-ever opener by an eventual champion; this game also remains the worst shutout loss ever suffered by an eventual champion. The 31–0 loss broke a record dating back more than 50 years and one that has barely been approached since. These are all of the blankings experienced by championship teams.

Year	PF	PA	Champion	Victor
2003	0	31	New England Patriots	at Buffalo Bills
1952	0	28	Detroit Lions	San Francisco 49ers
1960	0	24	Houston Oilers	at Dallas Texans (AFL)
1944	0	24	Green Bay Packers	at New York Giants
1944	0	21	Green Bay Packers	at Chicago Bears
1930	0	21	Green Bay Packers	at Chicago Bears
1974	0	17	Pittsburgh Steelers	Oakland Raiders
1937	0	14	Washington Redskins	Philadelphia Eagles
1946	0	14	Chicago Bears	at New York Giants
1933	0	10	Chicago Bears	at Boston Redskins
1934	0	9	New York Giants	at Detroit Lions
1934	0	6	New York Giants	at Philadelphia Eagles
1927	0	6	New York Giants	Cleveland Bulldogs
1950	0	6	Cleveland Browns	New York Giants

Year	PF	PA	Champion	Victor
1933	0	3	Chicago Bears	at New York Giants
1932	0	2	Chicago Bears	Green Bay Packers

The Bears' loss in 1932 came in the fourth game of the year, on the heels of three consecutive 0–0 ties. They would go on to set the record for most ties in a season with a 7–1–6 record. The next year would be the first that the NFL scheduled a championship game, and the Bears were in it, getting payback from the Giants for giving them one of their two shutout losses of 1933. The '34 Giants were also blanked two times and are the only championship team other than the '03 Patriots who were whitewashed on opening day.

The other team to lose by shutout twice in a season was the 1944 Packers, who have two of the six worst shutout beatings ever suffered by title-winning teams. In the first one, Sid Luckman was given shore leave by the Navy to play against Green Bay, and the Bears quarterback responded with two touchdown passes and scored a third via rush. Two weeks later, the Packers' high-flying passing attack was whitewashed again as the Giants stymied Don Hutson and prevailed 24–0 in front of 56,481 at the Polo Grounds. Those would be their only two losses in '44, as they would have their revenge against the Giants in the Championship Game, beating them 14–7 in a return to New York.

In fact, half the teams on this list went on to beat the team that shut them out later in the same season. Another five had already beaten the shutout team earlier in the season. Only the '27 Giants, '34 Giants, and '52 Lions could not claim a same-season victory against the team that zeroed them out.

The Most Consecutive Seasons with 10 or More Victories

The Patriots began something in 2003 that few teams have accomplished: winning in double figures for as many as eight years in a row. In fact, only 13 have managed the trick as many as five seasons in a row, although it was just about impossible to do in the first 40 years of pro football because of the shorter schedules.

It became more likely when the NFL switched to the 16-game schedule in 1978, although a few teams made the list playing 14 games per season. The Miami Dolphins of 1970 to 1975 are one such team. They also have the best winning percentage of all the double-figure-streak clubs listed below. Remarkably, their streak started in just their fifth year of existence, a year after they went 3–10–1. The current Patriots have the second-best winning percentage on this list, all the more impressive because their streak is one of the longest.

Years	Titles*	Team	From	To	W	L	T	Pct.
16	4	San Francisco 49ers	1983	1998	181	63	0	.742
9	1	Indianapolis Colts	2002	2010	109	35	0	.757
9	2	New England Patriots	2003	2011**	114	30	0	.792
7	1	Dallas Cowboys	1975	1981	80	26	0	.755
6	2	Miami Dolphins	1970	1975	67	16	1	.804
6	0	Los Angeles Rams	1973	1978	66	19	1	.773
6	1	Dallas Cowboys	1968	1973	64	19	1	.768
6	3	Dallas Cowboys	1991	1996	70	26	0	.729
5	1	Chicago Bears	1984	1988	62	17	0	.785
5	2	Pittsburgh Steelers	1972	1976	53	17	0	.757
5	0	Philadelphia Eagles	2000	2004	59	21	0	.738
5	1	Washington Redskins	1983	1987	58	21	0	.734
5	0	Philadelphia Eagles	1988	1992	52	28	0	.650

Titles won during this streak only.

**Active streak*

Seven other teams have won in double figures four years in a row. The best winning percentage among the four-year teams was achieved by the 1974–1977 Oakland Raiders, who went 47–9.

New England Patriots vs. Philadelphia Eagles

SUPER BOWL XXXIX
February 6, 2005

	1	2	3	4	F
Philadelphia Eagles	0	7	7	7	21
New England Patriots	0	7	7	10	24

Although it might seem strange to say about the defending champions, the 2004 Patriots were a much improved team over the 2003 installment. They posted their second consecutive 14–2 regular season record, but it did it in more convincing fashion than they had the year before. Playing against a much tougher schedule, New England increased its point differential from 110 to 177. The addition of Corey Dillon did wonders for the running game as the team average on yards per carry rose more than 20 percent. Dillon rushed 345 times for 1,635 yards, good for third in the league. Acquired from the Bengals for a second-round pick, the 30-year-old Dillon broke the team's single-season record for rushing yards and was named to the Pro Bowl.

Joe Andruzzi: When you've got a guy like that behind you, it makes our job easier. I'm not sure what happened in Cincinnati, but he had a bad rap out there. He got here and was a great teammate and knew what he wanted to do and what we were about.

Dan Koppen: Corey was one of those guys that came in and wanted to win—and he came into a locker room that wanted to win for and with him. To see that guy run—and to be able to block for a guy like that and how hard he ran—made it fun.

Dante Scarnecchia: Corey didn't have a whole lot to say about things. He wanted it; took it; and kept sticking it in there. He was a guy our linemen appreciated and liked to block for. If there was an opportunity, he was going to find it. If there was nothing, he'd come out with something anyway. You get him down on the goal line he was awful tough to keep out of the end zone. He was a pleasure to have around here.

Tom Brady had a similar season to 2003. The most noticeable improvement was in the all-important yards-per-throw category, where he jumped from 6.9 to 7.8. For the third year in a row, he threw about twice as many TD passes as interceptions.

Dan Koppen: [Offensive coordinator] Charlie Weis and Tom Brady were on the same page. Tom wasn't afraid to bounce ideas off of Charlie, and Charlie, being the coach, wasn't afraid to tell you what he thought. He demanded a lot out of his players, but he demanded a lot out of Brady more than anybody else. He wasn't afraid to yell when things weren't going well. Sometimes the meetings weren't fun. One thing about Charlie, he could call plays. You had trust in what he was doing.

With Deion Branch missing seven games due to injury, Brady's favorite targets were David Givens (56 catches) and David Patten (44). Patten was fifth in the league in yards per reception with 18.2. Of tight end Daniel Graham's 30 receptions, seven were for touchdowns. Patrick Pass, Kevin Faulk, Troy Brown, and Christian Fauria were viable targets as well. Linebacker Mike Vrabel repeated his Super Bowl offensive-touchdown trick not once but twice during the season.

Adam Vinatieri had a career year in 2004, which is saying something. He missed only two field goals in 33 tries, both from beyond 40 yards. His 93.9 percent success rate led the league, as did his 141 points. For the second time in his career, he was named All-Pro.

On the other side of the ball, Tedy Bruschi followed up his outstanding 2003 season with another fine outing, being named to the Pro Bowl for the first time in his career. Strong safety Rodney Harrison anchored the backfield, but cornerbacks Ty Law and Tyrone Poole were limited to seven and five games respectively. Asante Samuel and Randall Gay stepped into their shoes. There was turnover on the line from 2003. Both Bobby Hamilton and Ted Washington departed for Oakland. Rookie Vince Wilfork and veteran Keith Traylor handled the nose tackle spot in place of Washington, and Hamilton was replaced by second-year man Ty Warren.

Dynasty talk was becoming common, and with it one began to hear about something called "the Patriot Way."

Troy Brown: "The Patriot Way" just means do your job. Whatever is required of you, you do it. You don't worry about the next man's job or what's being said outside of your team and your organization. You just worry about yourself and what's going on with your football team and that's it. It's not a very difficult thing to design. Basically, do your job and stay humble. Say very little and do your job.

As defending champions, the Patriots were chosen to kick off the 2004 season and, naturally, drew a team designed to make for an interesting game.

Joe Andruzzi: Coming back, we knew it wasn't going to be easy. The league is going to want a tough match. They want a rivalry renewed: It's going to help the league. Once again we had to face Peyton Manning and the Colts and his firepower offense. It was a Thursday night game, in prime time. We also knew they had those good pass rushers, Dwight Freeney and Robert Mathis. We put together a good team and we were able to triumph again—but we knew we'd see them again.

Andruzzi and his line mates held the Colts to one sack, and Brady threw for 335 yards and three touchdowns as New England got past the Colts, 27–24. Four more wins followed, extending the team's regular-season winning streak to 17 and tying the record set 70 years earlier by the Chicago Bears. That record fell the following week when the Patriots bested the Jets 13–7. It wouldn't be on the books for long, however. Four years later, New England would break its own record with a 21-game winning streak that spanned late 2006 to early 2008.

A 19th straight win was never a possibility as the Steelers broke out on top 24–3 in week seven and never looked back. The 34–20 loss helped determine where the AFC title game would be played. It was also a bad day for the defensive backfield, who then had to worry about the next game against the Rams.

Troy Brown: Ty Law went down in the Pittsburgh game and we were looking like we were falling apart. How were we going to get past St. Louis? They weren't a great team anymore, but they were still the St. Louis Rams playing at home. They still had Isaac Bruce and Marshall Faulk. Bill's defensive plan was that I was going to play defensive back if somebody went down. And wouldn't you know it, Asante Samuel went down on the second play of the game and I had to go in there on defense. I was nervous as hell because I had to guard Isaac Bruce and Torry Holt and all these fast guys. I had a big target on my back. They came right after me. They tried to brush me off with some crossing routes. I dropped a couple of interceptions that hit me in the face, but we held them and were able to come out of there with a win. I inherited some more confidence from my teammates and my coach because I didn't want to give up any plays in that game; it was great. And I did catch a touchdown pass from Adam Vinatieri in that game!

That fake field goal play put the Patriots up 26–14 in a game they would eventually win 40–22 going away. Brady threw for two touchdowns, including one to Mike Vrabel, and Vinatieri hit on four field goals.

Now New England really began to take it to their opponents. They outgained the Bills 428 to 125 and beat them by 23. After a close one against the Chiefs, Bethel Johnson took the opening kickoff in Cleveland for a 93-yard touchdown ride, which soon became a 21–0 lead after two Corey Dillon touchdowns. The 3–8 Browns were no match for the Pats, eventually falling 42–15. Their only other misstep came two weeks later on a Monday night in Miami when they allowed the 2–11

Dolphins to erase an 11-point lead with under four minutes left to play. With Miami trailing 28–23, an ill-advised pass by Brady was intercepted, giving the Dolphins a shot at the winning touchdown on the New England 21, which they eventually got on a fourth-and-10 play with 1:23 to go. It was the first time in 32 games the Patriots had lost a game they led at halftime. Since they had already clinched the division, the game's cost appeared to be a shot at home-field advantage throughout the playoffs, although that proved to be moot when Pittsburgh ran the table and finished 15–1.

The Pats closed out the regular season with tune-up wins over the Jets and 49ers and spent the first week of the playoffs waiting to see who their opponent would be in the divisional playoffs. It turned out to be the Indianapolis Colts, a team that hadn't won on its last eight trips to New England dating back to 1994, including the previous year's AFC Championship. That was all in the past, though. What really mattered was the Colts' offense, which was easily the best in the NFL. They'd scored 522 points on the season, topping 40 points six times, including their 49–24 trouncing of Denver in the wild-card round of the playoffs.

Richard Seymour, Ty Law, and Tyrone Poole were all sidelined with injuries. This was good news for Manning and his talented trio of receivers, Marvin Harrison, Reggie Wayne, and Brandon Stokley, who caught 231 passes between them. For his part, Manning had the single best passer rating ever at 121.4. Working in the Patriots' favor, however, was the snow, which was damp and plentiful. The Patriots kept the Colts in check all day. Pro Bowler Edgerrin James was held to just 39 yards, and while Manning completed 27 passes, he was limited to less than six yards per attempt, a far cry from the 9.2 he'd racked up in the regular season.

Nick Cafardo: That was an incredible defensive performance. They had it all together. They were always a great defense, but that game was almost ridiculous. That's the only word I can use to describe it.

"Our game plan was to keep them on the sideline and do what we do best, which is run the football," said Patrick Pass after the game. The Pats' first scoring drive, for instance, consumed nine minutes. Corey

Dillon rolled up 144 yards on 23 carries and the defense held one of the highest-scoring teams of all time to a single field goal. It is, in its way, one of the more impressive victories of the Belichick era.

The Steelers, meanwhile, nearly capped their 15–1 season with a playoff loss to the Jets. They battled to tie the game at 17 in the fourth quarter and then held their collective breath as New York kicker Doug Brien missed two field goals in the waning moments of regulation, allowing Pittsburgh to walk off with the overtime 20–17 victory.

The AFC Championship matched two teams on incredible runs. Including the playoffs, the Steelers had won 15 straight and the Patriots had won 30 of their last 32. It was a testament to New England's reputation that they were favored even though they were on the road against a team on an extended winning streak that included a nifty takedown of the Patriots themselves.

The line makers were right. Ben Roethlisberger, coming off one of the best rookie seasons ever for a quarterback, was pressured into three interceptions by the Patriots, who hung him with the first loss of his career. Eugene Wilson had two of the picks and Rodney Harrison helped put the game out of reach when he returned an interception 87 yards for a touchdown in the second quarter, making the score 24–3. Brady was an efficient 14 for 21 for 207 yards and two touchdowns.

The Patriots had qualified for the big game by beating the two best teams in the league and were now in line to become the seventh team to win back-to-back Super Bowls.

THE EAGLES

The 2004 season marked the fifth consecutive season the Eagles made the postseason, and the fourth straight time they won the NFC East. Their previous four trips to the playoffs had ended in defeat, including three consecutive losses in the NFC Championship Game. The 2002 and 2003 exits were especially frustrating for Eagles fans, who saw their team lose home games in both years and score just 13 points in the two games combined.

Now in his sixth year as head coach, Andy Reid had taken over a team that Ray Rhodes had left in dire straits. Reid had cut his teeth as a college assistant for a decade before joining the Green Bay Packers as an offensive assistant in 1992. By 1997, he had been promoted to assistant head coach under Mike Holmgren. When he was hired by the Eagles in 1999, he had never been a head coach anywhere. Any doubts about his ability to lead were erased when he took a 3–13 team and cut 100 points off its scoring differential in the first year and had them in the playoffs by the second.

The NFC had a down year in 2004; few teams managed a positive point differential, and AFC teams bested them 44 games to 20 in interconference play. As the one truly good team in the conference, the Eagles plowed through this inferior competition. They didn't lose until week nine, and that was to the AFC's Steelers. They ran their record to 13–1, but started resting regulars in weeks 16 and 17 and lost their last two games to St. Louis and Cincinnati. Quarterback Donovan McNabb threw three passes against the Rams and didn't play at all against the Bengals.

In the playoffs, Philadelphia had no trouble pushing aside the Vikings, a team that had gone 8–8 in the regular season. For the third straight year, the Eagles were hosting the conference title game, and their opponent this time was a team that had outscored its opponents by only 3 points during the season, the Atlanta Falcons. Michael Vick and his mates Warrick Dunn and T.J. Duckett had rushed for 327 yards against the Rams in the first round of the playoffs, but the Eagle defense held them to just 99 on a frigid afternoon. McNabb had an efficient passing day and, for one of the few times all season, showed a willingness to get out of the pocket and run around like he had earlier in his career. The Eagles took an early lead and pulled away in the second half, getting to the Super Bowl for the second time. Their first trip came after the 1980 season, and resulted in a loss to the Oakland Raiders. They had last been NFL champions in the Patriots' inaugural season, beating the Green Bay Packers in the 1960 title game, 17–13.

The rise of the Eagles coincided directly with the arrival of Donovan McNabb, now playing in his sixth season. In 2004, though, he took his game to a new level, setting personal highs in touchdown passes, passer rating, and yards per throw. He had an outstanding 31:8 TD-to-interception ratio and would make the Pro Bowl for the fifth straight year. His favorite target was former 49er Terrell Owens, who caught 77 passes for 1,200 yards and 14 touchdowns. Fortunately for the Patriots, he had been lost in the 14th game of the season and was done for the year—or at least, so everyone, including his doctors, seemed to think. McNabb's other favorite target was Pro Bowler Brian Westbrook, who caught 73 passes for 703 yards, both of which led all NFL running backs. In addition, he gained 4.6 yards per carry when handed the ball. Tight ends L.J. Smith and Chad Lewis got plenty of action, while wide receivers Todd Pinkston and Freddie Mitchell had excellent yards-per-reception numbers. Pinkston ranked third in the league and Mitchell ninth, although those numbers mask the fact that neither was highly regarded in Philadelphia. The offensive line was anchored by Pro Bowler Tra Thomas and veteran tackle Jon Runyan.

On defense, the Eagles had two of the best backs in the league in left corner Lito Sheppard and safety Brian Dawkins. Sheppard had returned two interceptions for touchdowns and Dawkins had regained his powers after an injury-shortened 2003. Both were named All-Pros. On the left end of the line was former Titan Jevon Kearse. He had crashed the league with a bang five years before, running up 36 sacks in his first three seasons before being felled by a broken foot in the 2002 opener. He had come to the Eagles as a free agent with a record-breaking monster contract and, while he was not the one-man wrecking crew he had been when he first came into the league, he was still a force that needed minding on the outside.

Another Eagle whose best years were behind him but who still commanded respect was middle linebacker Jeremiah Trotter. Serving his second stint with the team after signing with the Redskins as a free agent, he was named to his third Pro Bowl for his 2004 efforts. Relegated to special teams in the early part of the season, he was reinstated as a starter in week 10, and it took the Eagles defense to a new level. On the whole, Philadelphia allowed the sixth-fewest yards per play on defense and tied with the Patriots with the second-fewest points allowed (260), albeit against much weaker competition than New England faced.

A third dimension the Eagles brought to the ballpark every Sunday was an outstanding special-teams unit. *Football Abstract* noted that it was good from year to year, whereas most top units did not stay on top for more than a season at a time. Like the Patriots' Larry Izzo, the Eagles'

Ike Reese was named to the Pro Bowl for his special-teams play. In David Akers, Philadelphia had a Pro Bowler and one of the most highly regarded kickers of his generation. His matchup with Adam Vinatieri marked the first time since Super Bowl II that both teams in the title game had Pro Bowl kickers, although the events of the game would render this auspicious matchup nearly moot.

THE GAME

One of the bemusements of the two-week runup to the Super Bowl was the status of Terrell Owens. He'd had two screws and a plate put in his damaged ankle six weeks before and, in spite of a lack of clearance from his surgeon, was insisting he was going to play in the big game.

"I got the best doctor that anyone can have," Owens told the *New York Times*. "That's God."

For their part, the Eagles resented the perception that they had no chance without Owens.

"T. O.'s a great player, no doubt about it, but to throw it in our face like without him we're chopped meat, that's not the case," said Eagles tackle Corey Simon.

Pundits might have been talking like that, but the Patriots certainly weren't. "You know, T. O. is not the whole team," said Asante Samuel. "They have gotten this far in the playoffs without him, so we are not going to worry about one player. We are focused on the whole team."

Still, New England was leaving nothing to chance. Said Rodney Harrison, "We're putting our game plan in regardless of whether T. O. plays or not. We're not going to change anything if Terrell Owens plays. I'm preparing as if he's going to be a major factor in the game."

In the end, Owens would play and play well.

The other great distraction was provided by a different and much less notable Eagles wide receiver, Freddie Mitchell. What he lacked in talent he more than compensated for with heaping doses of self-love. He is probably the only player in NFL history who had more self-bestowed nicknames than catches.

The grandfather of Super Bowl trash talking was Fred "The Hammer" Williamson, who spent the two weeks leading up to the very first

Super Bowl letting everyone know he did not fear the mighty Lombardi Packers. The difference between Williamson and Mitchell was that Williamson had proven himself a ballplayer of some merit. Mitchell, on the other hand, was a first-round pick who was widely considered a bust. In an interview with Dan Patrick, he repeatedly dissed the Patriots' secondary by feigning ignorance of their names. It only served to stir up a team that normally carried itself with comportment.

Rodney Harrison: As a football player and as a man you don't disrespect anybody. You don't call me or my teammates out because we work hard.

Rosevelt Colvin: I think some of it had to do with Freddie Mitchell ensuring he got his fifteen minutes of fame. That was his mentality, to talk. The problem was, he was talking to Hall of Famers and other good ball players. They take that stuff to heart.

Troy Brown: I don't know what Freddie was dealing with. He was trying to make a name for himself, I guess, but we were ready for him. He made a point to call me out. Down in Jacksonville, I sought him out, and he called me over to the car and was talking smack to me. I said to him, "We'll see you on Sunday."

Willie McGinest: Then you have Freddie Mitchell running off at that mouth, talking about what he was going to do. This was a guy who had been insignificant the whole year. We had heard they had already set up for the parade. All that stuff made us angry; like pouring gasoline on a fire. Made us want to go out and physically dominate them and hurt them and do everything we could in our power to win. Once all that stuff started coming out, there was no way we were going to let them beat us.

Rosevelt Colvin: All the things that Freddie Mitchell said created a small fire that was going to explode—and it didn't help his team.

Rodney Harrison: We were cool and it took a lot for me to humble myself and not respond to any of that. He was directly responsible for us raising our game. That was all the ammo that we needed. From a motivational standpoint he was solely responsible for us getting that victory.

Dan Koppen: Trash talking does you no good. You can talk and say what you want, but what really matters is what happens on Sunday. If you want to waste your energy, so be it. The guys in our locker room didn't care: We just wanted to play.

The other big story was that both of New England's coordinators were leaving after the Super Bowl. Romeo Crennel was in serious talks with the Cleveland Browns to become their head coach (a move that became official after the Super Bowl), and his offensive counterpart, Charlie Weis, was already slated to take on the head-coaching job at Notre Dame.

These moves were not seen as distractions, however, but rather as a natural progression of things. It only stood to reason that the men who had helped build a program as successful as New England's would be given the opportunity to run their own.

THE FIRST QUARTER

It was a clear night in Jacksonville, Florida's Alltel Stadium, with temperatures in the mid-fifties. At 6:38 P.M. local time, Adam Vinatieri put the boot to the ball and Roderick Hood gathered it in at his own 7. He went right up the middle for 32 yards to the Philadelphia 39, putting the Eagles in a good place to start their first possession. It didn't take long for the Patriots to announce they were going after McNabb. On the first play from scrimmage he was flushed from the pocket by a rampaging Willie McGinest and threw the ball away. On second down, the effectiveness of Owens was tested in game conditions and he quickly showed that, hardware in his foot or no, he was going to be a factor. Going in motion from left to right, he caught a short pass in the flat for 7 yards and seemed none the worse for wear.

On third and 3, Tedy Bruschi burst in on McNabb unimpeded and hit him a glancing blow that was hard enough to knock him to one knee. McNabb maintained his balance, though, and kept playing. The Patriots' hopes soared when he was then stripped by McGinest and lost the ball to Bruschi. Andy Reid challenged on the basis that McNabb was down, and the replays showed conclusively that he was, so the Eagles avoided an early issue.

Willie McGinest: McNabb presented some unique challenges to us because of his mobility. We knew they had a lot of weapons, but we came out in a totally different defense and they didn't know what to do.

So as to better contain McNabb, the Patriots had switched from a 3–4 base defense to a hybrid 4–3.

Ty Law: We'd been doing things like that all year long. You never knew what we were going to do and I think you have to give credit to Belichick and Romeo Crennel for that. We were always looking forward to coming in on Wednesday and getting the game plan and seeing what we were going to do that week. We had that much versatility and that much depth. Everyone knew how to play a multitude of positions. A lot of teams go out there and they play pretty much the same package, but we didn't have a true identity with the New England Patriots. Our base defense is wherever we're going to play this week. To play on our defense you needed to have as much brains as you did brawn.

Starting from their own 28, New England's first play from scrimmage resulted in a 16-yard pass to Deion Branch as he picked up where he had left off in Super Bowl XXXVIII. The most memorable thing about the play, however, was the spectacular block that Corey Dillon made on Jeremiah Trotter as he made a speedy beeline for Tom Brady. Dillon caught Trotter at full clip and sent him into the air, allowing Brady to hit Branch. After that, the Patriots went three and out, as did the Eagles on their next possession after being buried at the 7 by a beautiful Josh Miller coffin-corner punt.

The next time the Eagles got the ball, they finally got their initial first down of the day when McNabb dumped off a pass to Brian Westbrook good for 14 yards out to their own 40. L.J. Smith got them another first down with a nifty sliding grab out in the right flat. After a short pass to Westbrook put the Eagles in New England territory, McNabb found Owens going across the middle at the Patriots' 45 with room to run. He was pushed out of bounds at the 17, but Rosevelt Colvin was flagged for a late hit, bringing the ball to the 8-yard line.

With the Eagles knocking hard on the door, Colvin got immediate atonement for the unnecessary-roughness call by bursting through the line and forcing McNabb to retreat. By the time he was hauled down by Mike Vrabel, he had lost 16 yards on the play. McNabb responded by going straight to the end zone, lofting a pass to Owens on the right side. Rodney Harrison stepped in front of it and tipped the ball to Asante Samuel, who brought the ball out to the 32. It was for naught, however, as Roman Phifer was flagged for illegal contact. The Eagles were now reloaded with a first down at the 19. McNabb went to the other side this time, looking for Westbrook.

Vince Wilfork: We knew Donovan was going to take some shots down field. We wanted to contain him if not sack him. We knew if the ball was in the air for a long period of time, we had guys who could get it. We knew we had to capitalize on it and we did.

His pass was wobbly and seemed to die in midflight.

Rodney Harrison: I saw Westbrook spread out in the backfield and I saw that Bruschi was on him. I knew Donovan would take that match-up, so I ran to Westbrook and Donovan threw it. I *knew* he was going there. It was the most instinctual play I ever made. I came down with it.

Harrison was wrestled down at the three by veteran tight end Jeff Thomason, who was making his only appearance of the season, having been signed to a one-game contract just for the Super Bowl.

Rodney Harrison: To me it was my greatest play. I left the middle of the field and Belichick wanted to kick my butt for it, but I knew Donovan was going there and that's when I said to myself, "Trust your instincts." I made a huge play.

The Patriots' offense continued to sputter, and the Eagles got the ball back with excellent field position when Westbrook ran Miller's punt across midfield to the Patriots' 45. On first down, McNabb went for the gold, lofting one out to a streaking Pinkston at the 5. He overshot the mark, and the ball went right through the hands of Randall Gay. On second down, the Eagles tried play action, but when McNabb couldn't find anyone open, he took off to his right. Finding himself in space against Harrison, he tried a shoulder juke, but the Pats' safety didn't bite, and cut McNabb's legs out from under him. On third and 11, three New England defensive backs combined to make an excellent play. L.J. Smith caught a pass over the middle, 8 yards past the line of scrimmage, where he was grabbed and held by Harrison. While he struggled to break free, Randall Gay came up on him and popped the ball out, and Eugene Wilson recovered the fumble.

Rodney Harrison: I knew they were short for the first down. I just hit him and tried to hold him up and waited for my troops to rally and they did. I held him up and put him in position where other guys could tee up and knock his brains out or strip the ball from him, and Randall came and stripped the ball and it ended up being a huge play for us.

For the second year in a row, the first quarter had ended without a score.

THE SECOND QUARTER

The second quarter began with Brady getting dumped on third down for an 8-yard loss, with defensive end Derrick Burgess getting the sack. Miller came out for his fourth punt of the young game, already more than his per-game average during the regular season. This one was a boomer, putting the Eagles all the way back at their own 19.

On third and 8, Cunningham targeted Pinkston in the middle distance for 17 yards. Two plays later, the two hooked up again, only this time Pinkston had to make an impressive midair grab to take the ball right out of the waiting hands of Randall Gay. He fell to the turf at the

Patriots' 17. On the next play, Westbrook went around the left end and down the sideline for 11 yards. Two plays later, McNabb hit a diving L.J. Smith in the middle of the end zone.

Now trailing 7–0, the Patriots started from their own 13. They got moving when Brady threw two identical screen passes to Dillon, the first good for 13 yards and the second for 16. They immediately switched to the ground game, and Faulk totaled 13 yards on two carries to put the ball in Eagles territory. Brady then threw a quick slant to Givens coming from the left. He eluded a tacked at the 40 and was brought down at the 32, losing the ball to cornerback Sheldon Brown. Belichick challenged the call, though, and replays showed that Givens's knee was on the ground while he was still in possession.

Corey Dillon then tore off a 27-yard run that involved a lot of improvisation. When he got jammed up on the left side, he broke back toward the center. Troy Brown made a nice block on Sheldon Brown to open the field, and Dillon carried Brian Dawkins the last several yards before finally succumbing at the 7. It had been a near-perfect drive to that point, but it was about to end in futility. On second down, Brady and Faulk got crossed up on a handoff and the ball hit the ground. Brady almost seemed to have it under control, but Jevon Kearse fell on him and the mad scramble was on. When the wreckage was cleared, Eagles tackle Darwin Walker popped up with the ball.

The Patriots' defense negated the turnover in short order, swarming over everyone who dared touch the ball. The possession died when McNabb was chased from the pocket and threw away a short pass to avoid a sack. The ensuing punt by Dirk Johnson went no farther than the Eagles' 41, a 27-yard kick that Troy Brown returned four yards.

The drive that followed was ruthless in its efficiency. Brady completed five of six passes, the last of which was to Givens, who had gotten wide separation from Lito Sheppard on the right side of the end zone for the tying score.

The follow-up kickoff proved costly for New England. As J.R. Reid sped upfield on a nice return, Eugene Wilson extended his arm into the return man's churning legs, bringing him down. Unfortunately, it also broke Wilson's arm, putting him out of the Super Bowl for the second straight year.

THE THIRD QUARTER

The only other time a Super Bowl had been tied at halftime was after the 1988 season, when the 49ers and Bengals were locked at 3–3 in Super Bowl XXIII.

The Patriots' opening drive of the half pretty much boiled down to two men: Brady and Branch. They connected on passes of 8, 27, 15, and 21 yards to bring the ball down to the Eagles' 2-yard line. The wideouts retreated to the sideline, and in trotted Mike Vrabel. With Christian Fauria in motion, Vrabel was lined up on the left end, just as he had been the previous Super Bowl. He slipped through the charging Eagles line and cut to the left midway into the end zone as Jevon Kearse dropped back on coverage. Brady soft-tossed the ball and Kearse was all over Vrabel, poking him in the face—which drew a flag but did not break Vrabel's concentration. As Kearse fell away, Vrabel reached up and tapped the ball into the air with his right hand. He kept his eye on the ball and came down with it, cradling it as Quintin Mikell tackled him. It was not graceful, but it worked, and the Patriots had their first lead of the day, 14–7.

Things really seemed to be going the Patriots' way when the Eagles were held on their next possession and Troy Brown made a magnificent punt return that involved six changes of direction and ended at the Eagles' 40 yard-line. It was all for naught, though, as the ball was brought all the way back to the New England 8 because of a holding call. New England stalled and punted it away, and the Eagles got started at their own 26.

Suddenly, McNabb looked like a different player. He started throwing with authority. Balls were zinging to receivers on a line, not fluttering like moths in the arc lights, as they often had before. He started out by hitting Westbrook for 15 and then Owens for 8. Westbrook did some damage on the ground and Greg Lewis caught a 12-yarder. Then Westbrook did a nice job reaching back for a pass that went where he'd been instead of where he was going and pulled it in, giving the Eagles first and goal at the 10.

McNabb saved his best pass for the last play of the drive. While falling backwards, he drilled one right over the middle to Westbrook, threading the needle between Vrabel and Dexter Reid for the touchdown.

With the score now 14–14, Belichick was not pleased. NFL Films captured him going to his bench like a school principal and addressing members of the defensive unit in a firm but mildly perturbed tone.

"Look, let's spend a little more time focusing on our jobs and less time jawing and pushing them, okay? Just do our job and get on to the next play."

After Bethel Johnson brought the ball out to the Patriots' 34 with a 26-yard return, New England got things moving. Brady went back to the screen, this time dumping it off to Faulk, who worked his way for 13 yards. The quarter drew to a close after two nice runs, the first by Dillon for 9 yards and the second by Faulk for 8. New England was on the Philly 28 to start the final quarter.

THE FOURTH QUARTER

In two more firsts, no Super Bowl had ever been tied at the conclusion of each of its first three quarters, and no Super Bowl had ever been tied heading into the final quarter. As the curtain rose on the fourth, the Patriots seemed determined to make short work of that deadlock. The first play was a give to Faulk, who exploited a gaping hole in the line created by center Dan Koppen and right guard Stephen Neal for a 12-yard gain. On first and 10 from the 16, Brady looked to his left and then swiveled his head the other way and dumped the ball off to Faulk on a screen. He very nearly took it all the way; he tried to leap over Lito Sheppard while extending the ball inside the goal-line flag with his arm. Faulk was ruled out at the 2, setting up the next play, in which Dillon powered his way through Brian Dawkins and on into the end zone for the 21–14 lead.

Philadelphia's first play from scrimmage came at their own 22, and the Patriots' pass coverage was excellent. While McNabb had all kinds of time to throw, he couldn't find an open man and eventually made a low pass at Dorsey Levens's feet. It's probable that the old McNabb would have taken off with the ball under the same circumstances. On second down, Rosevelt Colvin fought off a block from Tra Thomas, got into the backfield, and hauled down Westbrook for a 6-yard loss. On third down, McNabb aired one out to Greg Lewis, but overthrew him out of bounds.

Bethel Johnson got the Patriots into Eagles territory with a 14-yard punt return. On second down, Deion Branch made his 11th catch of the day (which tied the Super Bowl record), a crafty piece of work in which he grabbed the ball away from Sheldon Brown in midair.

Joe Andruzzi: Branch is such an impact guy. He is a great route runner, and he fit our offense perfectly. He has a great relationship with Tom. He fit perfectly into the offense, which helped him become Super Bowl MVP.

Dante Scarnecchia: He's a guy that can get open and he and Tom were on the same page. There was cohesiveness between those two guys and it manifested itself in that game.

The play was good for 19 yards, which became 34 when Corey Simon was called for roughing the passer. (In Simon's defense, the hit did not seem especially late or egregious.) Corey Dillon churned up 12 yards on the next two plays, bringing the ball to the 4-yard line. With just over 10 minutes on the clock, the Eagles were going to have to dig in if they didn't want the game to get completely out of reach.

And that's just what they did, snuffing runs by Pass and Dillon, sandwiched around a pass that was knocked away by safety Michael Lewis. After three plays, New England was still at the 4, and Vinatieri was brought on to stretch the lead to 10.

Adam Vinatieri: The time you take an extra point or a 23-yard field goal for granted is the time that you miss it. I literally try and take every kick the same. You don't know if that is going to be the difference in the game. I look at it as every time I step on the field, I have to be perfect. I have to do my job every time. I don't get 50 plays. I don't get another chance: I either make it or that's it.

How would the Eagles respond? On second down, Terrell Owens made a catch-and-run that brought two things to mind: It made one wonder if he really had all that metal in his foot, and it also reminded everyone why so many teams have put up with all the baggage he carries. The play started with him going into the right flat and catching a short pass in front of Randall Gay. He then stopped on a dime, spun, changed direction, and shot down the field for a 36-yard gain. In a flash, Owens had put the Eagles at the Patriots' 36-yard line and given them hope with 7:27 still left on the clock.

When McNabb dropped back to pass on first down, Tedy Bruschi mirrored his drop-back on the other side of the line, falling back and camping out in the middle of the field. He never took his eyes off the Eagle quarterback, watching him all the way as he released a wobbly pass that was intended for L.J. Smith cutting over the middle. The ball floated over Smith's head and Bruschi had it all the way, hauling it in at the 24.

The script called for a long, grinding drive, but the Philadelphia defense had other ideas, holding Dillon to 5 yards on two carries and pressuring Brady into a quick throw and incompletion on third down. Punter Josh Miller came through with a long, high one, and deep man Lito Sheppard had no choice but call for a fair catch at the 21, some 50 yards from the point of origin.

There then followed one of the most perplexing possessions in Super Bowl history—perplexing, that is, to everyone but fans of the Eagles. For them, it was like watching their own deaths in slow motion. Trailing by two scores, McNabb and the Philadelphia offense played as though it was the opening drive of a preseason game. They sauntered out of huddle breaks and made no effort to get back to the line at the ends of plays.

Willie McGinest: The Eagles did not go hurry-up, which was kind of a shock to us. Maybe they were confident that they were going to score anyway. We didn't try and figure it out. We played what was thrown at us.

Dan Koppen: I don't know why they were going that slow. We actually had time to watch it on the big screen. We were saying on the sidelines, "Take your time."

Rodney Harrison: I looked at Bruschi and was like, "What the hell are these guys doing? They are playing like they have all day." He laughed and said, "Good for us." I laughed with him, but I couldn't believe it. I'm like, are they serious? I had to look at the clock again and wonder if we were doing something wrong. I thought they knew something we didn't know. I was totally surprised.

Rosevelt Colvin: They didn't want to give us a chance, having the greatest clutch kicker, to win the game, and they may have been trying to use up as much time as possible so they could win. They felt like they had enough time, I think.

Vince Wilfork: When they took their time we knew they were kind of screwed.

The Patriots seemed willing to let them have what they wanted underneath, so the Eagles were moving forward, but at too great an expenditure of time. Owens made a nice catch on a third-and-8 play to give them a first down, and the drive also included the last catch of Freddie Mitchell's short, loud NFL career.

By the two-minute warning, the Eagles had traveled to the New England 30, covering 50 yards in three minutes and 40 seconds. An indication of how much time they were burning is that the drive included three incompletions and a successful challenge, not to mention Owens getting out of bounds on his first-down catch, so there had been numerous stoppages. Coming back from the break, Richard Seymour nearly picked off McNabb at the line of scrimmage, but did succeed in batting it away. Then McNabb hurled one into the end zone and a leaping Greg Lewis came down with the ball making it a 24–21 game.

Andy Reid had to call for the onside kick. If the Eagles could come away from it with the ball, then their dawdling on the previous possession would be of no consequence. They'd be in great field position with two time-outs and enough time to get in field goal range if not more. If the Patriots recovered the kick, however, the Eagles would have to expend their time-outs and hope for a staunch defensive stand. Still, their odds lengthened considerably if the Patriots came away with the ball. If they'd showed some urgency on the previous drive, their situation wouldn't have been so dire.

When Akers popped the kick in the air, it was Christian Fauria who made a clean grab of it, nestling the ball at the Philadelphia 41. Three rushes by Faulk into the line produced little yardage but succeeded in making the Eagles use their final two time-outs. With 55 seconds on the clock, Josh Miller dropped a perfect pooch punt at the Philadelphia 15, where it hit and bounced slowly into the waiting arms of his team-mate Dexter Reid, who downed it at the 4.

McNabb was now operating out of his own end zone and getting harassed. He was able to avoid a safety at the hands of a hard-charging Richard Seymour on first down by dumping the ball off to Westbrook near the line of scrimmage. Given that he was surrounded by white jer-seys, Westbrook's best bet would have been to let the ball drop. Instead, he caught it for a 1-yard gain but a big expenditure of time. McNabb's second-down pass to Owens was off target, skidding harmlessly to the ground at the 25.

There were now 17 seconds left on the clock and the Eagles were a good 55 to 60 yards from the outer limits of Akers's range. This time, McNabb took a shotgun snap in the end zone and tried to connect with L.J. Smith down the middle at the 25. The ball was overthrown, however, and Smith just got his hands on it with a fully extended, twist-ing leap.

Rodney Harrison: I knew they felt the safeties were deep and we were outside. Donovan looked to the outside to try and make me bite. I knew he was coming back inside and I was just there.

It tipped right into to Harrison at the 28. He was tackled by, of all people, his pregame tormentor, Freddie Mitchell.

Rodney Harrison: I just said, "Thank you, big mouth!" He didn't say anything. During the game, the Eagles were very arrogant flapping the wings, but it felt good that they knew we were a better team than them.

Joe Andruzzi: We knew it was going to be tough again, but to be able to triumph and hold that trophy up again for the third time in four years . . . what an unbelievable stretch for us.

Troy Brown: And who makes the kick to win the game for us by three points? Adam Vinatieri. It wasn't a buzzer beater, but it won the game for us.

Romeo Crennel also recounted an end-of-an-era moment that took place after the game. He told *USA Today*, "Bill, Charlie and I huddled on the field. That kind of lets you know it was over and it was the last time we were going to coach together. It felt kind of different. A little strange. But if you have to go out a winner at the Super Bowl, that's a really special feeling."

"I'd like to take my hat off to Charlie and Romeo," Belichick said to the Associated Press. "I'm extremely grateful to them. They're two of the best coaches I've ever been around, and it's been a pleasure to work with them."

To a man, the coaches and their players would turn aside any post-game questions that asked them to define the team as dynastic.

"We've never proclaimed ourselves anything. It's not our style," Brady told *USA Today*.

"We've never used that word, but three out of four ain't bad," Charlie Weis added. "When you're doing it, you don't think about what you're doing. When you're talking about dynasties, you're talking about teams from 10 or 20 years ago. Maybe in 10 years people will be talk about this team that way."

Willie McGinest: I was blessed. I played against and with a lot of great guys and played for some really dynamic coaches. It was a lot of hard work, dedication, sacrifice, and commitment. Being around guys who were like your brothers, having coaches that understood you and brought guys that fit in with you—I think the stars aligned right for me. I have no regrets for my 12 years there. I think the one thing a player wants is to retire someplace, and that didn't happen, but I have no regrets. I had a ball. I've done things there multiple times that some players never get to do in their careers. I played the game the way it was supposed to be played. I respected the guys I played against. I respected everybody. I respected the logo. I was fortunate I played with a lot of great players, and they made my game better.

APPENDICES

The Biggest Mismatches in Super Bowl History

It has been the fate of the Patriots to have all seven of their Super Bowl appearances qualify for the table below, which shows the biggest on-paper mismatches in Super Bowl history. SRS stands for "Simple Rating System," a tool in use at pro-football-reference.com that assigns a number to teams based on their point differential and strength of schedule. It is a quick and dirty way to separate teams of divergent quality while taking into account the usual inequities of scheduling.

One thing to remember is that all of the low teams on this list, with the exception of the 1968 Jets, won at least two playoff games to get to the Super Bowl. So, while their regular-season performances were a good indication of their true quality heading into the playoffs, they might not necessarily paint an accurate picture of where that team was by the time they reached the big game.

In their first three Super Bowl appearances, the Patriots ran into teams of heightened historical merit. The '85 Bears are always in the conversation when people discuss the best team ever. Eddie Epstein names them number one in his book *Dominance: The Best Seasons of Pro Football's Greatest Teams.* He picked the Patriots' next Super Bowl opponent, the '96 Packers, as the sixth best of all time. His choice for 10th best was the 1999 Rams, and he wrote that the 2001 version—the Pats' Super Bowl XXXVI opponent—was even better but did not qualify for his best-of list because it included only champions, and the Patriots did away with them in the Super Bowl.

For New England's next four appearances, the shoe was on the other foot; yet all three of the lesser teams gave the Patriots all they could handle.

Is SRS foolproof as a predictive tool? Of course not, but note that the high team did win eight of the nine most egregious imbalances, the exception being of special infamy to Patriots fans.

Season	SB #	SRS Difference	High Team	SRS	Low Team	SRS	Result (High Team)
2007	XLII	16.8	New England Patriots	20.1	New York Giants	3.3	Lost
1991	XXVI	13.0	Washington Redskins	16.6	Buffalo Bills	3.6	Won
1979	XIV	12.5	Pittsburgh Steelers	11.9	Los Angeles Rams	−0.6	Won
2008	XLIII	11.7	Pittsburgh Steelers	9.8	Arizona Cardinals	−1.9	Won
1999	XXXIV	10.9	St. Louis Rams	11.9	Tennessee Titans	1.0	Won
1996	XXXI	10.2	Green Bay Packers	15.3	New England Patriots	5.1	Won
1985	XX	10.1	Chicago Bears	15.9	New England Patriots	5.8	Won
1975	X	10.1	Pittsburgh Steelers	14.2	Dallas Cowboys	4.1	Won
1968	III	10.0	Baltimore Colts	17.9	New York Jets	7.9	Lost
2001	XXXVI	9.1	St. Louis Rams	13.4	New England Patriots	4.3	Lost
1994	XXIX	8.0	San Francisco 49ers	11.6	San Diego Chargers	3.6	Won
2003	XXXVIII	7.8	New England Patriots	6.9	Carolina Panthers	-0.9	Won
2011	XLVI	7.7	New England Patriots	9.3	New York Giants	1.6	lost
2004	XXXIX	7.2	New England Patriots	12.8	Philadelphia Eagles	5.6	Won
1983	XVIII	7.1	Washington Redskins	13.9	Los Angeles Raiders	6.8	Lost

The Best Four-Season Runs in History

Below are all the teams that managed to play at .800 or better for a consecutive run of four seasons, along with their playoff records and the number of titles they won in that period. There is a pretty good spread of teams across the history of pro football represented here, except for more recent times. It appears to be getting harder to maintain excellence. Consider that only one of these teams—the 2004-2007 Patriots—played after 1990, although the 2007–2010 quartet of New England seasons just missed the cutoff, coming in at 51–13 and 797.

Team	From	To	W	L	T*	Pct.	Playoffs W	L	Titles
Chicago Bears	1940	1943	37	5	0	.881	4	1	3
Miami Dolphins	1971	1974	47	8	1	.848	8	2	2
Chicago Bears	1939	1942	37	7	0	.841	3	1	2
Oakland Raiders	1974	1977	47	9	0	.839	6	3	1
Cleveland Browns	1950	1953	40	8	0	.833	2	3	1
Oakland Raiders	1967	1970	45	8	3	.830	4	4	1**
Green Bay Packers	1929	1932	44	8	3	.827	0	0	3
Chicago Bears	1985	1988	52	11	0	.825	4	3	1
Oakland Raiders	1966	1969	45	9	2	.821	3	3	1**
New England Patriots	**2004**	**2007**	**52**	**12**	**0**	**.813**	**8**	**3**	**1**
Minnesota Vikings	1973	1976	45	10	1	.813	6	4	0
Decatur/Chicago Staleys/Bears	1920	1923	37	7	4	.813	0	0	1
Miami Dolphins	1982	1985	43	10	0	.811	6	4	0
San Francisco 49ers	1987	1990	51	12	0	.810	7	2	2
Green Bay Packers	1960	1963	43	10	1	.806	2	1	2
Baltimore Colts	1967	1970	43	9	4	.804	5	1	1

Ties are counted as half wins.

**AFL title. Lost Super Bowl II.*

New England Patriots at New York Giants

December 29, 2007

	1	2	3	4	F
New England Patriots	3	13	7	15	**38**
New York Giants	7	14	7	7	**35**

Had the New England Patriots lost this game to finish the season 15–1 and then beaten the Giants in Super Bowl XLII, there would be little to counter the boast that they were the greatest team of all time. Both games against the Giants were won by the same margin, and if they had simply been reversed, perception throughout history would have been forever altered, in spite of the blemish on the regular-season record. Instead, the Patriots' consolation prize is to have played the greatest regular season ever. If the NFL owners ever get their way and expand the schedule to 18 games, the already overwhelming odds against having a perfect season would only increase, making it very likely that the 2007 New England Patriots have played the last perfect schedule in pro football history.

THE PATRIOTS

In the two seasons since their last Super Bowl victory, the Patriots were finding out what the 49ers discovered before them in the NFL and the Atlanta Braves and latter-day New York Yankees had realized in baseball: You can make the playoffs every year, but you can't always be a champion. New England won the division both seasons, going 10–6 in 2005 and 12–4 in 2006. They lost in the divisional round of the playoffs in 2005 to an excellent Denver Broncos team and were bested in an AFC Championship Game barn burner by their archrivals, the Colts, in 2006. After an off year in '05, the New England defense had rebounded to post one if its best performances ever. The defense would hold its own in 2007, but it was the offense that was about to blast off to previously unimagined heights.

One of the keys to this improvement was the acquisition of wide receiver Randy Moss from the Oakland Raiders for a fourth-round draft choice. Moss had made his NFL debut with a similar high-flying offense, the 1998 Minnesota Vikings, a team that rung up 556 points, the most in NFL history through 2006. He had been named All-Pro three times in Minnesota, but after two years of nagging injuries and doubts about his interest level in Oakland, he was deemed expendable. As good as he'd been during his first six years as a Viking, what he and Tom Brady managed to do in 2007 eclipsed all that.

Another key acquisition was made when the Patriots sent two draft picks to the Dolphins for Wesley Welker, a receiver who would thrive in his new environment.

Dan Koppen: When those trades were made, it was like, "Oh boy— let's see what we can do with this!" We brought two great weapons into an already confident group and instantly we had that much more confidence in the offensive unit. It was fun.

Vince Wilfork: The type of talent we had on offense with a quarterback like we had, what can you get out of it? And you saw: A league MVP who broke passing records and Randy Moss, you saw what he did.

Rodney Harrison: We were practicing against these guys and we'd look over on the offensive side of the ball and we'd be like, "Wow, that's Randy Moss. Wow, that's Wes Welker. There's Kevin Faulk." We had weapons all over the place. And Tom Brady was so happy. He was like a kid at a toy store. He could pick out each toy he wanted and play with each toy. It was kind of amazing to go out there and practice against these guys. It made our defense better because we were going up against what ended up being the best offense in the National Football League. It was easier to face other teams knowing we had to face Welker, Moss, and Ben Watson in practice. I was excited about it, so you can you imagine how excited Tom Brady was about it.

For the first half of the 2007 season, the Patriots didn't just beat their opponents, they destroyed them. Their offense played as though they'd come down from a higher league, treating the NFL like some backwater developmental roster farm. New England won games one through eight by an average of 26 points, with the lowest margin of victory being 17. They were so dominant in winning their first eight games that they trailed only one time, a 7–3 deficit to Buffalo in week three that barely lasted into the second quarter.

In the second half of the season, they were more human, having to sweat out a few games, make some comebacks, and generally not see their enemies run before them as they had in the first half of the campaign. In week nine, they had their first close game in a much-anticipated showdown with the Colts, who were also undefeated. Indianapolis went up 20–10 with just under 10 minutes to play, but Tom Brady drove the Patriots to two touchdowns for the win. It would be the first and only time New England was outgained in the regular season. For one week they went back to annihilation mode and got their largest margin of victory of 2007, a 56–10 thrashing of the Bills in which Brady and Moss connected for four touchdowns.

Rodney Harrison: Belichick had us so focused and he had us what I would call "brainwashed." We didn't look ahead; we just looked at winning the next game. Each week after we'd beaten a team by 25 or 30 points, he'd show us all the negative plays. That was his way of keeping us humble and telling us we can always play better. One thing he preached that season was finishing. We were criticized for blowing people out and keeping our starters in, but he wanted to teach us to finish playing sixty minutes of football.

Vince Wilfork: We had a chance to do something special, but we didn't think about going undefeated. We thought about the big goal. We put our heads down. Bill was so tough on us every week—it was like a training camp every week, and we kept winning. We did a good job of blocking out everything. We went in, did our job, and went home.

There then followed two close calls. In week 12, the Eagles were 20-point underdogs, in part because they were reduced to using their backup quarterback, A.J. Feeley. With nothing to lose, they took a lot of chances and led 28–24 after three quarters before New England finally prevailed in the fourth. The 4–7 Baltimore Ravens then gave the Patriots their toughest game of the season, in inclement weather and with Don "Perfect Season" Shula sitting in the stands. Baltimore led 24–17 late in the fourth quarter, and appeared to stop the Pats on consecutive, game-deciding fourth-down plays. But each time, fate intervened: One play was nullified by a time-out called an instant before the snap, and the second by a defensive penalty. Given one last chance, the Patriots offense did what they'd done with ruthless efficiency all year: getting into the end zone. New England won it 27–24 with 44 seconds to go on a Brady–to–Jabar Gaffney touchdown pass that had to be reviewed.

Things eased up again for the next three weeks as they dispatched the Steelers 34–13, the Jets 20–10 (their lowest point total of the regular season), and the lowly Dolphins, 28–7. All that stood in the way of a perfect season was a visit to New Jersey to play the 10–5 Giants.

Heading into week 17, New England stood on the cusp of several offensive records. If Brady and Moss could connect on two scoring passes against New York, they'd become the most prolific touchdown passing combo in history. Brady's 48 TD passes (against just eight interceptions) were just one shy of the 49 Peyton Manning had thrown in 2004; and Moss's 21 touchdown catches were also one shy of Jerry Rice's record set in 1987, although Rice set the record in 12 games because of the strike that season. The team itself was just 6 points away from breaking Moss's Vikings' record for the most points ever in a season, although one record that was out of reach was the one for most points on a per-game basis, held by the 1950 Los Angeles Rams. In order to break it, the Patriots would have to score 70 points against the Giants, and that simply wasn't going to happen.

The juggernaut offense produced some impressive individual statistics. In addition to the Brady/Moss touchdown pass bonanza, Wes Welker led the NFL in yards after completion while catching 112 passes.

Combined with Moss's 98, they were one of the most productive receiving tandems ever. Kevin Faulk caught 47 passes out of the backfield, and Laurence Maroney averaged 4.5 yards per carry after taking over for the injured Sammy Morris, who had been equally proficient. The Patriots landed three offensive linemen in the Pro Bowl: left tackle Matt Light, left guard Logan Mankins, and center Dan Koppen. Moss and Brady were also so honored.

The defense was led by nose tackle Vince Wilfork and a group of veteran linebackers, including future Hall of Famer Junior Seau. The Pats D scored six touchdowns of their own and allowed the fourth-fewest points in the NFL. They were sixth in passing yards allowed. (Considering the leads they had in many games, it's surprising they didn't allow more junk passing yards.) Left cornerback Asante Samuel and left outside linebacker Mike Vrabel joined Wilfork as Pro Bowl selections.

Now in his eighth season as head coach of the Patriots, Bill Belichick had amassed an impressive 90–37 regular-season record through week 16 of the '07 season, and his Patriots teams was also 12–2 in the postseason through 2006. In 2007, Belichick had seemingly done the impossible: He had assembled a better team than the clubs that went 17–2 in consecutive years in 2003 and 2004. His was not a season free of controversy, however. Few stories in recent NFL history attracted more attention than the Patriots getting caught videotaping the Jets' signals prior to their season opener.

"Spygate," as it was called, personally cost Belichick a half-million dollars in the form of a fine from commissioner Roger Goodell, and was the result of a Patriots camera operator getting caught taping the signals of the Jets coaches prior to their first game of the season. Former Patriots defensive coordinator Eric Mangini, who had left in a bitter endgame to become the head coach of the Jets, became a public enemy in New England for his role in turning Belichick in. Like the Watergate scandal that inspired its name, it was an unnecessary breaking of the rules. Richard Nixon had the 1972 election sewed up without whatever intelligence was gained by breaking into the national headquarters of the Democratic Party. Likewise, the 2007 New England Patriots were good enough that they didn't need to resort to chicanery to succeed. As it turned out, the Patriots had been taping opponents' practices as a matter of course during the Belichick era. In his apology, Belichick insisted that he thought he'd been acting within the parameters of the rules and that he had never used the tapes to gain an unfair advantage. On this much, at least, NFL commissioner Roger Goodell agreed. Still, he fined Belichick $500,000 and the Patriots organization half that much. He also took away their first-round 2008 draft pick.

THE GIANTS

Tom Coughlin was in his fourth season with the Giants after building the expansion Jacksonville Jaguars from scratch. He had previously served a stint with the Giants as their wide-receivers coach from 1988 to 1990 at the same time Belichick had been New York's defensive coordinator. Coughlin was a notorious rules-and-regulations guy who had decided to soften his approach in 2007. He created an executive players council with whom he conferred regarding decisions that affected the rank and file.

New York had made the playoffs the previous two seasons, but bowed out in the first round both times, and they were headed back there again in 2007, having overcome a rough start and a dodgy patch in midseason to secure a wild-card berth. The Giants attack was led by Eli Manning, playing in his fourth year since being the first player named in the 2004 draft. Installed as the team's starter midway through his rookie year, he demonstrated many of the typical symptoms of a young quarterback who is required to come of age on the job. Consequently, he became a lightning rod for the frustrations of the fans and media who grew tired of watching him make ill-advised throws (he led the league in interceptions thrown in 2007 with 20) and occasionally lose his composure.

Manning's main target was Plaxico Burress, a veteran receiver who was so banged up that he did not attend practices until the final week of the season. His only time working with Manning came during pregame warm-ups. With that, they were able to connect 70 times for 12 touchdowns. It wasn't Brady to Moss, but it was fairly remarkable given the circumstances. Manning's other go-to wide receiver was Amani Toomer, the Giants' all-time leader in reception yards. Tight end Jeremy

Shockey caught 57 passes before being felled by injury and had been replaced by rookie Kevin Boss. The Giants' main running back was Brandon Jacobs, a man who would have been the biggest player in the NFL throughout most of its early history. At six-four and 255 pounds, he proved an effective force moving through the line, averaging 5.0 yards per carry.

New York was ranked 17th in the NFL in points allowed, with 351. Not all of that was on the defense, however, as 37 of them were scored while the offense or special teams were on the field. They allowed the seventh-fewest yards from scrimmage in the league. Their D line was a strength, with Michael Strahan and Osi Umenyiora especially effective coming off the ends. Third-year man Justin Tuck improved steadily as the season wore on. The unit was led on the field by middle linebacker Antonio Pierce.

The Giants' season started 0–2. The defense had given up 80 points in those first two games, and the New York media was calling for everybody's heads. When they fell behind the Redskins 17–3 at halftime in week three, it seemed as though the team was on a one-way trip to nowhere. In the second half, the New York defense shut down the Redskins, including a heroic, game-saving goal-line stand on first and goal from the 1-yard line in the fourth quarter. Meanwhile, the offense scored 21 unanswered points to record their first win of the season. Five consecutive victories followed and, after a bye week following their trip to London to play the Dolphins, the Giants were 6–2, good for second in the division behind Dallas, at 7–1.

From that point forward, there was no telling which Giants team would show up. They lost to the Cowboys for the second time again and just got past a fading Lions team, 16–10. Then came the low ebb of the season. The 4–6 Vikings came to town with one of the worst pass defenses in the league. All they did was run back three interceptions for touchdowns and beat the Giants 41–17. It was at this point that fan and media confidence in Eli Manning, which was never rock solid to begin with, dropped to perhaps its lowest point.

The Vikings debacle was followed up by a stirring 21–16, come-from-behind win in Chicago in which Manning led two fourth-quarter touchdown drives. They followed up with a win over Philadelphia, but came out flat against the Redskins and lost 22–10. In week 16, needing a win to clinch a playoff spot, the Giants traveled to Buffalo and quickly fell behind the Bills 14–0 before rallying for the win.

Rodney Harrison: I knew we would see a good Eli. Special players have a tendency to get up for big games.

Vince Wilfork: We felt Eli Manning was an average quarterback. He's not Tom Brady. He's not Peyton Manning. He's not Drew Brees. That night he looked like Tom Brady. He looked like Peyton. For some reason, he got it together from the last regular season game to the Super Bowl; he looked like a different quarterback. He carried that team and they walked away with the W. He got the job done.

THE GAME

We expect Super Bowls and conference championships to deliver drama. After all, they're designed with that in mind. But when a regular-season game rises above its station as just one of the 256 games on the ledger, isn't that more exciting in its own way?

With a playoff spot already clinched and many of their fans supposedly scalping tickets to Patriots rooters who wanted a chance to see their team go 16–0 in person, the Giants geared up for the final Saturday night of the season. While there was some concern in the media that Patriots fans were going to turn Giants Stadium into their house, the Giants players joked that they welcomed the opportunity to play another "road game."

"We play well on the road," Giants nose tackle Barry Cofield told the *New York Times*, referring to their 7–1 away mark, "If this is going to be Foxborough South for a week, we'll get through it."

Giants coach Tom Coughlin made the decision to play his starters. He later wrote, "Yes, it is a bit unusual to have an undefeated team as an opponent. Even so, it is a difficult decision. It becomes clear that the media and fans care about a playoff game and therefore don't want our first-teamers to play. But I feel differently."

The Giants players were all behind their coach's decision. They were in agreement with guard Rich Seubert, who said simply, "I wanted to be the team to beat them."

Justin Tuck: We were going to play them toe to toe. We knew they were going for history, and we wanted to make history by beating them.

Michael Strahan: I think there were two plans. Obviously, we weren't gonna go into the game with a big game plan about stopping the Patriots, because we didn't want to give away what we were gonna do in the playoffs to Tampa Bay, our next opponent. But we *were* gonna go into that game with a solid game plan and we were gonna play hard. And for us, it was a challenge, because they asked us [and we told them], "Of course we want to go play. We want to be the team that beats them. We don't go out there to roll over and give them a perfect season. I don't want those guys to be perfect. Are you kidding me? Bragging rights, man."

Vince Wilfork: There was no way in the world you sit back and relax. You can't do that. When history has a part in something, you had to let it play out. We play football for a living: let us keep this going.

Rodney Harrison: When you step on that field, you represent what you are about—not just the organization and the team. When you go out there, you go to compete—you don't go out there to lay down for anybody.

Michael Strahan: We went into that game with the mentality that we were out there to win. The Patriots weren't gonna pull their players; they were playing for something—so we were gonna play for something, too.

Dante Scarnecchia: I mean this as a compliment to the Giants: Neither team had anything to play for; their fate was cast and so was ours, yet they wanted to beat us as badly as we wanted to beat them. It came down to who was going to blink first. The desire to win the game was so strong on both sides. What a tribute to both teams.

Dan Koppen: We didn't publically announce it, but we wanted to keep winning to have an opportunity to get to sixteen-and-oh. It didn't wear on us, though, because our preparation level was out-standing. We practiced to win.

One thing that was not going to be a factor at the Meadowlands: the weather. In spite of it being the dead of winter, it was a beautiful, clear evening with temperatures in the mid-forties at kickoff. Another thing that soon became apparent: While this game would have no impact on the standings, it gave off the electricity of a playoff contest. When Eli Manning unloaded a 50-yard bomb to Plaxico Burress on the Giants' second play from scrimmage, the stadium erupted. It was an early sign that this game was going to live up to its promise.

Three plays later, Burress got the Giants another first down at the Patriots' 8-yard line. On second down, Manning went from the shotgun and spotted a pass to a slanting Jacobs. He was hit at the four by Tedy Bruschi and again at the two by Rodney Harrison, but managed to extend the ball across the goal line. It was 4:01 in and the Giants led 7–0.

Being perfect was not going to be easy.

Brady came out throwing, hitting Moss and Welker for 14 yards apiece before things slowed down, leaving the Patriots with a fourth and 2 on the Giants' 37. Unlike a lot of coaches, Belichick has always understood that a play like this is a worthy risk, because the chances of success are good and the downside of failure is not devastating—especially with a defense like New England's. Moss pushed off on Sam Madison, but it was apparently not flagrant enough to warrant a flag, and Brady drilled him for five yards and the first down.

With the Giants jamming up their running the game, the Patriots stuck to the air, but when tight end Ben Watson dropped his second pass of the night and Moss was blanketed in the end zone so that Brady had to throw it away long, they settled for Stephen Gostkowski's 37-yard field goal.

When the Patriots got the ball back via punt later in the quarter, the Giants defense had them on the ropes, sacking Brady on third and 14 for an 8-yard loss. New England was given new life, however, when Corey Webster was called for illegal contact downfield, so the sack was wiped from the books. It was then that the New York fans got their first real glimpse of the Patriot machine. Operating exclusively from the shotgun,

Brady nailed Donté Stallworth for 13 and then threw a flare to Welker, who was sprung by a Randy Moss block and made it 19 yards. Two plays later, he threw short to Faulk, who worked his way down to the 6 for a first and goal. At the tail end of the play, Moss was jacked up but good on a hit by safety Gibril Wilson, and had to be guided off the field.

After yet another run for minimal gain, Moss returned at the start of the second quarter and was Brady's target on the right side of the end zone, where he had gotten free of his entanglement with Aaron Ross. With this one catch, the Patriots broke the '98 Vikings record for most points, while Brady was tying Peyton Manning and Moss was doing same for Rice. Such was the Patriots' excitement, however, that a flag was thrown for excessive celebration, a penalty that would have immediate ramifications.

Now kicking off from his own 15, Gostkowski booted the ball to Domenik Hixon, who took it at the Giants' 26. Nobody touched him. Running right up the middle, he found a seam in the Patriots' coverage, broke left, and soon found himself in a footrace with the kicker, a race he won by 10 yards. The Giants were now up 14–10 as a good game just kept getting better.

The Patriots got their running game untracked while Brady was on a 12-completion streak. This led to 3-point payoffs on their next two possessions, with Gostkowski making good from 45 and 37 yards respectively. So successful had the Patriots offense been at capitalizing in the red zone that this was only the second time all season that Gostkowski had been called on to try as many as three field goals.

Now trailing 16–14, the Giants started from their own 15 with 1:54 to go in the half. In the five games leading up to this, Eli Manning appeared to be regressing as a quarterback, his comeback against the Bears notwithstanding. He'd lost four fumbles, thrown eight interceptions and only four touchdown passes, and had a 51.6 passer rating over that period. On this drive, though, he looked like a new man. He went straight to the shotgun and skillfully moved New York down the field. A falling, juggling catch by Amani Toomer was one of the key plays of the drive, as he atoned for an earlier drop. On the possession, Manning was 5 for 7 for 69 yards and ran for 11 himself. The capper was a 3-yard TD strike to tight end Kevin Boss, his fourth catch of the night. The half ended with the Giants leading 21–16, only the second time all year the Patriots were trailing at the midway point.

THE SECOND HALF

Dante Scarnecchia: Brady said, "I'm not coming out of this game."

Dan Koppen: When we'd clinched in years past, the starters got a rest. When our starters were still in after halftime, that's when we knew it was going the full length. It was when I realized it: This is for keeps.

The Pats started the third quarter with their first three and out of game. Brady did well to elude a hard-charging Reggie Torbor on third down, looping a pass downfield that Moss very nearly plucked off his shoe tops. Had he been able to hold on, it would have been one for the highlight reel. Still, it showed Brady's courage under fire and ability to improvise.

The Giants started from their own 40 and switched the aerial focus of the previous drive to the ground attack. Brandon Jacobs blasted through the line and amassed 35 yards on three carries. He was load enough hitting the line, but taking down his massive frame in the open field was a real chore. On third and 9 from the New England 19, the Giants put two receivers wide right. Asante Samuel moved up to cover the underneath route, leaving Plaxico Burress momentarily alone on the right side of the end zone. Manning hit him perfectly as Eugene Wilson arrived too late to stop the catch-and-foot-drag by Burress.

With 9:12 to go in the third quarter, the Patriots were looking at their greatest deficit of the season: 12 points. When reserve linebacker Gerris Wilkinson, filling in for Kawika Mitchell, who had gone out earlier with an injury, burst into the Patriots backfield and upended Kevin Faulk on first down, the crowd became even more energized. They started up the famous Giants "dee-fense" chant, which dated back to 1956 and which only grew louder when the next play produced just a handful of yards on a swing pass to Faulk.

And then Brady quieted the throng. With four straight completions, three of them to Wes Welker, he moved the Patriots 55 yards to the red zone. On second down from the 14, Wilkinson, who had started the series with such promise, was on deep coverage in the end zone against Randy Moss in something of a mismatch. Brady let fly, and Wilkinson never turned around. If he had, he may well have had a drive-busting pick, but instead the ball hit him in the back of his arm while he made contact with Moss, a sure way to get flagged.

Now with first and goal at the 1, the Patriots dusted off their old favorite, the Mike Vrabel goal-line play, only to be flagged themselves for an illegal formation. Brady reloaded from the 6 and handed off to Maroney, who went into the end zone standing up, thanks to a sealing block that Welker threw on safety James Butler.

The Giants went nowhere on their next two possessions, sandwiched around a Patriots series that ended on their own 28.

With 11:29 to go in the game, Brady stood to in the shotgun at his own 35-yard line. After an incompletion to Welker, he stepped back on second and unloaded a long one down the right side to Randy Moss. A few minutes earlier on the NFL Network telecast, the always astute Cris Collinsworth had just commented that the Patriots had had at least one pass play of more than 40 yards in every game so far but didn't have one against the Giants. With Gibril Wilson having fallen down on coverage and Moss standing all by himself at the 15, this appeared to be the play that was going to keep that streak alive. The throw was short, and Moss had to stop his momentum and take a step back toward Brady to catch it. As Patriots fans stood on the brink of celebration—everyone around the country knew that this catch would make NFL history, not to mention turning the tide of this critical game—the ball bounced of Moss's outstretched hands, kicking away to the turf.

On third and 10, Brady showed his confidence in the offense and his precision arm, throwing downfield again, this time with the knowledge that an incompletion would mean they would be forced to punt. This time, Brady's pass hit Moss in stride. Having blown past Butler, who seemed to give up on the coverage, Moss caught the ball at the 22 and eased in for the record-setting touchdown, his 23rd and Brady's 50th. Maroney went up the middle for the 2-point conversion, and the Patriots were back on top, 31–28, now with their names freshly added to the history books.

"I threw it about as far as I could," Brady would say later, "and he tracked it down."

The Giants gave the ball right back to New England when Manning threw into coverage trying to hit Burress on a sideline route and Ellis Hobbs snared it, falling out of bounds at the Patriots' 48. Time was that a team with a lead would siphon off the clock with a sustained ground attack, but that's not what the Patriots did. On first down, Brady stepped up in the pocket and found Donté Stallworth at the New York 35. The game's first sack of Brady only temporarily slowed the New England advance. The Patriots had the fifth-best sack percentage in the league that year, while the Giants defense led the league in sacks. Although they were playing with two subs on the right side of the line, Russ Hochstein and Ryan O'Callaghan, the Patriots were able to keep Strahan, Umenyiora, and Tuck at bay, although the running game continued to get the stonewall treatment. In the air, things were golden. Brady hit on his next four passes, setting up a Maroney touchdown run up the middle from the 5. With 4:36 to go, the Patriots had made it a two-score game.

After another good return from Hixon, New York commenced operations from their own 32. On first down, the tensions of the evening boiled over again and resulted in a 15-yard personal-foul call on Rodney Harrison. Brooking no such nonsense, Belichick immediately sent him to the bench.

Rodney Harrison: He was always talking about holding your composure and discipline, and he would call you out if you played like crap. Everyone got the same treatment and that's what I loved about him.

While the Giants began moving the ball, their use of the clock was reminiscent of the Eagles in Super Bowl XXXIX. After two consecutive completions, Manning let precious seconds go by while he made adjustments over center. On second and 10 from the 27, he found Jacobs in the left flat, but instead of heading out of bounds to stop the clock, the big back lowered his head and went for extra yards.

Manning ran a keeper to get the first down heading into the two-minute warning and came back from the respite with a toss over the middle to the rookie receiver Steve Smith. He caught it at the 14 and went wide to the left to avoid Harrison, now back in the game after his brief exile. Smith got past, but not without Harrison managing to lunge at his feet and get a hand on his ankle, leading to his eventual downfall at the 4. It was a trip-up that saved a touchdown, but what really hurt the Giants was their lack of urgency after the play. Smith hit the ground at 1:53 and the next play didn't go off until 1:22. Like the Eagles three years before, New York was putting itself in a position where the only way they could get the ball back was on an onside kick.

Manning missed Burress on a corner route and then David Tyree fell down after making a catch at the 4, forcing New York to use one of its two remaining timeouts. The Giants, who had done so much to frustrate New England's bid for perfection, were frittering away their chances for a dramatic comeback. Finally, with 1:08 on the clock, Burress broke to the right corner and Eugene Wilson fell down scrambling to cover the ground between them. Burress reached up with one hand and brought down the pass to make it 38–35.

Although Mike Vrabel had not been able to score on his one shot as a tight end, he was about to put his hands to use to ice the game and the perfect season. Lining up 5 yards behind the frontline four on the kickoff, he was in a perfect position to grab Lawrence Tynes's onsides attempt. It was all over but the kneeling.

No less than Don Shula had this to say after the game: "I know firsthand how difficult it is to win every game. And just as we did in 1972, the Patriots have done a great job of concentrating on each week's opponent and not letting distractions interrupt the focus."

Dante Scarnecchia: It was a game that was hyped nationally and it could have been the biggest clunker ever had we both given up and decided not to put our best guys out there. Instead, you absolutely got the best that both teams had to offer. You have one of the greatest games ever played and it came in the last week of the season. That game was special.

Troy Brown: Bringing Randy Moss on board definitely made it fun to watch. Watching his talent up close was just amazing. Having the opportunity to have him on the team was great. He came in wanting to win a championship, with a great attitude. The sheer amount of plays, record breaking, not being in a close game for a long time was a fantastic thing to see.

Rosevelt Colvin: After the Spygate thing, the fines, etcetera, I knew Bill wanted to prove a point to everyone: "I'm the best coach you've ever seen." And what he did with us that year proved it.

Dante Scarnecchia: I've heard the phrase "The Patriot Way," and I don't subscribe to any of that stuff. I just know that every year is different. We try to keep the same approach that we've always kept. We are going to practice a certain way. We're going to be very demanding. We're going to have schemes that fit our players' talents. We will try and get them to understand and embrace our system and ultimately play as well as they can within that system.

Kevin Faulk: Did that season even happen?

APPENDICES

The Best Point Differentials in the NFL Since World War II

No team since World War II dominated its opponents the way the Pats did in 2007, and only one club prior to 1946 put up a better per-game point differential: the 1941 Chicago Bears. Unlike the Pats, however, those Bears lost a regular-season game.

Per Game	Year	Team	Record	Point Differential
19.7	2007	New England Patriots	16–0	315
19.2	1949	Philadelphia Eagles	11–1	230
19.1	1962	Green Bay Packers	13–1	267
18.7	1948	Chicago Bears	10–2	224
18.4	1968	Baltimore Colts	13–1	258
18.3	1948	Philadelphia Eagles	9–2–1	220
17.8	1999	St. Louis Rams	13–3	284
17.6	1969	Minnesota Vikings	12–2	246
17.5	1968	Dallas Cowboys	12–2	245
16.3	1991	Washington Redskins	14–2	261

Where do the undefeated 1972 Miami Dolphins finish in this race? Fourteenth, at 15.3. True, 1972 was a less offensive year than 2007, but the '07 Pats have the best case for having the best regular season ever.

Perfection Denied

As of this writing, more than 1,900 attempts have been made at achieving a perfect NFL (and AFL) season, and the 1972 Miami Dolphins remain the sole team to manage that feat. Fourteen other teams have gone through a full season with but a single blemish on their records, whether it be a win or a tie. Listed here are those teams and the team that inflicted upon them that nonvictorious exception, along with the number of wins they had at the time their perfect season was marred. Two non–NFL/AFL teams did achieve perfection. The 1937 Los Angeles Bulldogs of the second version of the American Football League won all eight of their games, and the Cleveland Browns ran the table on a 14-game schedule in the 1948 All-America Football Conference and then blasted their way to a 49–7 victory over Buffalo in the championship game.

Year	Team	Total Wins	Wins when lost/tied	Spoiler, Score
2007	New England Patriots	18	18	New York Giants, 17–14*
1934	Chicago Bears	13	13	New York Giants, 30–13*
1985	Chicago Bears	18	12	Miami Dolphins, 38–24
1942	Chicago Bears	11	11	Washington Redskins, 14–6*
1962	Green Bay Packers	14	10	Detroit Lions, 26–14
1929	Green Bay Packers	12	10	Frankford Yellow Jackets, 0–0
1984	San Francisco 49ers	18	6	Pittsburgh Steelers, 20–17
1923	Canton Bulldogs	11	6	Buffalo All-Americans, 3–3
1941	Chicago Bears	12	5	Green Bay Packers, 14–6
1945	Cleveland Rams	10	4	Philadelphia Eagles, 28–14
1982	Washington Redskins	12	4	Dallas Cowboys, 24–10
1949	Philadelphia Eagles	12	3	Chicago Bears, 38–21
1976	Oakland Raiders	16	3	New England Patriots, 48–17
1942	Washington Redskins	11	1	New York Giants, 14–7

Indicates loss came in championship game.

Note: The Duluth Kelleys were 5–1 in 1924, losing only to the Green Bay Packers, 13–0.

Acknowledgments

This book would not have been possible without Peter Thomas Fornatale. It was he who introduced us right after Super Bowl XLII and set this all in motion, so it is he who must be thanked first. Pete also did most of the heavy lifting on the Snowplow Game chapter and the chapter on the 2001 postseason. Our editor at Bloomsbury USA, Benjamin Adams, took our original idea and made it into something different and better. We also thank him for his patience and understanding.

We assembled a team of researchers who did some digging for us: R. J. LaForce and Jack Moulds put in the most time, while Kevin Edelson, Mark Collins, Christopher Bond, and Will Moore pitched in as well. Cristina Zizza was our main transcriber and was always quick on the turnaround trigger.

We'd also like to thank our agent, Frank Scatoni of Venture Literary, Inc., for believing in us. Nate Knaebel at Bloomsbury USA came through once again, while Rob Neyer of SBNation.com proved himself an invaluable asset with his expertise and resources. Others who offered insight and assistance include David Schoenfield of ESPN.com, Allen Barra, and Dave Ringel. Raj Sidhu, Ron Marshall, and Scott Griffin were instrumental in getting us Patriots' game tapes.

We owe much to the following people: Dick Johnson and Rusty Sullivan with the New England Sports Museum, Ned Cully of the Gridiron Club of Greater Boston, Stacey James and Aaron Salkin of the New England Patriots, Luke Schanno of the Kansas City Chiefs, Harvey Greene of the Miami Dolphins; Dominick Rinelli of the Buffalo Bills, Tom Yewcic and Steve Thurlow of NFL Alumni, Todd Schmidt and Chris Willis of NFL Films, Bryan Morry of the Hall at Patriot Place, Fred Kirsch of *Patriots Weekly*, Billy Thompson of the Denver Broncos Alumni Association, Jack Grinold, Barbara Rizzo, Amy Palcic, Kirsten

Durocher, Michael Connelly, Mark Linehan, Sean Glennon, Kristen Kelly, Max Lane, Dean Boylan, Chris Wertz, Cathy Helms, Mia Boykin, Roger Homan, Joe Villapiano, and Mark van Eeghen.

Our eternal gratitude is also extended to all of the players, coaches, broadcasters, and writers who were gracious enough to share their recollections with us. A book of this sort cannot exist without the buy-in of these talented people and we were very fortunate to have so many of them participate.

The Voices

Joe Andruzzi: An undrafted free agent out of Division II Southern Connecticut State University, he earned his way onto the Green Bay Packers in 1998 and signed with the Patriots in 2000, becoming a starting guard on all three Super Bowl champion teams. He finished his career with the Cleveland Browns.

Houston Antwine: A six-time American Football League All-Star at defensive tackle, he was a member of the Patriots' famed "Boston Pops" front four. When the AFL merged with the NFL in 1970, he and Tom Sestak of the Buffalo Bills were named as the tackles on the All-Time AFL team. Antwine passed away on December 26, 2011.

Upton Bell: Broadcaster and executive, he had been the personnel director of the Baltimore Colts when he was hired to be general manager of the Patriots.

Raymond Berry: A Hall of Fame wide receiver for the Baltimore Colts. He served as the Patriots' receivers coach from 1978 to 1981 before becoming head coach from 1984 to 1989, compiling a record of 48–39.

Dean Boylan: A member of the Patriots' original ownership group, he is the retired president of Boston Sand and Gravel. He became one of the founders of the team at the recommendation of his lifelong friend former Red Sox center fielder Dom DiMaggio.

Troy Brown: The 198th pick of the 1993 NFL draft, he became known as "Mr. Patriot." He was an impact contributor as a wide receiver/ kick returner/punt returner, and also played as an emergency defensive back in 2004.

Nick Cafardo: A native of Hanson, Massachusetts, he was the *Boston Globe*'s Patriots beat writer from 1996 to 2004 and is one of the most prominent baseball columnists in America.

Gino Cappelletti: The "Duke" has been part of the Patriots organization for virtually its entire half-century history. He was a five-time AFL All-Star and the league's MVP in 1964. With 1,100 career points, he holds the AFL scoring record. He served as a wide receiver/ defensive back/placekicker. He remains the conscience of the New England franchise to this day as the longtime radio color analyst.

Raymond Clayborn: A shutdown career defensive back from 1977 to 1984, he was named to the Pro Bowl three times while setting the team's all-time interception mark with 36. His three kickoff returns for touchdowns in 1977 remains a team record.

Joe Collier: An original member of the Patriots coaching staff, he served as defensive back mentor under Lou Saban in 1960–61. Collier returned as defensive coordinator for head coach Dick MacPherson in 1991 and 1992. In between, he was head coach of the Buffalo Bills and spent two decades as defensive coordinator for the Denver Broncos.

Tony Collins: A second-round draft pick in 1981, he rushed for 4,647 yards and 32 touchdowns in his NFL career and added 261 receptions for 2,356 yards and 12 touchdown catches. He was an AFC All-Pro in 1983.

Rosevelt Colvin: As a Chicago Bears linebacker known for his pass-rushing skills, Colvin was pursued as a free agent by the Patriots and landed prior to the 2003 season. A shattered hip socket cost him that season and a starting position in 2004, but he battled back for three more productive years.

Larry Eisenhauer: A four-time AFL All-Star, the "Wild Man" racked up 45.5 sacks from his defensive end position. He was the first in a long line of Boston College linemen to go on to play for the Patriots, and was a member of the famed "Boston Pops" front four.

Kevin Faulk: A major all-purpose contributor to all three Patriots Super Bowl championship teams. He ranks in the top 10 on the Pats' all-time lists as both a rusher and receiver. In addition, he's the club's all-time kickoff return leader.

Christian Fauria: A member of the Patriots' 2003 and 2004 Super Bowl championship teams. A starter at tight end and also a special-teams member.

Tim Fox: One of three Patriots selected in the first round of the 1976 NFL draft. He was named an AFC Pro Bowl safety in 1980.

Larry Garron: An original Patriot, he came to the club as a free agent out of Western Illinois University. A four-time AFL All-Star at running back, Garron was an all-purpose standout (similar to Kevin Faulk, four decades later), amassing 2,981 rushing yards, 2,502 receiving yards, and 2,299 yards on kickoff returns from 1960 to 1968.

Jack Grinold: The longtime sports information director at Northeastern University, he was an original member of the Patriots' front office as a public relations coordinator.

Steve Grogan: Acknowledged as perhaps the toughest player in Patriots history. Grogan established nearly every early franchise passing record, throwing for 26,886 yards and 182 touchdowns. A fan favorite, he remains one of the Patriots' most beloved and respected players.

Ron Hall: A fixture at cornerback from 1961 to 1967. He was named an AFL All-Star in 1963, and his 29 career interceptions ranks third in team annals.

John Hannah: The first Patriot to be named to the Pro Football Hall of Fame, he was a Pro Bowl guard 10 consecutive times (1976 to 1985) during his 13-year career. "Hog" has often been cited as arguably the best of all time at his position.

Rodney Harrison: After a nine-year run with the Chargers, he was brought in by the Patriots in 2003 to solidify their pass coverage and responded with an All-Pro season. He spent five more years with New England before retiring. Bill Belichick called him the best practice player he ever saw and one of the best players he ever coached.

Mark Henderson: The central figure in the Snowplow Game, he was on a prison work release when he cleared a path for John Smith's game-winning field goal versus the Miami Dolphins on December 12, 1982.

Dan Koppen: After making the Patriots as a rookie fifth-round draft pick out of Boston College, he became starting center for the Super Bowl champions in 2003. Koppen has since started all but seven games (through 2010) and was named to the Pro Bowl in 2007.

Max Lane: A sixth-round pick out of Navy in 1994, he became a starter on the offensive line the following year. He played in 100 career regular-season games as a Patriot.

Ty Law: A fifteen-year veteran of the NFL, he spent the first ten seasons of his career with the Patriots, getting three Super Bowl rings. A five-time Pro Bowler and two-time All Pro at cornerback, he twice led the NFL in interceptions and totaled 53 for his career.

Willie McGinest: A standout at both the linebacker and defensive end positions for more than a decade, he was twice chosen for the Pro Bowl at both positions. He compiled 78 career sacks and was an integral core member of all three Patriot Super Bowl champion defenses.

Gene Mingo: The AFL's leading scorer in its inaugural season, he was a triple-threat running back, return man, and placekicker. He was the offensive standout of the first-ever AFL game for the Denver Broncos.

Leigh Montville: A best-selling sports biographer today, he covered the Patriots for the *Boston Globe* during the 1960s, 1970s, and 1980s.

Jon Morris: The anchor of the Patriots' offensive line at the center position for a decade (1964 to 1974). He was an AFL All-Star from 1964 to 1969 and an AFC Pro Bowler in 1970. Morris was named to the Patriots Hall of Fame in 2011.

Steve Nelson: A fearless, hard-hitting linebacking leader of the Patriots' defense from 1974 to 1987, he was the team's leading tackler eight times and a three-time AFC Pro Bowl selection. A Patriots Hall of famer, he had his number 57 retired by the team.

Babe Parilli: A veteran of the NFL and CFL before coming to the AFL Patriots in 1961, Parilli quarterbacked the Boston offense with his colorful, flamboyant style for the next seven seasons, earning AFL All-Star recognition three times. He finished his career backing up Joe Namath on the world champion New York Jets.

Ray Perkins: A two-time member of the Patriots' coaching staff. He first worked with the team under Chuck Fairbanks from 1974 to 1977 and then returned as offensive coordinator for Bill Parcells from 1993 to 1996.

Jack Rudolph: A second-round draft pick out of Georgia Tech in 1960, he became a member of the original Patriots at the linebacker position and remained with the team through the 1965 season.

Gil Santos: The radio voice of the Patriots for 35 of the past 46 seasons, he is tied with the Philadelphia Eagles' Merrill Reese as the longest-tenured radio broadcaster in the NFL. Santos has teamed with Patriots icon Gino Cappelletti in the booth for the past 21 years.

Dante Scarnecchia: He has been coaching football for more than four decades, more than half of that with the New England Patriots. Since 2000, he has been the team's assistant head coach, while also running the offensive line.

Chris Slade: A second-round pick in 1993, he became a starter at outside linebacker the following year. He remained a Patriot through the 2000 season, totaling 51 career sacks, and was named to the Pro Bowl in 1997.

John Smith: A free agent signed prior to the 1974 season, he was the team's placekicker for a decade. His career total of 692 points ranks third in the team record book.

Otis Smith: A starter at cornerback on the 1996 AFC championship team, he returned to the Patriots from the New York Jets and reclaimed a starting position for the 2001 Super Bowl champions.

Len St. Jean: The starter at offensive guard for 112 games from 1966 to 1973. He also played defensive end and linebacker during his decade as a Patriot and was named an AFL All-Star in 1966.

Michael Strahan: One of the most dominant defensive players of his era, he faced the Patriots in their quest-for-perfection game in 2007's week 17. Strahan has since become an analyst for Fox Sports.

Patrick Sullivan: The son of the Patriots' original owner, Billy Sullivan, he began his involvement with the ball club as a ball boy and worked his way up to general manager.

Mosi Tatupu: One of the most popular players and most versatile contributors in team history, the Hawaii native excelled both as a running back and on special teams. His heart, passion, and pride remain unmatched in team history, and the Patriots community was deeply saddened when he died suddenly in February 2010.

Justin Tuck: The defensive end for the New York Giants who faced the Patriots in the final game of the 2007 season. Off the field, he is known for his tireless philanthropic efforts.

Mark van Eeghen: He was a member of the Patriots' backfield in the

Snowplow Game, but had been on the other side of the ball as a member of the Raiders in the "Roughing the Passer" playoff game in 1976. His son-in-law is current Patriots center Dan Koppen.

Phil Villapiano: The first game of this Oakland Raider's career was also the first at Schaefer Stadium in 1971. He was a starring antagonist in the 1976 AFC divisional playoff, dueling Patriots tight end Russ Francis.

Adam Vinatieri: A free agent signee from NFL Europe in 1996, he became known as "Mr. Automatic" during his decade as the Patriots' placekicker. His last-minute field goals accounted for the game-winning points in Super Bowls XXVI and XXVIII. Despite those heroics, his signature moment remains the 46-yard game-tying field goal in the 2001 AFC divisional playoff Snow Bowl/Tuck Rule game at Foxboro Stadium. He is the team's all-time scoring leader with 1,158 points.

Vince Wilfork: The twenty-first player taken in the 2004 NFL Draft, he soon became one of the league's premier nose tackles. Although he'd only played five seasons to that point, he was named to the Patriots 50th anniversary team prior to the 2009 season.

Tom Yewcic: The young Patriots got talent from everywhere, including the Detroit Tigers' farm system. He played with them through 1959 before becoming the Patriot punter in 1961. He stayed with Boston through 1966, also serving as the team's backup quarterback to Babe Parilli. He retired with an impressive 5.9 yards per carry on his rushes.

Index

INDEX